INTERIORS IN DETAIL

Dominic Bradbury

Richard Powers
Principal Photographer

INTERIORS IN DETAIL

100
Contemporary
Rooms

The
Monacelli
Press

Contents

Introduction

When it comes to the subject of house and home, we are all – in a sense – interior designers.

In the world of design, interiors are unique because they are intrinsically linked to our daily lives and the way we think about aesthetics and visual delight. Inevitably, we shape the spaces around us, lending them various degrees of originality, personality and style, but how do we differentiate between a design that 'works' and one that does not?

A successful room can be a challenge. It is easy to criticize a space for its obvious shortcomings but no simple task to design and create a room that is welcoming, comfortable and functional as well as aesthetically rewarding and layered with personality and interest. It is no wonder we are constantly looking to professional interior designers, architects and innovators to elucidate the concepts and themes that we want to express in our homes.

Interiors in Detail is all about the process of unlocking ideas and providing inspiration. It not only gathers together one hundred interiors, created by some of the leading names in design and architecture, but also explores the attributes that make them successful. Importantly, the book embraces a breadth of design, both aesthetically and geographically. Grouped into ten thematic chapters, the entries include beach houses and cabins, apartments and penthouses, country idylls and tropical getaways in Bangkok, Sydney, Paris, London, New York and beyond.

There is something of a pick-and-mix philosophy to *Interiors in Detail*. Although the emphasis is on contemporary interiors, some of the designs have been created within a historical context. Naturally, some projects will fire your imagination more than others, depending on taste and outlook, but within the blend there are ideas that have broad application and relevance. As the masterful English interior designer David Hicks once said: 'Interior design is essentially the process of maximizing the potential of a space and what it contains.' The ambition of this book is to inspire you to do exactly that. And enjoy it.

KEY DESIGN PRINCIPLES

These principles provide guidance on the tenets that lie behind some of the most successful interiors. They are intended to be informative and thought provoking, rather than prescriptive.

[1] CONTEXT Context refers to the provenance and characteristics of a building's architecture but also to its broader setting and surroundings. For example, the consideration of a beach house – Rolf Ockert's rebuild in Sydney (see p.362) – and a sophisticated town house – Wells Mackereth's Urban Retreat in London (see p.46) – would be very different. Context also encompasses the notion of *genius loci*, or the spirit of a place.

[2] PROPORTION AND SCALE The physical dimensions of a room play a profound role in the understanding of interior design. The relationship between them is partly a matter of function but also of aesthetics, perspective and the way we place ourselves within a space. In Marc and Melissa Palazzo's Ranch House in California (see p.10), for example, close attention was also paid to the scale of individual elements.

[3] CLARITY AND SIMPLICITY There is a significant difference between a richly layered room and a confused space. A calm environment is generally one that speaks of clarity and restraint, with an assured vision and focus behind the design approach. Cluttered and overloaded rooms soon become overwhelming. David Kohn's Norfolk Stable Conversion (see p.266) and Fearon Hay's Tribeca Loft in New York (see p.346) are prime examples of considered interiors.

[4] SYMMETRY A key aspect of interiors, symmetry is one of the most important elements within the background fabric of a room. However, it also refers to the placement of furniture, artwork and other elements within a space, as seen in Carlos Aparicio's 1930s house in Miami (see p.332). Moments of asymmetry have a role within an interior, but tend to be limited for fear of creating a discordant home.

[5] FOCAL POINTS Key components within a space draw the eye and hold attention, becoming pivotal to the way in which a room is arranged. A classic example is the fireplace, which retains a powerful allure even in contemporary homes, such as Marc Newson's London apartment (see p.18). Other points of orientation can include a picture window framing an outstanding vista or a statement piece of furniture.

[6] COHESION The way in which the many elements of a room come together is facilitated by common threads that lend cohesion. These threads relate to texture, colour and tone more than period and provenance. In the Paris apartments of Pierre Frey (see p.286) and Frédéric Méchiche (see p.282), disparate features from a variety of periods are united by key characteristics and themes.

[7] BALANCE A balanced room is a harmonious one, in which its various aspects have a similar visual weight and aesthetic importance. The scale, colour and texture of all the components have a bearing on balance. At the same time, there needs to be an allowance for splashes of colour and more expressive accents, otherwise a room can become mundane. Adam Rolston's Forest Escape in New York State (see p.210) is a balancing act between contrast and cohesion.

[8] REPETITION The repetition of similar elements can provide a pleasing rhythm to a room as well as occasional moments of theatre. Twinning chairs and sofas is a standard method of achieving cohesion, for example, whereas repeated motifs – mirrors, lighting, clocks or artwork – can create engaging combinations that anchor a room. In Anthony Collett's London home (see p.106), the striking collection of ceramics draws the eye and unifies the space.

[9] NARRATIVE Every interior should have a story to tell, and ideally this narrative should reveal itself over time. Rooms layered with narrative and character are naturally engaging and invite a process of discovery, infused with delight. Samuel and Caitlin Dowe-Sandes's modest home in Marrakech (see p.94) is much like reading a good book, for example. Narrative threads may also relate to the *genius loci* or to a more original commonality that subtly pervades the space.

[10] FUNCTIONALITY Like all other strands of design, interior design is a combination of the aesthetic and the functional. However, in the pursuit of style, function and practicality can often be overlooked. Even the most stylish room will generally have to offer a variety of functions, and in open-plan and multipurpose living spaces, these practical considerations are more complex. They require considerable planning, particularly in relation to kitchens, bathrooms and service spaces, exemplified by Tim Gledstone's Infill House in London (see p.232) and Sefer Çağlar's minimalist apartment in Istanbul (see p.358).

[11] COMFORT Comfort is an essential element of interior design but it can sometimes be neglected. In addition to being practical and pleasing to the eye, a room should be welcoming and comfortable, as is evident in David Collins's Bangkok apartment (see p.396) and Studio Catoir's duplex in Saronno, Italy (see p.114). This does not mean adding a few enticing sofas; it is a matter of ergonomics and thinking about the daily enjoyment of each and every space, so that rooms do not fall into disfavour or become visual showcases.

[12] CHARACTER The idea of character is among the most subjective of design elements. Rather than relating it to a particular style, fashion or movement, it is better to consider character in more general terms and explore personality, individuality and originality. Indeed, sometimes it derives from the architecture itself, as seen in Antonie Kioes's Station Chalet near Gstaad in Switzerland (see p.172). Fortunately, character can be layered upon almost any space with imagination, creativity and a little free thinking.

Composition

FRIDA KAHLO/1907.2007

Ranch House

DESIGNERS	PAL + SMITH/TECHENTIN BUCKINGHAM ARCHITECTURE
COMPLETED	2006
LOCATION	ORANGE COUNTY, CALIFORNIA, USA

THIS SPACIOUS 1950S ranch-style residence is the home of interior designers Marc and Melissa Palazzo and their three children. The house was updated and modernized in collaboration with <u>Techentin Buckingham Architecture</u> and has a generous living space at its heart. This becomes the backdrop to a series of carefully organized zones and thoughtful compositions, full of colour and character.

Marc and Melissa Palazzo run their own design company, <u>Pal + Smith</u>, so the house is inevitably something of a testing ground for prototypes and new ideas. They share a strong eye for striking combinations and elegant compositions as well as a love of pattern and colour set against more muted wall tones and simple polished concrete floors.

The Palazzos bought the mid-century Ranch House just after the birth of their second child. They decided to remodel and extend the house quite radically and enlisted the help of architect Henry Buckingham. Together they added a new double-height family room on the ground floor and a dining room. An open-plan layout was retained for the main living spaces, and extra skylights were introduced, which enhanced the sense of connection between inside and out. The main living area features a number of zones. These include the custom kitchen, designed by Marc, and an office area by the open staircase. A lounge sits alongside, with two large Pal + Smith sofas, plus another seating area arranged around the fireplace. These zones are defined only by the composition of the furniture and other more subtle touches that help to delineate the space without the use of partitions.

This arrangement allows for great flexibility as to how the living spaces are used. Marc comes back now and again to find Melissa busily reinventing their home, by creating new combinations of furniture, art and lighting.

DESIGN INGREDIENTS

· Accents of colour

· Contrasting patterns

· Layering and zoning

· Playfulness

· Theatrical highlights

[1] ZONING SOLUTIONS

With neutral walls and ceilings and simple polished floors, the open-plan living space is a blank canvas for creating compositions that become rooms in miniature, floating within the space as a whole. A number of rugs are layered on the concrete floors to lightly delineate certain zones, and alcoves and other architectural features also help to define these rooms within a room. However, it is predominantly the careful placement of furniture – sofas, chairs, desks and tables – that gives these zones identity and purpose.

[2] **FEATURE WALL** The elegant Cole and Son wallpaper on the far wall of the alcove creates a striking splash of contrasting pattern and colour, which provides an anchor for the composition of furniture and artworks around the fireplace. The two matching green armchairs, in 1940s style, are Pal + Smith designs, and the large-scale picture is a pastel drawing by US artist Zaria Forman. The silver standing lamp is an iconic mid-century design by Achille and Pier Giacomo Castiglioni, known as the Arco lamp, and the Art Deco cabinet was bought on a trip to Italy.

[3] **DRAMATIC LIGHTING** Statement lighting and chandeliers add drama and interest throughout the house, and also help to delineate particular zones within the main living space. A period chandelier hangs over the two Pal + Smith sofas within the central lounge area. 'The chandelier really helps ground this space,' said Melissa Palazzo. 'And for hanging out as a family or talking to one another, having the two sofas facing each other like this is perfect.'

[4] **STANDOUT COLOUR** Against the muted backdrop of the white walls and ceilings, any splashes of colour and pattern stand out as vivid accents. The warm green of the small armchairs is particularly pleasing, and the hue is echoed elsewhere in the cushions on the twin sofas and the giant plant holder set in the corner against the feature wall. Within a neutral context, small amounts of colour and pattern introduce a playful element and draw the eye.

BEDROOM RETREAT

The master bedroom is a soothing space situated on the ground floor, alongside the main living area. The white diaphanous curtains have been hung to conceal large storage closets, but they also soften the space and create a striking backdrop for the black and white image by US photographer Rick Meoli. The generously sized bed was made by US firm Environment Furniture from reclaimed Brazilian timber and the pendant lights that drop on either side of the bed are from Plug Lighting, based in Los Angeles.

Wonder House

DESIGNER	WONDER
COMPLETED	2011
LOCATION	MELBOURNE, AUSTRALIA

THIS UPDATED EDWARDIAN HOUSE in
Melbourne offers a fusion of international design
influences within a seamless and sophisticated
composition. One of the most delightful spaces in
this freshly reinvented home is a generously scaled
kitchen and dining area, which forges an intimate
connection with the adjoining terrace and the lush
rear garden. This new family hub is full of ideas
and character.

Opera singer Natalie Taormina grew up in
California with a love of US mid-century design.
She met her Australian husband, Jeremy Creighton
– the owner of a design and branding agency – in
Manhattan and the two lived between the United
States and Australia for a number of years and
renovated three houses together. Eventually, with
two young children, Taormina and Creighton
decided to settle in Melbourne and bought an
inviting Edwardian property in the leafy Armadale
district of the city. The house had plenty of potential,
but many of the living spaces were modest in scale
and the sense of connection to the garden at
the back was very limited. The family turned to
Georgina Armstrong and Pip McCully of the newly
established design studio <u>Wonder</u> and began
collaborating on a significant modernization
of the period property.

   Three bedrooms were refurbished and refreshed
upstairs, but most of the work was concentrated on
the ground floor. Here, an old carport to one side of
the house was replaced by an enticing new master
bedroom and bathroom suite. On the other side of
the house, Wonder created a new wing containing
a large kitchen and dining space, opening up to the
courtyard garden.

   Large expanses of glass form a vibrant link
with the lush planting outside, while a long,
narrow skylight introduces natural sunlight directly
into the heart of the kitchen. The high-end custom
kitchen recalls the style of a farmhouse kitchen, but
with a contemporary twist and a pared-down
aesthetic. A separate laundry room and pantry clear
away everyday household clutter, while the long
kitchen island doubles as a breakfast bar and
serving counter for the more formal round dining
table nearby. This space also flows through to a
comfortable family lounge alongside, which can
be closed off using a sliding door, thereby creating
a highly flexible and fluid living arrangement.

DESIGN INGREDIENTS

· Graphic design

· Light and bright

· Multiple grids

· Points of contrast

· Practicality

[1] ISLAND LIVING Designed by Wonder, the kitchen and island are both practical and elegant. The island functions as a preparation area and breakfast bar, furnished with stools by Australian furniture designer Mark Tuckey. The mirror glass on one side aids the circulation of natural light and creates a visual game that plays with one's perception of the space. The use of bright white tiles and finishes helps to unify the design.

[2] WINDOW SEAT The window seat represents an old idea given new life. These seats have a romance all of their own, often associated with period country houses. Here, the custom-designed bench frames the room and offers a significant amount of additional seating without swallowing up valuable space. The cushions are made from vintage Tibetan blankets.

BEDROOM SANCTUARY

The master suite is a new addition to the house. Deliberately set apart from the children's rooms and guest quarters, this bedroom pavilion provides a grown-up sanctuary from the rest of the house and displays a strong connection to the verdant greenery of the back garden. The pendant lights that hang either side of the bed are from the Finnish design company Artek, while the stool is by British designer Tom Dixon. The colours of the softly textured rug and patterned bedspread sit well with the soothing palette of the walls and the oak floors.

[4] CIRCULAR TABLES Given the linear nature of the space as a whole and of many of the elements within it – the island, skylight, windows, rug, etc – the circular tables add a point of contrast. The interior dining table, by Mark Tuckey, softens the space and provides a welcome foil to the multiple grids. The dining chairs are a Hans J. Wegner design manufactured by Carl Hansen & Son.

[3] GRAPHIC PATTERN The large black and white Ikea rug covering the American oak floorboards lightly defines the more formal dining area and distinguishes it from the kitchen island alongside. Furthermore, the simple graphic design introduces another layer to the composition and echoes the grid pattern of the wall of windows and the French doors.

Sorting Office

DESIGNERS	MARC NEWSON/SQUIRE AND PARTNERS
COMPLETED	2010
LOCATION	LONDON, UK

DESIGNER MARC NEWSON created this dramatic and individual family home for himself, his wife and their two children on the second floor of an Edwardian building formerly used to sort mail in London. He was determined to create a tailored apartment that would not only suit family life but also would avoid the open expanses of urban lofts. Working with architects Squire and Partners, Newson opted for a fluid layout, but one that allowed for the creation of distinct areas and inviting retreats.

The key space in the apartment is the double-height living room, with its central fireplace set within a feature wall of rounded Canadian river stone. 'We wanted to preserve a sense of volume but at the same time create an atmosphere and warmth, which is quite difficult to achieve in such a large space,' said Newson.

A major point of inspiration was the design of alpine chalets and – more specifically – that depicted in Alfred Hitchcock's film *North by Northwest* (1959). 'Lofts are large and cold but the thing about chalets is that they are cosy no matter how big the space.' The high wall of stone, in particular, was inspired by the cinematic chalet. It introduces organic texture, character and drama, with the warmth provided by the open fireplace.

The living room flows through to a more intimate dining area, tucked under a mezzanine level, and then on into the kitchen space. Here, the kitchen was designed by Newson in a shade of pistachio green – one of the designer's favourite colours. There are other surprises hidden away in the three-bedroom apartment, and one of the most unexpected is a formal period-style timber-panelled library. This was a special request from Newson's wife, fashion stylist Charlotte Stockdale, who was fond of the library in her childhood home. The new library was made using salvaged oak panelling and shelving.

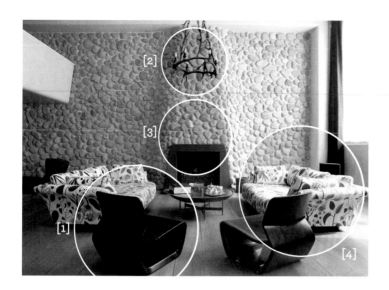

DESIGN INGREDIENTS

· Contrasting textures

· Feature wall

· Iconic furniture

· Incongruity

· Nature in the home

[1] NEWSON FURNITURE The living room contains some of Marc Newson's iconic designs. They include the Felt chair (below), which is produced by Italian firm Cappellini, and the two limited edition Micarta chairs designed for the Gagosian Gallery in New York. The designer's work spans interiors for Qantas jumbo jets to landmark furniture pieces such as the marble Voronoi shelf, which features elsewhere in the apartment.

[2] RUSTIC TOUCHES The river stone wall and the fireplace are important elements in achieving the warm and welcoming atmosphere that Newson desired, but so too are the wooden floors and other more unusual touches, such as the deer antler chandelier. These rustic elements contrast with the clean lines and sinuous curves of the architectural shell. The sitting room also features a grand piano and a grandfather clock.

[3] <u>RIVER STONE</u> The rounded river stone that has been utilized for the double-height fireplace and feature wall in the sitting room was specially imported from Nova Scotia, Canada. The vast scale of the wall, its inviting uneven texture and its obvious incongruity in such an urban setting all add to the heightened drama and appeal. A vibrant background to the arrangement of furniture, the stone wall provides an anchor for the space as a whole and it has a sensory quality that not only invites touch but also cannot fail to draw the eye.

MARBLE BATHROOM

The aesthetic of Newson's furniture is futuristic in style, with gentle curves and a sculptural quality. The same is true of the master bathroom in the Sorting Office. Designed by Newson, it has Carrara marble walls and flooring with rounded edges, as well as a highly sophisticated, crafted finish and exquisite detailing. This is one of Newson's favourite spaces in the apartment: 'It has a very zen kind of feel and the stripes in the marble work particularly well in the space. And I like getting wet.'

[4] <u>PLAYFUL PATTERN</u> Both the sofas and the sofa fabric were designed by Josef Frank for Swedish design house Svenskt Tenn. Playful and engaging, the green and white Windows pattern was one of a number of designs developed by Frank during his time as a visiting professor in New York in the 1940s. The plants featured in the design are common houseplants, with the leaves picked out in emerald green. The pattern stands out against the muted greys of the stone wall.

Provençal Modern

DESIGNER	STUDIO KO
COMPLETED	2007
LOCATION	LUBERON, PROVENCE, FRANCE

IT WAS THE QUIET beauty of the Luberon landscape that first attracted Thierry Gautier to the Provence region of France. Consequently, when he decided to build his own house here, it was essential that the design not only respected the surrounding countryside but also celebrated it. House G is not about statement architecture; it is more concerned with creating something that is contextual, subtle and considered. The layout of the main living spaces and the composition of the furniture and other elements are orientated around the extraordinary rural vista.

A director of jewelry company Van Cleef & Arpels, Gautier first discovered the charms of the Luberon during a holiday in the area and has come to know the region intimately. He bought a period farmhouse here, which he restored, but then decided that he wanted to build a contemporary house from the ground up. Eventually, he discovered a suitable plot of land in a tranquil setting and turned to architects Karl Fournier and Olivier Marty of Studio KO. 'We had the idea of designing the house as a "camera obscura" aimed at the landscape, with the closed side walls and then openings at the two ends of the house,' said Fournier. 'It needed to be a house that melts into the land.'

Guests have their own sanctuary within a discrete lower level, which leads directly out onto a terrace by the swimming pool. However, the main emphasis is on the upper level, which enjoys the best of the views. Here, an open-plan living space and kitchen are positioned at the front of the building, within a part of the house that pushes outwards over the terrace below and frames the vista with a series of floor-to-ceiling windows. The master bedroom is situated to the rear of the upper storey, with the bathroom and services contained in a crafted timber box that is centrally positioned within the floor plan.

The arrangement of furniture and seating in the main living area takes account of the views across the verdant landscape, encouraging an ongoing engagement with the surroundings. 'We wanted to magnify the view by using the furniture in quite a minimalist way,' said Gautier. 'I especially loved the way that Karl and Olivier used three mirrors in the living room to reflect parts of the landscape. You are inside the house but at the same time you feel outside because of the reflections.'

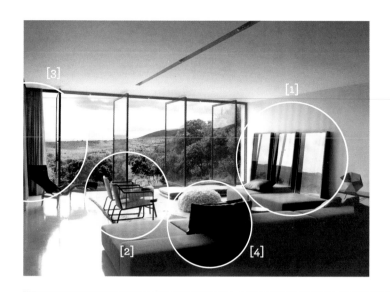

DESIGN INGREDIENTS

· Connecting with the landscape

· Craftsmanship

· Minimalist furniture design

· Repetition of forms

· Soft tones

[1] MIRROR TRIPTYCH

The three large mirrors leaning against one wall are custom-made designs by Studio KO. They help to reflect the natural light and also the landscape itself into the living room, while their repeated geometry echoes the rectangles of the pivoting windows. Repetition of these forms enhances the artistry of the composition. The versatile grey sofa and matching ottomans are by Italian upholsterers Living Divani. Mirror glass has also been used in the adjacent kitchen to provide another source of reflection.

[2] BERBER RUG
This Berber rug, from Morocco, is a hand-woven piece made from wool in the traditional manner. These crafted pieces are produced by artisans of the Beni Ourain tribes in northern Morocco. Although they remain prized possessions in North Africa, their reputation as high-quality furnishings has now spread internationally. The thick rug adds a softer texture to the living space and helps to define the seating zone within it. The long-haired woolly footstool that sits atop the rug is from the Caravane design shop in Paris.

CRAFTED KITCHEN

The kitchen, located alongside the main seating area, was custom designed by Studio KO in oak. It features a long island, complete with a breakfast and dining bar at one end with four chairs arranged around it, also designed by Studio KO. The rest of the kitchen is contained within the outline of a crafted timber box at the centre of the house. This also contains service spaces and the master bathroom; the generously sized master bedroom, also with a bank of floor-to ceiling windows, is located at the opposite end of the building.

[3] TRACK CURTAINS The SAHCO curtains are hung upon a concealed ceiling track. During the day, they hang against a wall to one side of the room, but at night they can be drawn across the long bank of windows. The grey tones of the curtains tie in with the colour of the sectional sofa and they also help to tone down the architectural purity of the space. In addition to the Berber rug and other pieces, they provide a layer of softer texture that contrasts with the hard surfaces of the polished concrete floor, the expanse of glass and the smooth walls.

[4] SEATING PLANS Naturally, the composition of the seating is arranged so that it faces out towards the landscape. The wall of windows was designed to maximize the view and to frame the open vista in the manner of a 'camera obscura'. This arrangement is anchored by the sectional grey sofa. The two durable armchairs are from outdoor furniture specialist Roda and the chaise longue is a vintage piece from Swedish designer and architect Bruno Mathsson; its sinuous form contrasts with the linear nature of the space and the geometrical sofa.

Rural Elegance

DESIGNERS   STEPHEN SILLS AND JAMES HUNIFORD

COMPLETED   1991

LOCATION   BEDFORD, NEW YORK, USA

THIS ELEGANT RESIDENCE on a hillside in Bedford was a major project for designers <u>Stephen Sills</u> and <u>James Huniford</u>, in which they explored an original take on US country style. The aesthetic is fresh and modern in feel, yet draws on period and European references and blends antiques and contemporary furniture. It also introduces modern art to the mix. The house was one of their most accomplished joint projects, although they have since gone on to establish individual design studios.

James Huniford calls the house a laboratory of ideas. The original building dates from the 1920s and was owned by gardener and author Helen Morgenthau Fox. By the time Sills and Huniford first visited the house, the building was crumbling and the gardens were lost, apart from some specimen trees. After taking on the house and gardens, which are located in a tranquil countryside setting, the designers decided to bide their time while they formulated their plans.

Initially, the pair rebuilt a neglected garage near the house as a guest lodge, which they lived in while they tackled the challenge of the main residence. 'It had a wonderful presence about it, but really there was nothing left,' said Sills. 'The house was totally dilapidated. We kept some of the architectural detailing, some of the original mouldings, but that was about all. We put the stone floors in, the fire surrounds are new and the plasterwork is our creation. We worked real hard at trying to keep a natural feeling to it.'

In the main living room, Egyptian columns mix with a Spanish refectory table, a mahogany chaise longue from the French Directory period and an English globe once owned by Rudolf Nureyev; there are also a number of self-designed pieces. The collection of modern art is a key element throughout the interiors, with notable works by Cy Twombly, Joan Miró and Robert Rauschenberg, among others. The bedroom furniture and furnishings are eclectic, yet sit together within melodic compositions.

The house has a calm, harmonious character, but is also full of individuality and invention. 'The great secret in decorating,' said Sills, 'lies in selecting objects within a space and looking at how they harmonize with one another. In the final analysis that's what decorating is really about.'

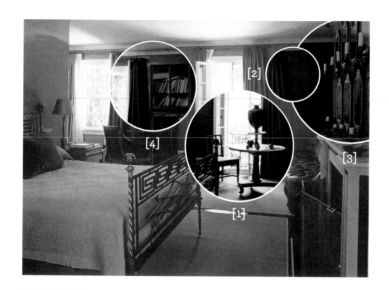

DESIGN INGREDIENTS

· Concentration of colour

· Country feel

· Eclecticism

· Harmonious arrangement
  of objects and furniture

· Period elements

[1] BEDROOM LOUNGE

The master bedroom is a soothing
retreat that has been designed as
a self-contained space set apart from
the more 'public' and open areas
of the house. It is spacious enough
for a comfortable seating area in
one corner and a *secretaire* between
the windows, which provides a
small work station. These elements
create a sanctuary, but also make
for a more inviting and welcoming
environment. In this way, the bedroom
becomes a multifaceted and restful
space that can be enjoyed at all times
of the day.

[2] ORGANIC COLOUR

The master bedroom is set apart
from the rest of the house by the
concentrated use of colour. Whereas
the walls throughout many of the
living spaces are decorated in neutral
tones, the bedroom is covered with
an enamel paint that Sills Huniford
labels 'pond scum green'. The earthy
tone is also utilized for the curtains
and other furnishings. This organic
colour is rich and evocative and ties
in well with the various green shades
of the towering trees outside the
windows. It has a suitably contextual
quality for its setting.

[3] **DELIGHTFUL REPETITION** A collection of 18th-century Dutch gilt-framed mirrors is arranged over the fireplace, which features a mantelpiece by English architect John Soane. The repetition of these mirrors creates a vivid tableau and a focal point in the bedroom. At the same time, the mirrors refract light through the space and their integrated candle holders promise a mesmerizing optical effect in the evenings.

[4] **HARMONIOUS FUSION** As in many other parts of the house, the bedroom features a range of furniture and other pieces sourced from a number of different periods and places: the Dutch mirrors, the 19th-century French *secretaire*, the late 18th-century French steel bed and a Russian chair by the circular 18th-century table, for example. Each feels correct and harmonious in its space according to its scale, positioning and finish.

BLUE NOTE

Within the context of the soothing cream walls in the living room, vibrant accents of colour stand out, such as the vivid blue sofa, which is a custom-made piece by Sills Huniford. The splash of blue brings a dynamic quality to the space and surprises the eye in a welcome way. Behind the sofa is a large drawing by Cy Twombly and the matching cabinets to either side are Louis XVI ammunition cabinets.

Mid-century Modern

DESIGNER	TRIP HAENISCH
COMPLETED	2011
LOCATION	LOS ANGELES, CALIFORNIA, USA

TRIP HAENISCH PREFERS to describe his interiors as 'curated' rather than decorated. For the Los Angeles-based designer, it is the hunt for standout pieces of furniture, photography and art that matters most, as well as the way in which they sit together within a well-proportioned space. The fun lies in defining the mix and setting up some unexpected compositions and juxtapositions of style, period, colour and texture, as seen here in his own mid-century home.

This house sits close to Mulholland Drive in Beverly Hills. The location is a special one: the building stands alone up in the hills, with views of the Santa Monica mountains. However, the designer can be in the centre of Los Angeles in no time at all and at his office in only ten minutes. It is the perfect combination of escapism and accessibility.

The one-storey house dates from 1958 and was a gem that Trip Haenisch had known about for years. When he heard that the property was finally coming on to the market he seized the opportunity. The bones and structure of the house were in good shape with a strong, fluid relationship between outside and inside living spaces, as would be expected in a well-designed house in California. However, Haenisch was determined to make a few changes before he began organizing his personal space. 'I'm kind of picky so I did do a big update on the house but I kept the same footprint,' he said. 'We changed all the floors inside and got random-width, oak plank floorboards and there was brick paving out by the pool that we replaced with a textured concrete with pebbles. We updated the bathrooms and the kitchen was closed off so we made a cut-out that opens the kitchen to the living room.'

Walls were painted in calming whites or off-whites, thereby creating a neutral backdrop. Haenisch could then begin the enjoyable process of layering with colour and texture through his choice of furniture and art. He is an inveterate collector and always hunting, although his taste is wide-ranging. For his own house, the preference was for 20th-century pieces, including a good mix of mid-century furniture by Mario Bellini, Eero Aarnio and others. The dining area includes vintage designs by Hans J. Wegner and Vico Magistretti, arranged around a sturdy dining table, which anchors the space.

[1]

[3]

[4]

[2]

DESIGN INGREDIENTS

· Contrasting timbers
· Flamboyant display of art and curios
· Neutral backdrop
· Outdoor rooms
· Sociable living

[1] PENDANT LIGHTING

Statement lighting helps to define a room or a particular zone within a more open floor plan. Sculptural pieces such as this striking pendant light for Italian design company Oluce introduce drama to the home and create an opportunity to add an engaging layer of surprise in terms of shape and scale. Here, the design by Vico Magistretti is reminiscent of the space age flying saucers that were a repeated motif of the mid-century period, when a passion for futurism combined with a love of sinuous forms.

[2] ANCHOR PIECES

Eye-catching pieces of furniture with a sense of grandeur anchor particular areas within the house. They also serve to define the purpose of the spaces and make them practical. Here, the size and shape of the timber and stone dining table – sourced from US furniture company Holly Hunt – sit well within the proportions of this part of the home and create a focal point around which other items of furniture and lighting revolve. The six matching dining chairs are vintage pieces by Hans J. Wegner.

INDOOR–OUTDOOR DINING

The interior dining area features floor-to-ceiling glass walls and sliding doors that open out onto a covered veranda. Here, Haenisch has created one of a number of complementary outdoor rooms. This particular space serves as a summer dining room, complete with a gas fireplace to warm up colder nights. Full-length curtains on tracks can be pulled across to 'wrap' the veranda, offering shade or creating a more intimate atmosphere in the evenings. The slatted dining chairs are vintage pieces by Norwegian designer Hans Brattrud.

[3] **VERTICAL LIVING** Oak floorboards and clapboard walls and ceilings – painted white – provide a muted and cohesive backdrop within the interconnected living spaces at the heart of the house. The vertical configuration of the clapboard accentuates the sense of height and volume in the dining zone in particular. Splashes of vibrant colour also stand out within this context, including the iconic *Cow* screen-print by Andy Warhol and the red leather bar cart by US furniture designer Eric Brand. The upended target table, positioned in the corner like a work of sculpture, is a vintage bull's eye sectional design by the Italian Studio 65.

[4] **SERVING HATCH** Within the original layout of the house, the kitchen was separated completely from the dining area and the interconnected sitting room. However, Haenisch decided to open up the space and to create a large hatch to the custom-designed kitchen. This allows the kitchen to exist as a clearly defined room but also invites a visual, social and practical connection between the two areas. The new counter of the hatch becomes a breakfast bar and a serving area for the dining zone nearby. 'I feel that the kitchen is the soul of the house,' said Haenisch. 'When I have a party I look up and find that everybody is in the kitchen.'

Pirate House

DESIGNER   O'CONNOR AND HOULE
ARCHITECTURE

COMPLETED   2011

LOCATION   PIRATES BAY, MORNINGTON
PENINSULA, AUSTRALIA

THE HOUSE THAT architects <u>Annick Houle</u> and <u>Stephen O'Connor</u> have built for themselves at Pirates Bay nestles among a grove of sculpted tea trees. They are a protected species on the Mornington Peninsula, which is a place of extraordinary natural beauty blessed with a mesmerizing coastline, much of it set within a national park. This family weekend and holiday home was designed to sit softly within this landscape and it does its best to connect with its surroundings as intimately as it can.

Pirate House has an organic, crafted, calming quality and the design is beautifully composed and executed. It is arranged around an open, bush 'courtyard' with a floating timber deck sitting among the tea trees. The main body of the house is L-shaped, with the master suite at one end and the children's bedrooms at the other. Between the two, at the heart of the space, sits an open-plan living area leading out onto a long terrace, partially sheltered by the overhanging roof line. The studio is a separate pavilion, connected to the main building via a timber walkway, and it can be used as guest accommodation or as an office.

'This house is really about getting back to basics,' said Houle. 'It's about escaping the city and getting back to nature. So maximizing the connections between indoors and outdoors was very important to us and that Japanese influence of bringing the calmness of the landscape right into the plan of the house.' The living zone is welcoming and warm, holding a custom kitchen at one end, the sitting area at the other and a dining zone at the centre. Generously scaled glass doors slide back to open the room to the deck and courtyard beyond, while natural light is drawn in from a series of high transom windows on the opposite wall. The timber-framed walls below these high windows double as display shelving for pictures and curios.

The character and warmth of the timber floors, walls and ceiling shine through and contrast with the concrete bricks that were used to build the fireplace and hearth, which anchor the space and form a focal point for the seating area. 'What really pleases us most about the house is that it was built to our often unreasonably exacting standards. It took a true craftsman carpenter.'

DESIGN INGREDIENTS

· Cohesion

· Fluid connection with
  outdoor space

· Geometric forms

· Organic textures

· Repeated highlights

[1] DISPLAY NICHES Although the timber
wall is structural, within the room it forms an
eye-catching geometrical lattice-like series of
niches. These shelves serve as elegant frames
for the collections of artworks, photographs and
family treasures. Tallow wood (a native species
of eucalyptus) was used for most of the internal
flooring and wall panelling, as well as for the
decking outside.

[2] FEATURE FIREPLACE At the far end
of the living room, the fireplace anchors the
space and draws the eye to the hearth. It is made
with dark grey bricks fabricated from concrete by
Australian construction and building materials
supplier Boral, with light-coloured mortar for a more
dramatic effect. The tone and texture of these bricks
contrast with the warm timber used for the walls,
floors and ceilings.

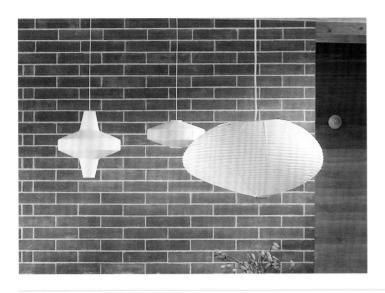

[3] REPEATED MOTIFS Japanese paper lanterns, some of which were designed by Isamu Noguchi, float over the dining table and the seating zone around the fireplace. Their sinuous, rounded shapes are evocative and pleasing, introducing a fresh element to the linear space. The repetition of the lanterns creates a more vivid composition and ties the space together. Paper lanterns saw a revival during the mid-century period, in the work of designers such as Noguchi and Danish furniture company Le Klint, and they remain popular today.

[4] SYMMETRICAL COMPOSITION There is a strong sense of geometry in the living space, with its timber grid walls and linear character. Within this ordered context, symmetry becomes particularly important, as seen in the arrangement of the Hans J. Wegner chairs around the Fritz Hansen dining table, and the pair of Mark Tuckey armchairs positioned on either side of the fireplace. At the same time, there are small touches elsewhere – such as the floating pendant lights – that prevent the space becoming entirely symmetrical and over-regulated.

CRAFTED BATHROOM

The master bathroom is another highly organic and crafted space, with an immediate sense of connection with the outdoors via a floor-to-ceiling sliding window. There is a clear Japanese-influenced purity to the room, with unity provided by the timber surfaces throughout and a steep-sided *ofuro* bathtub designed by Houle and O'Connor. The warm minimalism is enhanced by thoughtful touches, such as the Scandinavian Vola bath taps and spout emerging directly from the timber wall with no extraneous pipe work.

Silver Lake Cottage

DESIGNERS	STEVEN JOHANKNECHT/COMMUNE
COMPLETED	2005
LOCATION	LOS ANGELES, CALIFORNIA, USA

DESIGNER STEVEN JOHANKNECHT has made his home in a characterful cottage in a leafy corner of the Silver Lake district of Los Angeles. Built in 1928 in a wooded enclave, the house is one of four Tudor-style cottages that were originally constructed by Disney Studios for its script writers. Johanknecht was drawn to the cottage shortly after making the move from New York to Los Angeles and co-founding the Commune design studio.

'The house had all the quirky charm of an English cottage,' said Johanknecht, 'and incorporated great aspects of indoor–outdoor California living. It was important to me that it had not been over-renovated and still had all the original details. At the same time, I was looking for something that was the antithesis to my previous life in a New York high-rise.' Within the cottage itself, the layout is largely original. The ground floor is graced with a den, painted in a refreshing custom blend of Benjamin Moore's chrome green and Pacific Sea teal, but the majority of the floor plan is devoted to the open-plan living, dining and kitchen area, which combines period elements, mid-century treasures and custom designs. Here, Johanknecht was keen to preserve original features such as the brick and timber fireplace. The walls and ceilings were painted a crisp white, while the timber floors were treated with a piano-finish paint.

Johanknecht layered the interiors with texture, colour and a blend of furniture and lighting, featuring a number of vintage designs brought from his former home in New York, including the white leather chair and mid-century sofa. Other pieces, such as the coffee table and the fire screen, are original designs by Johanknecht for Commune. 'Many of the furniture pieces have been with me for a long time and started out in my 1960s apartment off Washington Square,' said Johanknecht. 'I appreciate them much more in this environment and love the juxtaposition with the style of the house.'

· Complementary colours

· Graphic qualities

· Individuality

· Juxtaposition

· Layering of textures

[1] GRAPHIC ELEMENTS The white walls and ceilings contrast with the near-black floors, which have been treated with a lacquered and reflective finish. This black and white combination creates a graphic quality in the space, enhanced by the dark fireplace surround and the exposed wooden beams. It is the perfect base for Johanknecht's layered interiors and compositions, enhanced by a diverse range of furniture and textiles in the dining alcove and sitting room alongside.

[2] POPPY RED KITCHEN Johanknecht revived the original kitchen within an imaginative and colourful treatment. The poppy red units work well with the terracotta tile detailing around the sink area and the warm timber worktops elsewhere. Linoleum floors were replaced with the same dark timber that unites the open-plan living area. 'The almost black floors, white walls and the red cabinets of the kitchen – I find that everything looks great with that combination,' said Johanknecht.

[3] MID-CENTURY TOUCHES

The eclectic blend of furniture includes a number of mid-century pieces, such as the vintage sofa, the AJ wall sconce by Arne Jacobsen and the woven Danish dining chairs by Peter Hvidt. Such items sit comfortably within the open proportions of the space and work well in juxtaposition with period elements, such as the brick and timber fireplace, thereby reaffirming the versatility of these 1950s and 1960s designs. The stainless steel and white leather MR lounge chair is by Ludwig Mies van der Rohe for Knoll.

[4] TEXTURAL BLEND

The interiors of the main living space are layered with a variety of textures, including sheepskin rugs and hand-woven kilims on the timber floorboards as well as the mid-century sofa upholstered in a linen from Pindler & Pindler. Cushions, throws, floor coverings and artworks – such as the 1950s Italian painting on the mantelpiece – offer a range of red and burnt orange accents that tie in well with the earthy brickwork of the fireplace and the more vivid red of the painted kitchen units nearby.

OUTDOOR LIVING

Johanknecht created an inviting outdoor sitting room in the garden, with a built-in sofa bench surrounded by succulents, hanging plants and a sunburst sculpture by Curtis Jeré on the timber wall. 'It really makes the outdoor spaces become part of the living area and it can be used all year round,' said Johanknecht. The dining area flows out into this sheltered garden area via a set of French doors, creating a smooth transition between outside and in, and introducing natural light and fresh air to the interiors of the cottage.

Hamptons Glamour

DESIGNER	MAISON 24
COMPLETED	2001
LOCATION	LONG ISLAND, NEW YORK, USA

ALLISON JULIUS AND LOUIS MARRA have a stronger and more creative relationship than most sisters and brothers. They work together and design together – as <u>Maison 24</u> – and so when it came to finding a weekend house out in the Hamptons, on Long Island, it was natural that they would share the project.

Allison's husband, Zachary, did the initial house hunt and came up with a shortlist of eight houses, which was whittled down by Allison to a final three. The house they selected is set in a calm green enclave surrounded by woodland. However, the former owners had preferred a traditional aesthetic, which felt out of place with the modern architecture of the building, so an update was required.

At Casa B, the walls, kitchen and bathrooms are all a neat, neutral white, which has allowed Allison and Louis to add colour, texture and pattern throughout. The house revolves around a double-height living room, opening onto the rear terrace and swimming pool. The dining area and kitchen sit to one side, and guest bedrooms are set apart in a wing of their own. Allison and Zachary claimed the master suite on the ground floor and Louis took the bedroom, bathroom and mezzanine loft within a modest upper level. 'The layout does work really well and we all meet in the middle and end up in the kitchen,' said Allison. 'The most appealing thing when we were looking at the house was that the guest rooms are at the far end so people can just do their own thing. We just peeled away the country aesthetic, stained the floors dark and painted it white top to bottom – and outside as well – so that it became a clean backdrop to our furnishings.'

Nothing stays still for long at Casa B. This is a house where ideas are constantly in motion and collections are frequently added to and rearranged. 'The great benefit – or the major pitfall – of what we do,' said Allison, 'is that we are constantly redecorating. We just can't help ourselves. It's a job hazard, but a fun one.'

DESIGN INGREDIENTS

· Cohesion

· Distinctive layering

· Dramatic lighting

· Playful motifs

· Prominent displays of art

[1] PATTERN AND TEXTURE With its soaring ceilings, crisp white walls and generous sense of proportion and scale, the living room makes a perfect canvas for a layered decorative approach. Within the mix, texture and pattern play a crucial role. Standout pieces include the teal sofas, the graphic curtains (with a pattern from Duralee Fabrics) and the soft, textured cream rug, which frames the seating area. The vintage Lucite and glass cocktail table adds drama.

[2] EYE-CATCHING CHANDELIER Statement chandeliers are not only the preserve of grand period-style houses. They also have a role to play within more contemporary interiors, adding drama and delight. Mid-century and contemporary chandeliers become focal points and create visual anchors for the room. Here, the black hand-blown Venetian glass stands out all the more against the white walls. The lighting fixture above the dining table is an Artichoke lamp by Poul Henningsen.

[3] FORNASETTI TOUCHES

Piero Fornasetti was one of the most engaging and imaginative of the Italian mid-century master designers. In recent years interest in his work has been revived, fuelled by the designer's distinctive love of pattern, theatre and playful motifs. Here, the square cushion on the sofa offers an emblematic touch of the Italian maestro. In the formal dining area alongside the main living room, a black and white Fornasetti wallpaper creates a vivid backdrop to the dining table and refurbished chairs.

[4] COMPLEMENTARY COMPOSITIONS

Within such a large room there are clear opportunities to create secondary and complementary compositions. Here, a blank wall surface to one side of the room invites not only artwork (an image by US photographer Steven Klein from a shoot for *W* magazine) but also a tableau comprising a polished chrome console table, a pair of hand-turned gold geode lamps and upholstered stools with Lucite bases by Maison 24.

DINING BY DESIGN

Although the dining area adjoins the living room, it is clearly defined by its low ceiling and a shift in proportion and scale. This helps to create a more intimate space suited to evening dining and entertaining. The Gustavo Olivieri Lucite dining table is the standout piece and the malachite wallpaper picks out the display alcove with buffet behind it. The Chippendale-style chairs were resprayed with a teal car paint, which lends them a fresh and more contemporary feel, while also tying in with the teal tones of the Maison 24 George sofas in the living room.

Urban Retreat

DESIGNER	WELLS MACKERETH
COMPLETED	2011
LOCATION	LONDON, UK

ARRANGED AROUND A HIDDEN courtyard garden, this north London home is an urban sanctuary with highly crafted interiors. The house is arranged in two distinct parts, with the newly built portion holding the main living spaces and a Victorian coach house hosting a generous master suite. The principal living area is an open-plan space, with a strong sense of connection to the secret garden, which forms a welcoming outdoor room.

The house was commissioned by an actor and property developer, who had wanted to create a home for some time but had struggled to find a suitable site with a complementary outdoor space. Eventually he came across the coach house with a ramshackle workshop behind it and asked architect Sally Mackereth of Wells Mackereth to create a scheme for the site. Her client was more interested in the idea of creating a sophisticated and highly tailored home with generous proportions than in maximizing the number of bedrooms. In fact, the coach house contains the only bedroom, with a bathroom floating above the sleeping area on a mezzanine level with a glass balcony. Here, the panelled walls are painted a soothing grey and the floor has been relaid with salvaged parquet.

Towards the back of the site, the workshop was pulled down, but both architect and client had been seduced by the open volume of the shed and also its semi-industrial attributes. These qualities served as key influences in the design of the new living areas, with a generous, double-height space opening onto the courtyard via two vast glass doors. This room features a seating area arranged around a fireplace at one end and a dining area anchored by a George Nakashima table at the other. An open kitchen sits to one side, defined by a shift in floor level and a change in ceiling height, created by the mezzanine directly above it.

There is a focus on texture and tailor-made elements throughout. One wall of the living room is clad in porcelain tiles and another, at the opposite end to the glazed doors, features a distressed paint finish by London-based artist Harvey Woodward that recalls the industrial flavours of the workshop. Among the many specially designed features are the lighting gantries over the seating area and the custom chandelier that floats above the sculptural dining table.

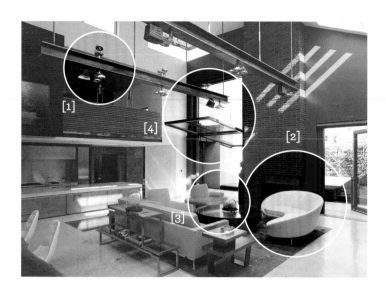

DESIGN INGREDIENTS

· Combination of directional
  and natural lighting

· Complementary textures

· Exposed industrial elements

· Inside–outside connection

· Scale and proportion

[1] CUSTOM LIGHTING Given the height
and scale of the living room, suitable off-the-shelf
lighting fixtures would have been difficult to source.
Sally Mackereth's solution was to design made-to-
order lighting features, such as the dramatic
chandelier over the dining table, which can be
lowered or raised with a pulley system. The gantries
above the main seating zone are also custom pieces,
and they hold directional lighting that helps define
the ambience of the space below.

[2] CONTRASTING TEXTURES The space is
enriched by many contrasting textures and finishes.
These include the concrete floors, the ridged tiles on
the rear wall and the black brick used to build the
fireplace and chimney. Softer textures are provided
by the rug and furnishings, including the Bruno
Triplet mohair used to cover the matching pair of
1940s armchairs. The semi-circular, biomorphic
white sofa is a 1950s piece by Italian architect and
designer Ico Parisi.

BEDROOM COCOON

The industrial character of the main living spaces is juxtaposed with the more traditional and insular quality of the original coach house. This building has been updated and restored sensitively to provide a generous master suite with a bathroom on a mezzanine level. Extensive wall panelling, parquet floors, cast iron radiators and a fireplace reflect the period character of this part of the house, which is accessed via a secret door behind the kitchen. A pulley system allows a television to be winched up to the bathroom level and viewed while in the tub.

[3] COFFEE TABLE COMPOSITION
The seating is arranged in front of the fireplace and partially defined by the Draw rug by Kate Blee at Christopher Farr. The circular coffee table at the centre of the composition provides a visual anchor around which the other pieces radiate. At the same time, the aluminium table by Barber Osgerby for Established & Sons is a sculptural statement in itself and worthy of its central position.

[4] **FEATURE WINDOWS** Large skylights and high clerestory windows introduce natural light from a number of directions, and also filter light down to a modest basement level via a glass floor panel. The two heavy glass doors that connect to the garden are features in themselves, particularly the larger of the two, which opens on hydraulic pistons at the touch of a button and turns on a central pivot to form a glass canopy stretching out into the garden.

Structure

Town House Retreat

DESIGNER	JULIAN KING ARCHITECT
COMPLETED	2012
LOCATION	MANHATTAN, NEW YORK, USA

WHEN TELEVISION-COMMERCIAL PRODUCER
George Fares set out to design a duplex apartment
for himself in the neighbourhood of Chelsea
in Manhattan he wanted to create a feeling of
tranquillity. He was aiming for a true escape from
the hectic pace and buzz of day-to-day urban
living. Working with architect <u>Julian King</u>, Fares
has achieved his goal: the apartment has been
enhanced by a new layout and the atmosphere
is now calm and relaxed.

George Fares had owned this 19th-century building
for a number of years before he began the
renovation project. Initially, the house was divided
into rental apartments, but when his tenants vacated
the ground and lower-ground floors, Fares decided
to create a duplex apartment for himself. He turned
to architect Julian King, with whom he had worked
in the past, to design a living space tailored to his
needs and ambitions.

While both architect and client shared a
preference for restrained, minimalist spaces, they
also admired the period detailing that had survived
in the house, particularly on the ground floor. This
included ornate stone fireplaces dating back to the
1860s and elaborate ceiling mouldings. 'It's rare
to have this level of period detail in such a well-
preserved condition,' said King. 'Even though I do
generally shun decoration, when I saw this place I
thought it was really beautiful and that every effort
should be made to preserve it.'

Period features were retained and restored, and
the pine floorboards stripped back in the ground-
floor sitting room. The walls were painted a crisp
white, which allows the detailing of the cornices and
mouldings to shine through. In terms of layout and
structure, King planned a number of key changes.
A bedroom towards the rear of the ground floor
was redesigned as a kitchen and dining area. Below,
the old kitchen was replaced by a new master suite,
which offers a very direct sense of connection with
the leafy garden outside.

53

DESIGN INGREDIENTS

· Connection with the outdoors

· Emphasis on light and space

· Grand gestures

· Intricate detailing

· Period elements

[1] MIRROR GLASS The use of mirror glass is a highly effective way to bounce natural light through a space, and also forms a feature in itself. Here, the large fitted period mirrors over the original fireplaces and between the floor-to-ceiling windows add another dimension to the room, increasing the impression of the size of the space and suggesting an enhanced sense of scale and openness.

[2] ACCENT COLOURS The white walls and stripped, bleached floorboards create a restrained and neutral backdrop against which splashes of colour can shine. Printed cushions provide bold accents of colour, as does Fares's collection of Australian aboriginal art. Even modest touches of pattern make a significant impact in this minimalist context.

[3] ZONING SOLUTIONS The sitting room is a generously proportioned space, enhanced by its high ceilings and intricate mouldings that imbue the room with a sense of grandeur. The area has been broken down into more manageable and intimate zones largely through the arrangement of the furniture and rugs. The L-shaped sofa is from B&B Italia, as are the armchairs, and the coffee table is by Eero Saarinen for Knoll. At one end, the room flows through into a kitchen via period double doors in timber and etched glass.

[4] GRAND MOMENTS The original period detailing draws the eye to certain areas of the duplex. This is particularly true of the pair of exuberant carved stone fireplaces in the sitting room. They are focal points and stand out against the less elaborate materials elsewhere and the neutral colour scheme throughout.

CUSTOM KITCHEN

The kitchen is positioned opposite a sequence of tall windows overlooking the back garden. The guiding principle behind its design was that it should recede into the more structural elements of the room overall, in order to allow plenty of space for circulation and for a dining area. The refrigerator has been slotted into an existing niche in one wall and storage units and a long counter have been pushed into another wall. An island adds a contemporary element and doubles as a breakfast bar.

Tropical Living

DESIGNER	STUDIO ARTHUR CASAS
COMPLETED	2005
LOCATION	GUARUJÁ, BRAZIL

TUCKED AWAY IN THE tropical greenery of Brazil's Atlantic Forest, not far from the coast, this seductive getaway was intended to connect with nature and the verdant surroundings. The house was designed by Brazilian architect <u>Arthur Casas</u> for himself and his family as a welcoming retreat, located about two hours' drive from São Paulo. The open-plan, double-height living area at the heart of the building enjoys a direct and extraordinarily intimate relationship with the jungle to either side.

'I have always wanted a house in the middle of the forest – a place where I can recharge,' said Arthur Casas. 'There's a balance between the generosity of the living spaces and the surroundings that gives this sense of meditative calm and intimacy.'

Certainly, the atmosphere that Casas created here is restful, with a powerful synergy between interior and exterior spaces. The house is centred on an open-plan living space, which features vast banks of sliding glass doors on both sides. When these doors are moved back, this part of the house is transformed into an open pavilion, where the greenery seems to become part of the interior. Even when the doors are closed, the space retains a dynamic transparency that brings the building alive via its direct relationship with nature.

The open-plan area is, of course, the hub of the home, around which other spaces and functions revolve. A suspended fireplace draws the eye, and custom-designed sofas and vintage pieces are arranged around it, all sitting upon a large rug on the timber floor. The outline of this rug helps to suggest the notion of a room within a room, with the spaces around its edges left free for circulation. An entrance terrace lies to one side of this living zone and a large deck to the other – devoted to fresh air living – complete with a custom-made outdoor dining table and a Japanese-style barbecue.

A ground-floor studio and a guest bedroom sit within one wing of the house and the kitchen and service spaces within the other; two further bedrooms and a home theatre are located on an upper storey on either side of the double-height hub, with a glass bridge connecting these two distinct zones. Interior and exterior finishes are largely in Cumaru timber, a strong native teak that can survive the tropical conditions and provides an all-pervasive sense of organic warmth and texture.

DESIGN INGREDIENTS

· Context

· Framing the views

· Informal styling

· Inside and outside living

· Simple symmetry

[1] PENDANT FIREPLACE

Traditionally, fireplaces and hearths offer a place around which to gather and to enjoy company in the home, as well as a practical source of warmth. In contemporary interiors, warmth is usually supplied by other sources of heating, too, but the fireplace often remains an important focal point for the design of a sitting room in particular, and it has a strong emotional and poetic resonance. Here, the pendant fireplace is centrally positioned. Its sculptural modern form contrasts with the linear quality and purity of the architecture.

[2] GLASS BRIDGE
Transparency is a key element in the space as a whole, allowing the eye to pass through the centre of the house and connect with the tropical greenery all around. A bridge was required to connect the upper storey rooms to either side of the double-height living area, but a solid bridge would have compromised the theme of transparency. The architect decided, therefore, to use glass balustrades, which preserve the see-through quality of the space and provide a safe structural solution to securing the bridge.

[3] STAIRWAY SOLUTIONS

The stairway is often a design statement in itself, full of drama and resonance. Here, the focus is on creating an open, transparent space that connects with the natural surroundings, so the staircase is given a very different treatment. A series of cantilevered timber steps climbs one wall, with a discreet banister alongside. This minimal but beautifully engineered dark wood stair assumes a subtle presence. At the same time, it has an abstract and geometric artistry to it, reminiscent of an installation by US sculptor Donald Judd.

[4] FURNITURE COMBINATIONS

Casas is a successful furniture designer as well as an architect, and he designed the sofas and the coffee table, made with reclaimed cinnamon wood. These made-to-order elements add personality to the space, but flea market finds and vintage pieces come into the mix too, adding layers of character and contrasting textures. One of Casas's favourite pieces is the vintage 1970s leather armchair and footstool, designed for New Zealand furniture company Forma by Martin Eisler.

DINING OPTIONS

A good deal of entertaining at the house happens outside on the terrace, which has a tailor-made dining table and a barbecue grill of its own. However, there is also an indoor dining area to one corner of the central, open-plan living area. Here, there is another custom dining table, designed by Casas and made with composite stone set on an aluminium base; the table also extends into the adjoining kitchen where it hosts the cooktop. The arrangement allows for easy conversation between the kitchen and both dining zones.

Ocean House

DESIGNERS	GORLIN ARCHITECTS/DAVID SCOTT INTERIORS
COMPLETED	2008
LOCATION	SOUTHAMPTON, NEW YORK, USA

THIS STRIKING OCEAN-FRONT HOUSE enjoys views of both the Atlantic and – in the opposite direction – the calmer waters of a tidal bay. Sitting on a narrow ribbon of land, the house makes the most of this dual aspect by placing the most important rooms on the upper storey. This allows for an open vista over the top of the dunes, while the arrangement of the public rooms on this floor also draws the best of the light into the social spaces. A roof deck on top of the building makes for a powerful viewing platform.

The house is a collaboration between architect Alexander Gorlin and interior designer David Scott. They were approached to create a new weekend home and summer retreat for a client based in New York. For many years the family had owned a 1970s house on the same site, but eventually decided to replace it with a more contemporary home.

One key issue was how to maximize the views and the relationship of the house with the beach and the ocean, while taking into account the undulating dunes at the front of the site. The solution was an 'upside-down' floor plan, which positions all of the main living spaces – plus the master suite – on the upper level of the building. Banks of glass not only connect with the vista but also feed out onto an elevated terrace and pool area at the front of the house, which offer a strong sense of connection with the surroundings. Additional bedrooms, a media room and service spaces are located on the lower level of the house.

The main living area is arranged in an open-plan formation, with an easy flow through to the pool terrace alongside. A custom fireplace helps to divide the seating and dining areas, while the kitchen nearby features hatches with sliding screens. These allow the kitchen to be connected to the living area or sectioned off as required. A large skylight above the seating zone introduces natural light.

The interiors by David Scott present a calming palette of soft blues and sandy tones that sit well with the character of a beach house. 'I wanted the architecture and furnishings to be integrated, so I made sure to use warm-coloured materials and high-quality pieces with graceful lines to counter the sharp angles of the building,' said Scott. 'The more organic additions to the design – textiles, rugs and accessories inspired by sea, glass and driftwood – bring out the softer side of the minimalist interiors.'

DESIGN INGREDIENTS

· Harmony inside and out

· Maximizing the ocean vista

· Organic textures

· Public spaces on the upper level

· Rhythm

[1] DOUBLE-SIDED FIREPLACE

The buff-coloured limestone fireplace forms a focal point in the living room, and also helps to separate the seating area from the dining zone beyond. Its double-sided design provides comfort and warmth for both spaces at the same time. 'The fireplace divides the space but being open to both sides it becomes rather like the house itself, which has views in both directions,' said Alexander Gorlin. The aluminium and oak dining table is by New York-based John Houshmand while the upholstered dining chairs are by US design firm Holly Hunt.

[2] FEATURE SKYLIGHT

The large skylight enhances the rich quality of natural light within the main living area of the house. The design of this ceiling aperture also reinforces the outline of the seating zone below, which is delineated by the custom-designed, hand-made rug from New York-based Carini Lang, as well as by the careful positioning of the furniture. The pair of sofas are from a collection by Hutton Home and upholstered in a Holly Hunt fabric, whereas the club chairs are by New York designer Roman Thomas.

[3] MATERIAL PALETTE The sandy tones of the upholstery directly echo those of the beach and the dunes as well as the Bulgarian limestone in which the fireplace is clad. These colours sit well with the pale blue ocean hues of the silk and wool rug and the accent blues of the cushions and artworks. The floors are laid with Afromosia, which is a type of African teak.

[4] INSIDE–OUTSIDE SYNERGY In a house set at such a good vantage point over the beach, in an environment full of natural beauty, a strong inside–outside relationship is vital. Here, in the main living space, there is direct access out to the terrace via a wall of glass doors, while the sequence of floor-to-ceiling glazing frames the panoramic ocean view.

ROOF DECK

The roof of the building has been utilized fully to create not only a viewing platform looking out over the ocean, but also a space that doubles as an additional outdoor room. Seating is arranged around the monolithic chimney that emerges from the floor below and provides the opportunity to create a fully functioning exterior fireplace. An outdoor kitchenette has also been built on the roof, making for easy entertaining during long summer evenings. The roof terrace furniture is from outdoor furniture specialists Walters Wicker.

Woodland Living

DESIGNER	KRAUS SCHOENBERG ARCHITECTS
COMPLETED	2007
LOCATION	HAMBURG, GERMANY

SITUATED ON THE LEAFY edges of Hamburg, Haus W is an award-winning eco-friendly new home designed for Henning and Ana Wachsmuth and their two children. The modestly scaled two-storey house is cut into the garden site, surrounded by mature trees, with both levels designed around a central, double-height atrium that becomes the focal point of the building. In this way, the house offers a powerful sense of connection with its green surroundings.

Henning and Ana Wachsmuth, who run an IT recruitment company, share a strong interest in architecture and design and had long dreamed of building a home for themselves. They lived in an apartment in Hamburg for many years before they began hunting for a suitable site to build their family home. Eventually they came across a tranquil spot on the edge of the city.

The clients turned to Anglo-German practice Kraus Schoenberg Architects to design the building, working to a relatively limited budget. Height restrictions placed upon the site presented another challenge, and it required some imaginative thinking to create a two-storey house. Kraus Schoenberg's solution was to sink the entire building partially into the ground – to allow for two full levels – with the main, open-plan living zone on the lower level and the bedrooms above.

The lower storey was built with a concrete base forming a plinth, which supports the rest of the house above, and a series of supporting steel columns. The upper level was put together quickly on site using a system of prefabricated, super-insulated timber panels. Between the concrete base and the timber panels runs a generous band of glass, which opens up the interiors to the gardens.

On the inside, the house is arranged around the double-height atrium, with the stairs slotted in behind a tall bookcase that spans the two levels of the room. Internal windows from the bedrooms above and also the bathroom look down into the atrium and connect with the floor below. The careful positioning of these windows, complemented by the shifting floor levels of the upper storey, allows for privacy while still permitting natural light to circulate throughout the house. At the same time the atrium and its windows help to create a more communal and informal spirit within the family home.

DESIGN INGREDIENTS

· Art and culture

· Eco-friendly building methods and materials

· Juxtaposition of old and new

· Vertical accents

· Zoning

[1] HIGH LIBRARY The design of the entire house revolves around the double-height living space, which lends structure and clarity to the interiors. The introduction of a floor-to-ceiling library wall – with the staircase discreetly built in behind it – creates a functional bank of storage, but naturally a home library is much more than a practical solution. The wall of books not only effortlessly introduces colour, texture and character, but also reveals much about the interests and passions of the owners.

[2] INTERNAL WINDOWS The use of internal windows is an effective way of circulating light through a building. At the same time these indoor apertures serve other purposes, providing a sense of connection between spaces and avoiding a more typical cellular and introspective style of home, in which living spaces are isolated and cut off from one another. The internal windows create an informal and sociable environment, and also offer a greater perception of space and openness in a smaller scale house.

PREFABRICATED LIVING

Prefabrication continues to be an effective way of building homes quickly and cheaply. Here, the structural timber panels used to create the upper level were installed rapidly, and the construction period for the entire house lasted only four months. Prefabrication is also seen as an eco-friendly method of construction, because it cuts down on time spent on site and on the transportation of people and materials. Haus W features top of the range insulation and glazing, as well as a ground source heat pump, which mean year-round low energy bills for the owners.

[3] INDUSTRIAL CHIC
The kitchen has been designed with a simple aesthetic, reminiscent of commercial kitchens and industrial spaces. The various elements of the kitchen have been stripped back to create a vivid structural framework, with some pieces sitting on wheels (including the sofas and chairs nearby) so they can be moved around easily, thereby keeping the composition adaptable. The kitchen island and the matching storage unit are designed by bulthaup, whereas the stools and breakfast table are by German designer Silvio Rohrmoser.

[4] ART TREASURES
The two oil paintings hanging on the floating wall above the kitchen island are 18th-century portraits from Henning Wachsmuth's family. Their presence is quite unexpected in a house of such modern design. The positioning of these family heirlooms creates an intriguing juxtaposition between old and new. At the same time, the historic artworks add a whole new layer of character, identity and interest to the interior spaces and stand out all the more against the well-illuminated and crisp white walls of the living space.

Hamptons Modern

DESIGNERS	BATES MASI + ARCHITECTS/ DANIELLE ROBERTS INTERIORS
COMPLETED	2009
LOCATION	AMAGANSETT, NEW YORK, USA

THIS HOUSE IN THE HAMPTONS by <u>Bates Masi + Architects</u> is all about subtle surprises and challenging expectation. The architects took their inspiration, in part, from their clients' collection of contemporary art, and a range of pieces has been integrated into the interiors. The key room in the house is the double-height living room, with soaring ceilings and a gallery-like quality, combined with a careful choice of furniture and a flood of natural light.

In the beginning, Bates Masi's clients were looking to build a traditional Hamptons retreat. Yet their art collection suggested an experimental and free-thinking approach, which ultimately helped to inspire the design of a more adventurous weekend and summer escape.

On the one hand, the house needed to accommodate the collection, including a number of large-scale works by artists such as Vik Muniz and Cindy Wright. On the other hand, a key theme of many of the pieces of art is the idea of illusion and of exploring the unexpected. The architects embraced this theme in a number of ways, particularly in their unusual choice of materials. At first glance, the outward appearance of the house suggests a shingle-clad home with a crisp, contemporary outline. Yet the 'shingles' on the lower level are actually lattices of simple wooden survey stakes, or pickets, arranged horizontally. The chimney stack at one end appears heavy and solid, but was constructed with light and slim cement panels.

The textural and material surprises continue within the house. The lower portion of the central staircase features a wall composed of thousands of white shells encased in glass. The reflective steel fire surround in the living room is, in fact, a custom-made composition of shiny metal tags. These are features that contribute fresh layers of texture and meaning, adding to the 'narrative' of the building. The living room is a multifunctional space, with a comfortable seating area arranged around the fireplace plus a dining zone, positioned close to the adjoining kitchen, which sits within a single-storey spur at one side of the house. Natural light is drawn from multiple directions: high and low window openings, plus sliding glass doors to one side that lead to a sheltered veranda, which becomes an outdoor room in the summer.

DESIGN INGREDIENTS

· Contrast of textures

· Idiosyncratic collection of art

· Outdoor rooms

· Reflective surfaces

· Unexpected twists

[1] ARTWORK DISPLAY Key artworks have been woven into the design of the interiors, including pieces on the staircase and in the main living room. The two large works in this room are *The Poppy Field at Argenteuil, after Claude Monet* (2005, below) by Vik Muniz and *Baconcube 4* (2006) by Cindy Wright. 'The home was designed to display the clients' collection as well as conduct a dialogue with the type of art that is collected,' said architect Paul Masi. '[Their] art was unique because it had deeper meaning. I really liked that multilayered concept.'

[2] REFLECTIVE FIREPLACE The fireplace is a traditional feature for a sitting room and retains a powerful allure. Here, the fireplace becomes a dramatic feature in itself, framed by a reflective wall made up of segments of shining steel. At closer inspection the segments reveal themselves to be military-style dog tags, thus defying expectations and introducing an unexpected reference point.

[3] CONTRASTING TEXTURES

Furnishings were selected by <u>Danielle Roberts</u>, and they include an irregular timber coffee table by David Stine Woodworking, a custom sofa and a sculptural plywood chair. They sit on a soft textured rug upon Brazilian walnut floorboards. Together, these various and contrasting textures add up to a richly layered combination that is stimulating both to the touch and to the eye. The steel hearth forms an axis point for the arrangement of the furniture within the seating zone at this end of the space.

[4] INSIDE–OUTSIDE

Sliding glass doors to one side of the living room connect to the veranda outside. This is a fully furnished outdoor room, complete with a dining area and lounge seating. The veranda also helps frame the view of the gardens, pool and surrounding woodland. The swimming pool, positioned just beyond the veranda, was a particular request of the owners, one of whom used to be a competitive swimmer. The three-legged CH07 plywood chair is a classic design from the 1960s by Hans J. Wegner, produced by Carl Hansen & Son.

KITCHEN PLAN

Although open-plan living has become a staple of contemporary homes, the inclusion of a kitchen within one fluid living space can create some practical issues. There is potential visual and sensory 'overflow' between two areas: one that needs to be highly functional and one that is dedicated to relaxation and escape. Here, Bates Masi positioned the kitchen within an interconnected space to one side of the main living area, which projects outwards from the side of the building. The kitchen 'wing' still allows for easy circulation yet creates a subtle degree of separation. 'It does create a range of spatial experiences,' said Masi, 'with low ceilings in the kitchen and high [ones] in the entertaining areas.'

Coastal Contemporary

DESIGNER	NORD ARCHITECTURE
COMPLETED	2011
LOCATION	DUNGENESS, KENT, UK

INSPIRED BY THE EXAMPLE of local fishermen's huts and cabins, Shingle House in Dungeness is a considered and contemporary response to a unique setting and context. The house is an assembly of interconnected spaces, which echo the former buildings on the site and respond to the powerful views of the sea and the vast shingle beach. The interiors have an endearing warmth and an inbuilt sense of character, making Shingle House a perfect ambassador for thoughtful modern design.

Living Architecture is an organization founded by Swiss philosopher and writer Alain de Botton with the aim of promoting the best of modern architecture and design. The organization runs a growing collection of holiday homes around the United Kingdom, created by leading architects such as Peter Zumthor and Michael Hopkins. One of the many successful projects to date is Shingle House on the Kent coast, designed by Nord Architecture.

Dungeness provides a unique and fascinating setting. This particular stretch of headland features

one of the largest shingle beaches in the world. An English desert, it is a place of great character and natural beauty, but it is also the site of a nuclear power station. Dungeness has long attracted the attention of writers, artists and architects, including writer and film maker Derek Jarman, who are drawn to the special personality of the area.

Development at Dungeness is tightly controlled and the majority of the houses here are modest, low-slung buildings, protected by coats of black pine tar. Some have been updated or rebuilt with contemporary designs, as has Shingle House. The new house replaces a ramshackle fisherman's cabin, workshop, garage and smokehouse. Echoes of these different forms remain within the structure of the building.

The main body of the house holds the sitting room, four bedrooms and a loft-style lounge over two storeys. The interiors have been carefully thought through, combining Shaker-style simplicity, organic textures and soft notes of colour within an informal but sophisticated coastal aesthetic.

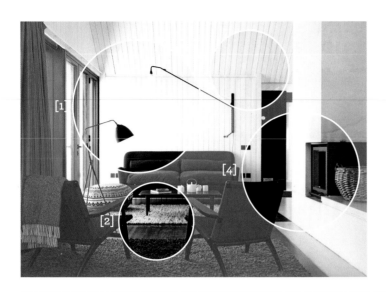

DESIGN INGREDIENTS

· Accents of colour

· Asymmetrical plan

· Beach house aesthetic

· In harmony with the surroundings

· Light and bright

[1] **STATEMENT LIGHTING** The swivelling Potence wall light fitted above the sofa is by French designer Jean Prouvé, originally designed for his Maison Tropique of 1950, and it is a classic mid-century design. The two Lean floor lamps by Swedish firm Orsjö Belysning are contemporary designs with a retro feel. Together, these sculptural statement lights add a new dimension to the space and also provide task lighting that allows for the creation of different moods within the seating area.

[2] **WARM COLOURS** The floors in the sitting room and kitchen are made of durable purpleheart timber. As the name suggests, this rich wood has a subtle vein of purple colouring, which adds warmth to the room and echoes the purple viper's-bugloss that flowers in abundance on the shingle beach in August. Concrete was used for the nearby entrance hall, stairs and chimney, thereby creating a strong contrast between organic and more industrial materials.

[3] SHAKER SIMPLICITY The clapboard timber walls and ceilings, painted white throughout, help to unify the different spaces and keep the interiors light and bright. The crafted simplicity of the walls, which feature integrated timber pegs in certain parts of the house, recalls the honest, organic craftsmanship of Shaker furniture and farmhouses. The concrete staircase and white interiors also offer a vivid contrast to the tarred black shingles used for the exteriors.

[4] SOPHISTICATED COMFORT With a comfortable, sink-in sofa, heavily textured rugs and a warm, welcoming fireplace, the sitting room of Shingle House offers a seductive degree of comfort and visual warmth. Although the architectural concept is strong and individual, a lot of thought has been given to the interiors and how visitors will utilize and enjoy the spaces throughout the seasons. Using a contrasting material palette of concrete and timber, Nord Architecture has created a house that shows that modernity and comfort are not mutually exclusive.

BEACH HOUSES

The traditional aesthetic of the beach house is one of informality and relative playfulness, compared to everyday residences. This also applies to more contemporary examples of the genre, such as Shingle House, which has a refreshing air of freedom tied to a sense of place. Although the modest mezzanine landing level offers additional living space, it is all about the vista. The large picture window is positioned low down, where the entrance to the net loft used to be, in order to maximize the view across the windswept beach and horizon.

Furniture House

DESIGNERS	SHIGERU BAN/SHAMIR SHAH
COMPLETED	2006
LOCATION	SAGAPONACK, NEW YORK, USA

SURROUNDED BY WOODLAND in a quiet enclave of Long Island, the Furniture House is a collaboration between innovative Japanese architect <u>Shigeru Ban</u> and New York-based designer <u>Shamir Shah</u>. The house employs a series of eighty maple-fronted cupboards to help organize the building and support the roof. Shah added another layer of interest to the interiors with a carefully assembled collection of furniture, art and installations.

Shigeru Ban is internationally renowned for his innovative use of materials and imaginative approach to the structure and engineering of his buildings. Some of his most experimental house projects have been built using structural cardboard tubes and semi-transparent polycarbonate walls. This property, situated among the tranquil woodlands of Sagaponack, is one of a sequence of Furniture Houses, which utilize furniture – specifically timber-fronted cupboards – as a key structural element. The heavy-duty cupboards not only provide storage but also form the partition walls.

The house is arranged in a U-shaped formation wrapped around a large swimming pool, with a processional entrance zone consisting of a long covered walkway. It is predominantly a single-storey dwelling, with the exception of a basement containing a studio and service spaces. The property was acquired from developers by an admirer of Ban's work, who was drawn to the open spaces within and the sense of connection to the surroundings. When the building was bought, it was incomplete in parts and the interior walls were dominated by the maple cupboard surfaces, which made it a challenge to incorporate the owner's art collection effectively.

Shamir Shah was commissioned to complete the interiors and to integrate a number of key works of art. Here, mid-century furniture mixes with contemporary pieces and vintage finds, such as the large Moroccan Berber rug.

DESIGN INGREDIENTS

· Contrasting timbers

· Innovative structure

· Integrated artworks

· Neutral palette

· Scandinavian influence

[1] CONTRASTING TEXTURES Shamir Shah's introduction of carpeting, rugs and softer furnishings has brought a fresh layer of texture to the house, which softens the architectural precision of the clean lines and the large expanses of maple-fronted cupboards. Furniture choices include a comfortable sofa designed by Edward Wormley and a pair of 1940s armchairs. The Berber rug sitting upon the flagstone floor introduces a warm textural presence underfoot. The soft textures contrast with the hard look of the side table by San Juan Ventures, based in Chicago.

[2] ART INSTALLATIONS Shah was careful to maintain the fluidity of the layout when hanging the art collection. A butterfly installation by US artist Paul Villinski, made from recycled beer cans, occupies one wall of the sitting room, introducing both texture and an abstract focal point. Large artworks also feature in other parts of the house, standing out against the maple cupboards. They include two floor-to-ceiling pieces by US artist Nathaniel Price, which hang side by side in the sitting room. They are complemented by a soothing, calm and neutral palette throughout.

[3] SKYLIGHTS A large skylight above the entrance hallway, alongside the sitting room, introduces an alternative and indirect source of natural light, which complements the sunlight that filters through the windows. When natural light is drawn in from different directions, heights and sources, it makes for a far more inviting home environment, because these various layers of light reduce any reliance on artificial lighting. Indirect sources of light are kinder to artworks, and here a large painting by Hawaiian artist Weston Teruya hangs above a tailor-made bench by Shah. The beams of the skylight echo the stripes of the rug.

[4] MID-CENTURY FURNITURE Furniture of the 1950s and 1960s remains much in demand and is represented in the Furniture House by Hans J. Wegner's endearing Papa Bear armchair (above) and Arne Jacobsen's classic Egg chair. Such pieces have assumed the status of design icons, beloved for their sculptural qualities, playful character, warm materials and ergonomic curves as well as for their emblematic power as expressions of sophisticated post-war modernity. Prototypes and original mid-century furniture are highly collectable, while many designs of the period have never gone out of production or have been reissued in recent years.

FIREPLACE AND HEARTH

The large corner fireplace, in painted brickwork, is one of the few structural elements in the house that is not made of timber. The simple design of the fireplace and hearth, with its combined use of brick and stone, is an interesting mix of Japanese-inspired purity and Scandinavian-influenced organic warmth. When lit, the fire introduces both literal and metaphorical warmth into the home. 'The house could have been cold but instead it is now warm, inviting and elegant,' said the owner.

Rural Idyll

DESIGNER   LARSON AND PAUL ARCHITECTS

COMPLETED   2006

LOCATION   DUTCHESS COUNTY, NEW YORK, USA

IT MAY BE A MODESTLY SCALED HOUSE, but Douglas and Victoria Larson's country home is rich in charm. Although the period farmhouse has only two bedrooms, it was given a touch of grandeur during the 19th century when a neoclassical porch with Doric columns was added to the building. Architect Douglas Larson has updated the house in contemporary style, while seeking to preserve the unique character of this small but perfectly formed rural retreat.

Initially, Larson was hunting for a suitable piece of land in upstate New York on which to build a new house from scratch. However, when nothing turned up at a reasonable price, he started to look for a worn-out house that he could update and transform into a peaceful country retreat for himself, his wife, Victoria, and their son. Eventually he stumbled across a semi-derelict farmhouse in Dutchess County.

The property had certainly seen better days, and Larson started by clearing the house and garden of many years' worth of accumulated junk and by stripping away some of the rotten woodwork. He then began to formulate plans for the post-and-beam building, which comprised a lower part that had been built in the 18th century and a taller section with a porch that had been added later. The plans were substantial and involved a number of alterations to the structure and layout. In the lower section, Larson removed most of the ceilings and opened up the space to create an open-plan family domain devoted to the kitchen and an eating area, with room enough for a comfortable sofa to one side. The gable end of the living area was replaced by a wall of windows, with sliding glass doors leading out to a substantial raised deck, facing north towards the mountains.

In the 19th-century section of the house, Larson removed a partition wall downstairs to create a single spacious living and dining room, arranged around the fireplace and the stairway to one side. Furnishings include a number of classic mid-century pieces with vibrant touches of colour and pattern that stand out against the white walls throughout. 'You start with a light background and then bring in your pieces of furniture – antique or modern – and they will work well with that neutral background,' said Larson. 'It's more of a gallery-like approach, which I prefer to a more decorated approach where everything matches.'

· Dramatic juxtapositions

· *Genius loci*

· High roof line

· Multipurpose living areas

· Outside rooms

[1] HOME HUB The lower portion of the house has been made into a multipurpose pavilion, with high ceilings and a wealth of natural light. The space is just large enough to accommodate a kitchen – built using adapted units from Ikea – as well as a long dining table and a sofa against one wall. The pavilion is the hub of family life and also offers an immediate connection with the deck in front of the house and the large garden beyond. The adjustable Leonardo dining table is a 1940s design by Achille Castiglioni, produced by Zanotta.

[2] EXPOSED HISTORY

The exposed timber beams in all parts of the house – including the kitchen and living room – are reminders of the original structure and history of the farmhouse. They carry with them a rich patina and texture, thus creating a dramatic juxtaposition with the smooth surfaces of the freshly finished walls, and the colours and textures of the more contemporary elements and materials. This considered contrast between old and new is highly effective throughout the interior, across both levels of the building.

[3] DYNAMIC PATTERN Douglas and Victoria have a love of mid-century Scandinavian design, including the fabrics of legendary designer Josef Frank. His fabric is used on the sofa in the kitchen and a Frank pattern appears on the headboard in the master bedroom. Frank created the sofa fabric, titled Vegetable Tree, for Stockholm-based company Svenskt Tenn when he was living in New York between 1941 and 1946. It was part of a series of organic, vibrant designs. Here, the colourful elements of the pattern stand out against the neutral surroundings.

OUTDOOR ROOMS

For the owners of this country house, the importance of being able to enjoy meaningful connections with the surroundings was paramount. Larson created two outdoor rooms that reinforce the building's relationship with its rural setting. One is arranged on the generous deck in front of the pavilion and the other sits upon the covered porch. The outdoor furniture on the deck is by Restoration Furniture, and the colourful armchairs on the porch are modern versions of the classic Adirondack chair.

[4] SOARING CEILINGS By removing the original ceiling and the attic space above the kitchen pavilion, Larson created a high roof line, which has a profound impact on the perception of the space. There may be no practical benefit in terms of floor area, but there is a dramatic difference in terms of volume and the feeling of a more generous, open and liberated space. The little internal window at high level looks down from the small bedroom belonging to the Larsons' son.

Mission House

DESIGNER	ADAM RICHARDS ARCHITECTS
COMPLETED	2011
LOCATION	PLAISTOW, WEST SUSSEX, UK

THIS STRIKING NEW RESIDENCE is built on the site of a converted chapel – or mission hall – on the edge of a quiet village in West Sussex. The original chapel was undermined by subsidence, but the owners managed to turn the disaster into an opportunity and commissioned a contemporary two-storey building in its place. The main living spaces are arranged on the upper level, in order to make the most of the views across the open countryside, while custom-made storage and shelving units help to partition this free-flowing space into distinct zones according to their functions.

The large oak tree that sits next to Mission House may be beautiful but it has been problematic. It was the roots of this majestic oak that caused the subsidence of the late Victorian chapel and adjoining cottage, owned by Dean Wheeler and Nick Taylor. However, a settlement from their insurers – together with the proceeds from the sale of their former apartment in London – gave them just enough money to build a replacement house on the same site.

Wheeler and Taylor commissioned architect Adam Richards to design the new Mission House. Its distinctive shape and formation echo the original combination of the single-level chapel and cottage, but the planning authorities granted permission to create a two-storey building, which significantly increased the available floor area. The new house sits upon a floating foundation, or raft, supported by a series of pilings screwed into the ground, which allows for any future ground movement. One portion of the building is rounded, with a shape reminiscent of a church nave or the bow of a ship; this part of the house has been re-clad in tiles reclaimed from the original chapel. The other interconnected portion of the house is more linear in form.

The entrance hallway and bedrooms are positioned on the lower floor, while a sweeping spiral staircase inhabits the rounded 'bow' of the building. The upper level is essentially one large, open-plan living space with big windows overlooking the fields nearby. 'We do have this great vantage point for the views,' said Wheeler, 'and we really make the most of the light and the landscape. We can see the weather pouring in and hear the barn owls hooting in the trees at night. We are right in the middle of it all.'

DESIGN INGREDIENTS

· Contrast between linear and rounded forms

· Main living spaces on upper level

· Picture windows

· Storage solutions

· Warm timbers

[1] PENDANT LIGHTING

Pendant lights help to define a particular zone within an open-plan space, and also provide valuable task and mood lighting. Here, a pair of large pendant lights (the Caravaggio model from Lightyears in Denmark) frame the dining table below and add another layer of interest to the interiors. The dining table is from the General Trading Company in London while the antique chairs were bought in Petworth in West Sussex. The landscape painting is by Canadian artist Peter Burega.

[2] STORAGE SOLUTIONS

Adam Richards designed two large storage and shelving units for the main living area that partition off the kitchen and study. In addition to these two tailor-made pieces, the design of the house subtly incorporates a large amount of built-in storage. The low units behind the dining table continue a sequence of custom-made cupboards that starts at the top of the staircase. Painted a crisp white, like the surrounding walls, they appear to recess into the space as a whole, thereby disguising their purpose.

[3] STRUCTURAL FURNITURE Richards specially designed two very large pieces of furniture for the upper storey of Mission House. Crafted in walnut, these tall units echo the proportions of the slice of space that they inhabit but on a rather smaller scale. They do not touch the ceiling or the side walls, thereby allowing people to move around them. These tailor-made pieces help to separate the study and kitchen from the rest of the open-plan living space, lending structure and order, but without the need for solid or more formal partitioning.

[4] STATEMENT STAIRCASE

A staircase is more than a functional and structural element; it can also be a dynamic centrepiece in itself. Many Victorian and Georgian residences placed the staircase at the heart of the house, and contemporary architects and designers have often revisited the notion of the statement staircase, as seen in Richards's custom-made curving design. The banister is made of medium-density fibreboard (MDF) and the stair treads are oak.

UPPER LEVEL

The idea of a *piano nobile* is rooted in classical and neoclassical architecture, in which the main living spaces were on an upper level, in order to make the most of the views, with the ground floor dedicated to secondary spaces. This feature is being adopted by contemporary architects who are interested in breaking away from the Western convention of placing the bedrooms on the upper storey and making better use of the prime vantage points in the house to frame views.

21st-century Victorian

DESIGNERS	FOUND ASSOCIATES/ JAMIE THEAKSTON
COMPLETED	2012
LOCATION	LONDON, UK

A DRAMATIC OPEN-PLAN EXTENSION has added a whole new dimension to this elegant Victorian house in Chiswick, London. The contemporary addition offers an immediate sense of connection to the walled back garden and creates a fresh hub for family life, housing the kitchen, dining area and a relaxation zone within one generous and inviting space.

Television and radio host <u>Jamie Theakston</u> has a passion for design and has therefore become something of a serial renovator. This period house in west London is one of his most ambitious projects to date, involving the radical reinvention and updating of a five-bedroom property for himself, his wife, Sophie – a jewelry designer – and their two children.

Theakston was drawn to the double-fronted property by its elegance, proportion and scale, as well as by the generously sized rear garden. He turned to architect Richard Found of <u>Found Associates</u> to help him open up the house on the ground floor, thereby creating a more fluid and casual layout well suited to 21st-century living.

They kept as many original features as possible, including the tiled hallway and the original staircase at the centre of the villa. However, the most challenging aspect of the project was how to address two poorly designed extensions at the back of the building: a ballroom added in the 1930s and a garden room. Eventually, Theakston and Found decided to demolish both and create a substantial new addition, with a wall of glazing and sliding glass doors, thus establishing a strong relationship between the living spaces inside and the terrace and garden outside. 'Once we had taken the decision to put the extension on the back and to glaze the section towards the garden, everything else fell into place,' said Theakston. 'Although it is a modern extension of an old house, for me it really feels as though this is the way that the house was meant to be.'

· Flow

· Multifunctional and practical

· Old and new

· Pavilion style

· Seamless indoor
and outdoor living

[1] OPEN PLAN The open-plan structure of the extension offers a fluid and flexible space, which sits in contrast to many of the more traditionally modular rooms throughout the rest of the period house. There is ample space for the kitchen at one end and a seating zone at the other, thus creating a key area in which the entire family can come together. The L-shaped B&B Italia sofa offers contemporary comfort, while the period dining table and chairs provide a foil to the modern aesthetic and clean lines of the architecture.

[2] INSIDE–OUTSIDE A key factor in the decision to design and build the extension was to provide a more intimate and immediate sense of connection with the spacious rear garden, which has been restored and re-landscaped. There is now a seamless transition between the new extension at the back of the house and the adjoining terrace, as they share the same floor level. The terrace is used as an outdoor room in summer, offering another key family living space, while the walled garden provides a secure and inviting play zone for the children.

[3] LIGHT AND SPACE A long skylight was inserted above the junction between the main body of the house and the extension and subtly demarcates the boundary between old and new. Here, the original period brickwork provides a wall of texture that offers a vivid contrast to the crisp outline of the new pavilion. In addition to providing a connection with the garden, the huge expanse of glazing across the back of the house offers a generous quantity of natural light, and the open-plan design helps to pull the light through into other adjoining rooms.

[4] KITCHEN CONFIDENTIAL The design of the kitchen at the far end of the space allows for a good deal of flexibility and practicality. A bank of timber doors conceals storage areas, as well as the stove and fan, so that the entire process of preparation and cooking can be tucked away out of sight. At the same time, the elegant and sculptural marble island – with a discreet sunken sink – provides a surface for preparation that also doubles as a breakfast bar. The industrial-style factory lights over the island and dining table add character and personality to the space.

THROUGH ROOMS

In addition to creating the extension, Theakston and Found altered the layout of the downstairs rooms in the original part of the house. By knocking two rooms together, they created a double sitting room with a parquet floor and high ceiling. The room plays host to a number of pieces of both contemporary and mid-century furniture, which Theakston collected over the years. Two items that stand out are the 1970s chandelier by Italian designer Gaetano Sciolari and the leather sofa by Swiss company de Sede.

Colour

Urban Blues

DESIGNER	POPHAM DESIGN
COMPLETED	2012
LOCATION	MARRAKECH, MOROCCO

THIS 1930S BUNGALOW, in the Guéliz district of Marrakech, was reinvented as a fresh family home by US designers Samuel and Caitlin Dowe-Sandes of <u>Popham Design</u>. The couple created a house full of colour, partly inspired by the Moroccan coastline and the beach-side houses of Essaouira, which they often visit with their young daughter. The floors are laid with tiles from the Popham collection, all of which are hand-made in Marrakech.

Samuel and Caitlin Dowe-Sandes first settled in Marrakech in 2006 and initially based themselves in the city's bustling medina, or old town, in a converted town house. Their traditional riad was arranged around a central courtyard and updated with plenty of colour and pattern. However, daily life in the medina – where access through the narrow streets is restricted and it is usually a fair hike to get to your car – can be difficult and draining, especially with a young child. Consequently, the family swapped the medina for Guéliz – a leafy part of Marrakech laid out by the French in the early years of the 20th century and still known as the 'new town'. Here, the boulevards are broad and open and residents can park their cars outside their houses. It feels like a world away from the dusty dynamism of the busy medina.

The bungalow itself was built in the French style, but on a modest scale, with a central entrance hallway, two reception rooms to one side and two bedrooms to the other. At the back of the house was an internal courtyard, which the designers enclosed to create a spacious dining room adjoining the kitchen area.

Despite the modest size of the house, the proportions of the rooms are welcoming and the height of the ceilings makes the spaces feel more generous, particularly the two sitting rooms front and back, which are interconnected by folding French doors. Caitlin and Samuel agonized over colour choices and experimented with a number of custom paint blends before deciding on the final palette. For a number of years, they had shared a dream of owning a home on the coast and so decided to introduce the colours of the sea into the bungalow to remind them of the ocean. This is manifested in a range of fresh blues and blue-greens for the main living spaces and a bold blue and white horizontal stripe for the hallway.

DESIGN INGREDIENTS

· Art assemblies

· Eclectic choices

· Flow

· Geometric patterns

· Inspired by the coast

[1] PICTURE GROUPS The sitting room is enriched by collections of prints and paintings. These assemblies are loosely connected by colours and themes and together become an abstract artwork in themselves, with far greater resonance than a single picture on an open expanse of wall. The quartet of black and white bird images by Samuel's father, Roger Sandes, is particularly striking against the vibrant blue walls.

[2] FLOOR PATTERNS The two living spaces are drawn together by the striking tiling, which spans both rooms. These tiles were designed by Caitlin and Samuel Dowe-Sandes as part of a range of tiles made locally that combine traditional Moroccan influences with a contemporary aesthetic. The vivid and colourful geometrical patterns bring dynamism and energy to the space and they are also used elsewhere, as wall tiles in the kitchen and bathroom for example.

[3] HARMONIOUS PAIRINGS

The interconnected living rooms are painted in two very different custom shades of blue: a pale blue-green for the space at the front of the house, which has better natural light, and a darker teal blue for the room at the centre of the building, which lends itself more to evening use. The colours are quite distinct and therefore give identity to these two individual spaces. However, by choosing colours within a similar spectrum the designers have reinforced the complementary nature of the two rooms.

[4] WELCOME SURPRISES

There is a welcoming, playful quality to these interiors, reinforced by the use of colour, shape and pattern. Furniture choices are eclectic and include items sourced in Marrakech and others bought at auction in Paris. Within the mix are more incongruous touches that add to the delight of the spaces, such as the green parrot on the marble mantelpiece. These unexpected pieces are key elements within layered homes that have a real sense of personality and individuality.

LIGHT WELL SPACES

The traditional internal courtyard to the rear of the bungalow was covered with a large skylight to create an additional indoor living area, which serves as a family dining room and kitchen. However, the white-washed space retains a parallel purpose as a light well, introducing sunlight to the enclosed rear of the house, which lacks any windows to the exterior. Internal windows between this dining space and adjoining rooms help to circulate natural light around the house.

Citrus Green

DESIGNER	BURO KORAY DUMAN
COMPLETED	2012
LOCATION	MANHATTAN, NEW YORK, USA

SITUATED ON THE BORDERS of the Chinatown and SoHo districts of Manhattan, architect <u>Koray Duman</u>'s apartment is a tailored space lifted by a spine wall painted lime green. This sculptural, twisting form begins as a sequence of wardrobes in the bedroom and travels through the apartment into the open-plan living area, where it frames the space and introduces a vibrant citrus tone throughout. Its sinuous quality softens and enriches the entire apartment.

Born in Turkey, Duman has made New York City his home for many years. Having studied architecture in Ankara, he furthered his education in California before moving to Manhattan. He first owned an apartment in East Village, but wanted to move further downtown and finally came across a three-bedroom apartment on the fifth floor of a corner building dating from 1910. 'The bedrooms were very small and the window frames were smaller so it felt very dark, even though it's on a corner with light from two sides,' said Duman. 'It felt quite claustrophobic so I stripped everything out: floors, ceilings, windows, partition walls, everything. It was a blank space.'

The original brickwork exterior walls were left exposed in their raw state and treated with a white sealant. Duman introduced white oak floors throughout, which were treated with a white bleach that took away the orange-yellow tones of the timber and gave it a purer, fresher finish. The layout was ordered from scratch, with three bedrooms reduced down to one that has more open proportions and light pouring in from two tall windows. A custom-built shower room floats within this space, picked out in white tile, with only two large panes of glass forming a transparent enclosure for the shower jets.

The green wall begins here and extends into the main open-plan living area, enclosing a small powder room and utility spaces. This sinuous element defines the entry zone and continues onwards as a lowered ceiling unit, holding a film projector and sheltering a custom-made work station below. 'The lime wall holds all the storage in the apartment,' said Duman. 'But it also helps define the sitting area and softens the whole space, with its curving, twisting form. I like things to be minimal but I also think that the architecture should be more than a backdrop. The lime wall adds a lot and, of course, introduces colour.'

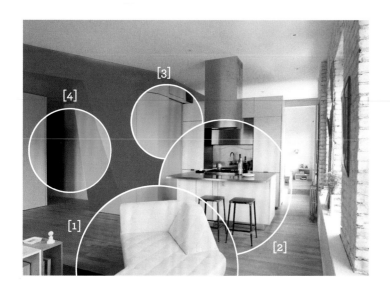

DESIGN INGREDIENTS

· Accent colour
· Asymmetry
· Cohesion
· Exposed brickwork
· Minimalism

[1] TWO-PART SOFA Duman was struggling to find a suitable sofa for the apartment, so decided to design his own with the help of interior designer Carol Egan. They collaborated on custom seating, which can be combined into one large unit or split into complementary twins. This design lends a degree of flexibility to the space and how it is used. The coffee table is from Design Within Reach.

[2] FLOATING KITCHEN In the centre of the floor plan sits the kitchen area, a custom design by Duman, using steel components and a ceiling-mounted extractor fabricated in nearby Chinatown. The units stop at three-quarter height, thereby allowing light to spill through from the bedroom beyond, which enhances the perception of space and volume. The kitchen island also functions as a dining table and breakfast bar.

FLOATING SHOWER

The shower 'room' to one side of the bedroom is another device that enhances the sense of open space and volume. Instead of creating a partitioned bathroom, Duman framed the shower and twin sinks in white tilework, while two panes of glass and a sunken shower floor prevent water spilling out into the bedroom. The transparency of the space creates a room within a room. Its design is reminiscent of that of a wet room, where every surface is waterproof and there is a slight angle to the tiling to direct the water towards the drain set into the floor.

[3] <u>STORAGE SOLUTIONS</u> In addition to framing the entrance hall, the citrus wall contains storage space, services and a guest toilet. The provision of such a generous amount of concealed storage, including in the bedroom, means that most of the daily clutter can be kept out of sight. This complements the minimalist purity of the space, together with its textures and detailing.

[4] <u>WORK STATION</u> A fitted desk with shelving is tucked underneath the citrus spine, anchored to the exposed brick wall to one side of the apartment. With cupboards to either side, framing the desk, it provides a useful home work station that is space efficient and does not intrude upon the rest of the living area.

Ladybird Red

DESIGNER	NEESON MURCUTT ARCHITECTS
COMPLETED	2009
LOCATION	SYDNEY, AUSTRALIA

ARCHITECTS NICHOLAS MURCUTT and Rachel Neeson designed this striking house in Sydney for a family of five. It sits on a plateau at the foot of a modest rock cliff, and the lower section of the house features an open-plan living area with a strong sense of connection to the garden plateau. The upper level holds four bedrooms and the main entrance, accessed via a bridge at the summit of the cliff. A vibrant shade of red is used prominently in the kitchen, standing out against the concrete and timber finishes.

Neeson Murcutt's clients purchased the site complete with a small cottage that they intended to replace. The location is an inviting and elevated spot upon the Woolwich peninsula, where the waters of Lane Cove River and the Parramatta River meet and flow into Sydney Harbour. 'We loved the site because of its privacy and the water views, as well as the north-west aspect, which gives us sunshine all day,' said the owners. Having spent some time living in the original cottage and getting to know their surroundings, the owners approached Neeson Murcutt with a detailed brief. They wanted a house that made the most of the connections to the gardens and the views, with a fluid relationship between indoor and outdoor living. In addition to a detailed specification, their sensory brief included a list of words, such as 'secluded', 'calm', 'retreat', 'modern', 'warm' and 'non-conformist'.

The house is effectively a combination of two interconnected rectangles, one floating upon the other. The upper volume, clad in timber, runs parallel to the cliff nearby and shelters outdoor rooms below its extended run. The lower pavilion pushes outwards towards the water, almost at right angles to the cliff. This lower storey, faced in concrete, serves as the hub for family life. The owners requested an open-plan space, with a kitchen and dining zone at one end and then a step down to a seating zone at the other. A sequence of sliding glass windows offers a free-flowing relationship with the gardens.

The wall of units in the custom kitchen is lacquered with a vivid ladybird red that contrasts with the concrete and is offset by other tones and textures. In select parts of the interiors, the same colour appears as a repeated motif for doors and cupboards; it is used extensively on the balcony of the entrance bridge.

DESIGN INGREDIENTS

· Concrete pavilion

· Distinct zones

· Easy flow between inside
  and outside

· Practical surfaces

· Warm accents

[1] BRIGHT RED ACCENTS

The reflective sheen of the lacquered paintwork on the ladybird red kitchen units adds to the intensity of the colour, which stands out dramatically against the neutral tones of the floor, ceiling and walls, as well as the bright white of the dining furniture nearby. This fiery shade of red warms the space, but here – as elsewhere in the house – it is used as a fulsome accent colour. In this way it never becomes overpowering. 'We landed on red,' said Neeson Murcutt's client, 'because it inspires positivity.'

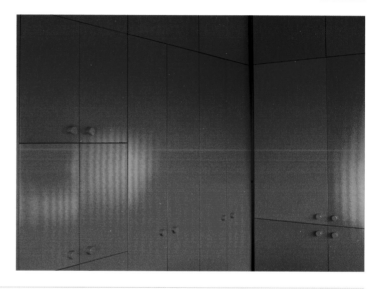

[2] SHIFTING LEVELS

A shift in floor level is an effective way of differentiating between various zones within an open-plan living space. Here, a single step is enough to create a degree of separation between the kitchen and dining area on the one hand and the seating zone on the other. At the same time, the strong relationship between inside and outside is maintained and promoted, with an easy transition between the two. The circular dining table is from Knoll and the classic Series 7™ white plywood chairs are by Arne Jacobsen.

[3] ISLAND CONTRAST The natural timber finish of the kitchen island helps to offset the use of such intense colour and provides an immediate point of contrast within the concrete pavilion. Vivid colour in an open living space can easily dominate, so it has been confined to one end of the room.

OUTDOOR LIVING

The upper level of the house projects over the plinth-like form of the lower level, thereby creating a perfect spot for an outdoor dining room underneath the overhang. This fresh air space benefits from a degree of shelter and shade, while the face of the cliff behind provides a dramatic natural background. The greens of the dining chairs complement the verdant lawn and foliage.

[4] TRACK LIGHTING
The simple track system fitted to the ceiling above the kitchen offers directional lighting, which is particularly useful in a functional space such as a kitchen where good lighting is essential. The lights can not only be moved along the track but also angled to the desired position and direction, serving as task lighting to delineate particular parts of the room as well as ambient lighting that illuminates the overall space at night. During the day, natural light floods in through the wall of windows to one side.

Golden Touch

DESIGNER	ANTHONY COLLETT
COMPLETED	1988
LOCATION	LONDON, UK

ARCHITECT AND INTERIOR DESIGNER Anthony Collett transformed this Victorian terraced house into a contemporary home, introducing touches of theatre and a wealth of evocative colours. The eclectic interiors fuse classical principles, modern art, Arts and Crafts Movement influences and custom pieces within a singular vision full of exuberance and delight. An accomplished collection of 19th-century studio pottery stands out against the gold leaf walls of the living room, which is also enriched by contemporary art by Gilbert & George and others.

Looking around Collett's home, so rich in colour and texture, it is extraordinary to think that the designer was once afraid of colour. Although he studied fine art and sculpture at Hornsey College and then design at the Royal College of Art, Collett still retained a degree of reticence about colour. Then, in the early 1980s, he began collecting English ceramics produced by the Moorcroft, Bretby and Ruskin potteries – characterized by their vibrant glazes – and his attitude began to shift.

Collett bought this large period house in the 1980s and set about reinventing the interiors. Previously, the lower-ground level had been divided off from the rest of the house and turned into a separate apartment, but the architect reclaimed it and created a generously sized kitchen and dining room with a strong Arts and Crafts flavour and elegant detailing. On the ground floor, he spliced together two rooms to form a large living and dining space with walls coated in golden schlagmetal leaf. Furniture, lighting and artworks were introduced along with a glorious profusion of studio pottery, which claims almost every surface in the room and offers a vivid display.

Some years later Collett was able to buy some adjoining land and extended the garden. He also created a new studio separate to the main house. This offers a welcoming summer room, which houses a collection of pewter ware.

DESIGN INGREDIENTS

· Colour theory

· Craftsmanship

· Dramatic lighting

· Eclecticism

· Reflective surfaces

PANELLED BATHROOM

The enticing master bathroom was used as a kitchen by the previous occupants of the house. Collett retained the tongue and groove panelling and added a salvaged claw-foot bath. The generous scale of the space and its inviting aesthetic allow it to double as a dressing room and relaxation zone, with a comfortable seating area as well as functional bathroom elements.

[1] COLOUR GROUPING With the gold leaf walls acting as a shimmering and dynamic backdrop, the colourful collection of studio pottery occupies a complex arrangement of wall sconces and shelving units. The ceramics are in groupings according to shape, height and colour. These considered compositions form pleasing patterns and offer some unexpected surprises and juxtapositions, too.

[2] COMPLEMENTARY
COLOURS 'Collecting these vases
made me realize that if colours were
good then they could be put together,'
said Collett. In colour theory, the term
'complementary colours' usually
refers to opposites, which provide the
greatest contrast and would combine
to make black if mixed on an artist's
palette. On a traditional colour wheel
diagram, gold and yellow would
naturally sit close together while blue
and red are opposites. Looking at the
ceramic displays, this helps to explain
why the red pottery leaps out when
placed near the blue vases.

[3] **ARTISTIC DISPLAY** Great attention is
paid to all the surface displays in the room. Collett
sourced a number of the ornamental display sconces
from antique and junk shops, while others were
especially designed for the living space. Displaying
the pieces upon the walls, like works of abstract art,
means they are viewed more clearly. At the same
time, the reflective quality of the walls allows their
lustre to become more brilliant.

[4] **STANDOUT LIGHTING** The living and
dining space includes an iconic Pallucco tripod
standing light, based on an original design by
Mariano Fortuny in 1909, by the window. Collett
designed the dramatic ceiling light above the
dining table himself. The circular forms of the
two lights echo one another and together they
create an arresting sculptural presence at one
end of the room.

Black Manhattan

DESIGNERS	WINKA DUBBELDAM/ ARCHI-TECTONICS
COMPLETED	2010
LOCATION	TRIBECA, NEW YORK, USA

ARCHITECT <u>WINKA DUBBELDAM</u> crafted this atmospheric Manhattan sanctuary as part of a mixed-use project. She bought the concrete-framed 1920s corner building in Tribeca to house her architectural practice, which has since moved to the Financial District, but also took the opportunity to create a tailored home for herself, with a large open-plan living space towards the front of the building and two bedrooms at the rear. With an expanse of windows facing the street and plenty of natural light, the space allowed her to experiment with dark materials and colours.

The building was originally used as a factory workshop for making airplane parts and then by a company that leased and restored telephone booths. At first, Dubbeldam and her team at <u>Archi-tectonics</u> moved their offices around the building as one space after another was converted and completed. When the business areas were finished, she turned her attention to the apartment that had been slotted in above the workshop and set about updating and remodelling the space.

The layout offers a neat division between the open-plan living space – combining seating and dining areas with a custom-built kitchen – and the bedrooms positioned on a secondary level, thus creating a duplex arrangement. 'The configuration is good,' said Dubbeldam, who grew up in the Netherlands but has been based in New York for many years. 'It gives good privacy to the bedroom areas and plenty of light in the living room. It is fabulous to have so much light.'

Full of character, the apartment is warmed by the use of striking materials, such as the beautifully grained palisander flooring in the living room made with recycled timber. Dubbeldam designed the custom kitchen using Trespa, a heavy duty material more often employed for cladding the outside of buildings and skyscrapers. The kitchen units were tailored with a self-designed pattern cut into the Trespa, and the black sink, black tap and black appliances were sourced to continue the sophisticated tone of the apartment. Furniture choices mix vibrant new pieces from Italian firm Moroso and Dutch designers Moooi with an antique Knoll leather sofa and other vintage finds. The master bedroom has a comfortable, more secluded feel, enhanced by the luxury of a generously sized en-suite bathroom and walls painted in a soothing Chelsea grey.

DESIGN INGREDIENTS

· Atmosphere

· Detailed textures

· Innovative use of materials

· Matt finishes

· Sophisticated tone

[1] DARK MATTER Given the rich quality of natural light in the living room, Dubbeldam had total freedom to opt for any colour spectrum. She decided on a matt black finish for the walls, complemented by the dark timber floors. These colour choices create a more intimate quality in the living area, holding it together, and a particularly atmospheric feeling in the evenings. The ceilings are painted white for contrast and to help promote a sense of height within the space.

[2] ACCENT PATTERN Although the kitchen island introduces a subtle pattern, furniture choices provide more characterful bursts of pattern and colour. In addition to the geometric Moroso rug, the ottomans and armchairs introduce visual variety and engaging sculptural shapes. The chairs and ottomans are also by Moroso.

[3] ORGANIC MATERIALS The space is given warmth and character through the use of organic, natural materials such as the palisander floor, made with recycled timber sourced from derelict Balinese boats. The kitchen units and island also have warmth and patina, although the material here is Trespa – a composite blend of wood fibre and resin. The units were designed by Dubbeldam with a milled pattern ingrained into the Trespa island.

[4] FEATURE LIGHTING Feature lamps and lighting add another dimension to the space, particularly at night. The suspended mirrored light is by Tom Dixon and the wall light from Italian manufacturer Artemide. The lights hovering over the kitchen are from Pallucco, and their sculptural shapes and reflective surfaces draw the eye.

[5] HOME WORK Although the separate office spaces are located downstairs, Dubbeldam furnished the apartment so that it was also possible to work from home. A neat and discreet work space is provided by the matt black Moooi dining table, which features a hidden work station accessed by a folding timber leaf at one end. When closed, the leaf hides away a laptop and paperwork. The dining chairs, known as Carbon chairs, are also by Moooi, an innovative product design firm founded in 2001 by Marcel Wanders and Casper Vissers.

Midnight Blue

DESIGNER   STUDIO CATOIR

COMPLETED   2014

LOCATION   SARONNO, ITALY

THIS SOPHISTICATED DUPLEX apartment, designed by <u>Studio Catoir,</u> is situated in the city of Saronno. A substantial new home arranged over two floors, the apartment and its roof terrace enjoy views of the Alps and are used by the owner as his main residence all year round. The colours of both winter and summer pervade the apartment, with bursts of vibrant yellow in the main sitting room combined with wintry greys and blues that dominate a number of other areas. Among them is the master bedroom: an elegant masculine space where midnight blue is the dominant colour.

Situated a short distance from Milan, Saronno is a picturesque city that is well known for its *amaretti* biscuits and the Museo Giuseppe Gianetti, which houses an impressive collection of porcelain and ceramics. Not far from the historic city of Como and the Swiss border, Saronno looks out towards the mountains, with Monte Rosa and the Matterhorn in the east and the peaks of the Engadin to the west. Studio Catoir's client – an entrepreneur working in the lighting industry – bought this three-bedroom apartment at the top of a luxury condominium and gave the designers carte blanche.

Elisa and Michael Catoir found inspiration from a number of sources, including the dramatic seasonal shifts experienced in the surrounding Lombardy region, where the summers are hot and the winters bring snow and temperatures as low as -15°Celsius (5°F). The Alfred Hitchcock film *To Catch a Thief* (1955), starring Cary Grant and Grace Kelly, provided a particular influence, too, and the duplex interiors splice together a touch of the mid-century Riviera glamour of the film and a more contemporary outlook.

The apartment features a series of terraces and outdoor rooms – with mountain vistas – and a range of crafted living spaces within, lifted by bold colours, playful touches and many custom-designed elements throughout. Rich colours, contrasting textures and tailor-made furnishings also resonate in the master bedroom and bathroom. The en-suite bathroom is a striking space in itself, with an individual geometric pattern inlaid into the maple wood panelling, which frames the sculpted Agape bath tub. The room continues the idea of a highly tailored residence, full of personality and individuality, attuned to the needs of the owner and the context of Saronno itself.

DESIGN INGREDIENTS

· Bold pattern
· Dynamic detailing
· Glamorous styling
· Natural materials
· Sculptural forms

[1] TEXTURE AND COLOUR

The character of the bedroom derives not only from a dynamic use of colour, but also from the richness of the contrasting textures within the space. These include the fabric-covered walls, the velvet curtains, the custom-made rug and the leather headboard. Soft and tactile surfaces contrast vividly with the harder surfaces of the timber floors and the desk. 'The space was inspired by an elegant man's suit,' said Elisa Catoir. 'We combined the blues and greys from a masculine wardrobe with natural leather and fabric accents.'

[2] CUSTOM DESK

With a rounded kidney bean top combined with angular base legs, the writing desk is one of many custom pieces. The apartment features a number of designs and here the wish was to have the desk right at the centre of the room, creating an amalgam of bedroom and study. The unique design allows for cables to be hidden in the legs and power points to be concealed in the two leather satchels. 'The client loves writing desks,' said Elisa, 'so we designed a collection of desks for him including this one, which is called Alessandra.'

VIBRANT BATHING

The en-suite bathroom is an imaginative and arresting space. The custom wall and ceiling panelling – with an inlay of grey stained burr maple and a stained oak set into maple boards – creates an enticing pattern that enriches the bathroom and lends it individuality. With the Carrara marble floors and basin, and the timber walls and ceiling, the room has an organic quality, somewhat reminiscent of a highly sophisticated Alpine chalet.

[3] **GEOMETRIC PATTERN** The custom-made rug in wool and silk introduces colour and vivid pattern to the master bedroom. Its geometry is reminiscent of Op art from the 1960s and 1970s, including the work of artists Bridget Riley and Victor Vasarely. The design brings a sense of both dynamic movement and optical excitement.

[4] **SCULPTED BED** The bed is a custom design by Studio Catoir, made with a striking headboard of woven leather. The enclosing curves of this feature headboard create the impression of enfolding arms, lending security and comfort, yet they also soften the linear outline of the room itself. Here, the wall behind the bed is coated in a hand-woven finish of natural fibres in midnight blue, while the rug in blues and greys is another Studio Catoir design. The blue velvet curtains and chair upholstery reinforce the dominant colour scheme.

White House

DESIGNER	STUDIO OCTOPI
COMPLETED	2012
LOCATION	LONDON, UK

STEPPING THROUGH THE DOOR of this south London home is like walking into a small slice of Scandinavia. This is a house of light, with a calm fusion of white walls, painted floorboards and an enticing assembly of Scandinavian sofas and furniture. Artwork and a collection of brightly coloured Swedish ceramics stand out against this relaxed, welcoming backdrop formed by opening up and reinventing a traditional Victorian terraced house.

Previously, the owners had lived in a loft in Clerkenwell, London, but they decided to move to Battersea to a larger family home with a garden. Although the house met all their requirements it required modernization, so the family turned to architect Chris Romer-Lee of Studio Octopi. The brief that they gave him was a loose one, but it included the idea of loft-style living, large expanses of white and plenty of places to display ceramics and artwork.

Most of the building work was focused on the ground floor, which was opened up dramatically to create a living room that leads straight through to the freshly extended kitchen. This connects directly to the garden via a sequence of glass doors. Natural light is circulated through the entire space by the use of fresh colours and materials, a good amount of mirrored glass in the kitchen and a large skylight over the Danish dining table at the back of the house. This arrangement also allows sunlight to wash over a recessed niche on the wall nearby, which displays a sequence of five colourful posters by German graphic designer Otl Aicher.

The point at which the living room and kitchen meet is marked by a step down, as well as by a change from white painted floorboards to Italian Pietra Serena sandstone tiles. There is also a made-to-order display unit here, holding part of a substantial collection of colour-coordinated ceramics, mostly from the 1950s, 1960s and 1970s. 'Clients with collections are delightful,' said Romer-Lee, who calls the house the Vitt Hus, or White House. 'Our clients have a very good eye for beautiful objects and the idea of displaying them was treated as part of the everyday make-up of the house. The simple palette of colours really worked because of the richly coloured and textural nature of the ceramic collection and the preferential treatment of the Aicher posters.'

DESIGN INGREDIENTS

· Art and ceramics

· Bright whites

· Circulation of light

· Harmonious living

· Rhythmic flow

[1] FLUID SPACES The period terraced house has been completely modernized and updated, with a series of cellular rooms opened up to create a fluid procession of family-friendly spaces. The cosy living room at the front of the house leads effortlessly through to the kitchen and dining area. This allows the free-flowing movement of the family and the natural light as well as the eye, which traverses the expansive perspective and savours the sense of open delight. At the same time the identity of each individual space has been preserved within the home.

[2] SKYLIGHT AND MIRRORS A key element of the welcoming atmosphere of the combined dining area and kitchen is the healthy distribution of natural light. A long skylight to one side and the large windows to the rear garden draw in a good deal of sunlight from different directions. This combination of sources enhances the overall quality of the light. In addition, a sequence of mirror glass above the kitchen counter helps to bounce the light through the space, aided by the white walls, white ceilings and white surfaces.

ATTIC STUDY

A home office was created in a small attic space at the top of the house. This study is tucked under the eaves, making good use of an area that would be redundant in many similar period homes. The slanted ceilings are low and the space limited, but the room has the inviting quality of a cocoon, with a large skylight and window seat helping to make the study space both practical and welcoming. The wallpaper is a design by Cole and Son and the clock mounted on the back wall is by George Nelson.

[3] **COLOURFUL ART** The white walls and muted colours employed throughout form a neutral backdrop for displaying artworks and ceramics. The vibrant colours of the posters – designed by Aicher for the Olympic Games in Munich in 1972 – stand out vividly in this context, forming an enticing burst of colour that enriches this part of the house.

[4] **CERAMIC DISPLAY** A shelving unit at the far end of the kitchen, close to the junction with the sitting room, offers a perfect display opportunity for the owners' collection of mid-century Scandinavian ceramics, assembled over many years. The majority of these colourful objects were produced by the Swedish company Upsala Ekeby.

Vibrant Teal

DESIGNER	GUILHERME TORRES
COMPLETED	2010
LOCATION	SÃO PAULO, BRAZIL

AFTER TEN YEARS OF WORKING as an architect and designer in Londrina in the southern region of Brazil, Guilherme Torres decided to relocate to São Paulo. He began hunting for a house in the leafy and affluent Jardins district of the city and eventually found a modestly scaled house dating from the 1940s hidden away behind high walls and a courtyard garden. Torres updated and redesigned the building to create a highly individual home, full of fresh colours and playful touches.

Torres suggests that the architect within him is a minimalist, while the designer and decorator inside is something of a compulsive maximalist. His work and his home splice together these two impulses within spaces that have a clear architectural framework and strong bones. The rooms are layered with pattern, colour, artworks and personality. 'I love houses that are like old ladies rather than minimal,' said Torres. 'I have a romantic approach to modernism.'

His reinvented house is full of character, while the layout is clearly defined and flexible. The latticed wooden front door sits beyond a walled garden that creates a private border and a processional entrance from the street. Visitors step across the threshold directly into a long, open-plan living area that combines a study with a lounge, enriched by teal blue walls and a sofa in matching azure tones. The space continues through to the back of the house, where Torres has transformed an internal courtyard – protected by a glass roof – into a dining area with its own indoor garden and healthy young trees. The kitchen sits alongside: it is a custom design with orange Corian worktops and cabinets decorated in arresting patterns by artist friends.

Upstairs, the designer also utilizes plenty of bold colour. The master bedroom is painted a glowing peach pink and looks down into the courtyard below via an internal window. The master bathroom sits within a mezzanine level floating above the kitchen, shrouded by verdant greenery that spills out and trails down over the courtyard garden. 'I use all the rooms in the house and every one of them is a favourite,' said Torres, 'just as a mother loves all her children. I really do use the entire house all the time. Normally, people who design in a minimalist way live in minimalist spaces, but that is definitely not me.'

DESIGN INGREDIENTS

· Bringing the outside in

· Colour repeats

· Informality

· Large-scale artworks

· Playful highlights

[1] **TEAL REPEATS** The fresh, inviting teal blue is used for the upholstery of the sofa and the rug in the seating zone at the centre of the house, where the walls are a neutral, creamy white and match the poured concrete floors. The shade is echoed in the walls around the main entrance and stairwell. Colour is employed selectively rather than exclusively, and it is reinforced by its repeated use in various ways, thereby creating a sense of cohesion. The teal has a refreshing quality, reminiscent of the sea and sky, and it lifts the house above and beyond its urban setting.

[2] **STUDY ZONE** Flexibility is important to the design of the space, and the main living zone has a multifaceted quality. The table extends into the room to provide a desk for home working, with library shelving alongside, but when the computer is put away the desk becomes a dining table for more formal entertaining. This piece of furniture was designed by Torres and the steel dining chairs are from Italian design brand Magis. A second dining and breakfast area is located in the internal courtyard adjacent to the kitchen.

[3] FOCAL LIGHTBOX The lightbox artwork by Brazilian artist Pinky Wainer references *Las Meninas* (1656) by Diego Velázquez. Its illuminated surface is particularly powerful in the evening, when the piece becomes a focal point in the space. A neon work by Wainer hangs on the facade and artworks by other artists feature throughout the house.

INDOOR GARDEN

A small back yard was converted into a light-filled dining area and kitchen, arranged around an internal garden planted with young trees beneath a large skylight. This courtyard introduces sunlight and nature into the midst of the living spaces. 'I decided to plant the trees because it's always been my dream to eat while the branches of the trees protect me,' said Torres, who designed the vibrantly coloured kitchen and the long table with the fitted cooktop at one end. 'I love that sensation.'

[4] CUSTOM FURNITURE
Much of the furniture in the house was specially designed by Torres, including the breakfast table (made from recycled timber), the sofa and the matching ottoman. These key pieces focus attention on the different living zones on the ground floor. They are complemented by hand-picked artworks and supplementary furniture by other designers, including a number of playful pieces. These include the black Chair_ONE chairs around the breakfast table produced by German designer Konstantin Grcic for Magis.

Chocolate Brown

DESIGNER	JONATHAN ADLER
COMPLETED	2001
LOCATION	MANHATTAN, NEW YORK, USA

ALWAYS CHANGING and never static, <u>Jonathan Adler</u>'s homes are laboratories where the multitalented designer can experiment at will. At his apartment in New York City, he brings in new pieces of furniture from his collection and gives them a test drive, or perhaps decides to shake things up with a ping pong table coated in a Cole and Son wallpaper. His husband, Simon Doonan, an author and creative director of Barneys department store, remains constantly patient and accepting. The master bedroom is particularly rich in colour, with walls painted 'choccy brown' and burnt orange accents.

Doonan bought one half of their Manhattan home seventeen years ago. Then Adler snapped up the apartment next door in 2001 and they knocked both spaces together. The greatest surprise has to be the two vast barrel-vaulted rooms at the heart of the home, with their high moulded ceilings and soaring windows that usher in a wealth of sunlight. 'It is a legendary building in downtown New York because it does have these large volumes of space,' said Adler. 'It's very rare to find rooms with this kind of height and volume in downtown New York. The ceiling mouldings were there – and the fireplaces – but we added all the wall mouldings.'

Adler created a carefully detailed white shell, complete with white painted floorboards, which serves as a canvas for his distinctive 'happy chic' approach. This involves plenty of colour, a variety of patterns and a blend of his own designs with mid-century pieces by George Nelson, Joe Colombo, Richard Schultz and others. There is a rich mixture of playful, considered kitsch and 1970s-style glamour throughout, and this has become the Adler hallmark. 'I grew up in a mid-century house and I now realize that my apartment is in many ways a perfect reflection of the house that I grew up in,' he said.

The master bedroom is designed as more of an evening retreat, with walls not painted white this time but a deep shade of chocolate brown. There is still plenty of pattern, particularly in the form of the vibrant wallpaper, the wardrobe panelling and the flooring. 'In our bedroom we wanted something squishy and comfy,' Adler said. 'The anchor is the David Hicks carpet. Hicks was a big influence on me, not just because of the groovy geometrics, but for his sense of abandon and boldness in design.'

DESIGN INGREDIENTS

· Contrasting patterns
· Eclectic decoration
· Organic colour
· Playful storage solutions
· Surprising retro touches

[1] **EARTHY COLOURS** Autumnal colours are well suited to an evening and nighttime space, yet the bright white ceilings create an impression of height and volume. The bedroom walls are painted a deep, rich shade of brown complemented by the addition of burnt orange damask fabric for the niche behind the bed, the main light shade and the wardrobe panels on either side of the bed. The various patterned pillows and white owl ceramic on the bedside table are by Jonathan Adler and the circular Raindrop mirror is a mid-century design by Curtis Jeré.

[2] **ORANGE ALCOVE** Picked out in a vibrant shade of orange, the alcove behind the bed resembles a giant headboard tucked into the wall, with fitted wardrobes on either side. The bold pattern stands out brilliantly against the chocolate brown backdrop. 'We thought it would be fun to upholster the niche and also use the fabric in other places in the room,' said Adler. 'A lot of the elements in the room are kind of traditional, like the fabric and some of the furniture, but keeping to a restrained use of pattern and colour, the room becomes more modern.'

[3] GEOMETRIC PATTERN The geometric Colony carpet by Hicks is laid in the bedroom, on the landing and on the stairs. Earning fame in the 1970s for his ground-breaking, eclectic and colourful approach, Hicks made a big impact upon Adler and many other designers of his generation. The geometry and colours of the carpet are echoed in a custom wallpaper on the slim staircase that connects the bedroom to the rest of the apartment.

[4] STATEMENT STORAGE The fitted and free-standing wardrobes in the bedroom become features in themselves, decorated with panels of colourful fabric set in frames of crisp white woodwork. These layers of pattern and colour enrich functional pieces of furniture that might otherwise appear mundane, or even cumbersome. Instead, Adler has used them as a way to add to the playful quality of the master bedroom.

RETRO STYLE

Mid-century designers have been a major influence on Adler's work as a potter and designer, and many of his pieces have a retro quality. The sitting room features a number of Adler designs – the sofa, the rug and the pair of striped chairs by the window – with retro touches and bold colours. There are also vintage mid-century furniture designs such as the sculptural green and white armchair by Joe Colombo. The marble Jumbo coffee table is by Italian designer Gae Aulenti for Knoll.

Verdant Greens

DESIGNER	AGNÈS EMERY
COMPLETED	1996
LOCATION	BRUSSELS, BELGIUM

DESIGNER AGNÈS EMERY has a masterful understanding of the way colours harmonize with one another in glorious synergy. Her homes in Brussels and Marrakech are her 'embassies': personal galleries that express her love of colours and patterns inspired by nature. The Brussels town house is replete with inspired design and decorating ideas, with each space flowing effortlessly into the next. One of the most engaging rooms in the house is the kitchen, with its delightful amalgam of greens and accent blues.

Emery grew up with a love of colour and beautiful design. Her grandfather was an artist and her parents were ceramists. She studied architecture in Brussels, although her love of pattern, ornament and the decorative style of the Arts and Crafts Movement was at odds with her teachers' emphasis on modernist purity. Emery began to move in a different direction, taking on interiors projects and then founding her own company, Emery & Cie, which creates ranges of paints, tiles and textiles. Her paint colours are produced in Belgium, whereas her tiles are made in Marrakech, where Emery has kept a second home for many years.

The Brussels town house is a 19th-century building, in which many original period features have been preserved, including the stairs and mouldings. It had hardly been touched since the 1950s and Emery was careful to retain as many period elements as she could. The ground floor is dominated by the kitchen, which flows into a dining room alongside. Here, the colours are a decidedly organic range of blues and greens.

The kitchen offers a harmonious collection of associated colours, with various different shades of green for the woodwork, walls and tiles, the last of which form eye-catching splashbacks. The synergy between these colours is soothing and restful, but also full of delight and interest. The adjoining hallway and dining room are also decorated in shades of green.

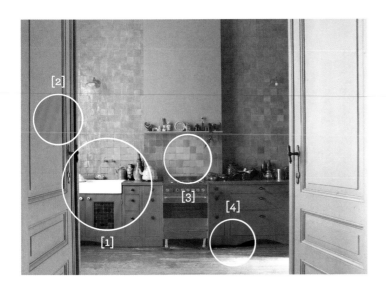

· Continuity

· Contrast of finishes

· Harmonious detailing

· Organic colours

· Rugged textures

[1] COLOUR SYNERGY Emery's use of colour is subtle and sophisticated. The shifts in gradation and tone between the variety of greens used in the kitchen are relatively modest, creating a harmonious effect. However, each shift is carefully thought out and picks out a particular element of the kitchen, as seen in the darker greens used for the woodwork of the kitchen units compared to the pearlescent greens of the tiles.

[2] COMPLEMENTARY LAYERING For Emery, colour is not simply a matter of consideration for walls, fabrics and surfaces. Painted furniture in the kitchen also picks up on a green and yellow spectrum, while ceramics and utensils sit well with the foundation colours of the room. Upstairs, in the library/study, Emery's books are arranged according to the colour of their spines to great effect.

SOOTHING SUITE

The upper storey of the house marks a transition from natural greens to sky blues. In the master bedroom, the designer wanted to orient the high bed towards the window and the light, so she created a custom-made headboard in the form of a half-height floating wall, painted the same soothing shade of blue as the walls. This addition anchors the bed but still allows the space to be read as a whole; it also shelters the doorway behind to the adjoining dressing room.

[3] ACCENT COLOURS Although the downstairs rooms are dominated by organic tones, there are also accent colours that draw the eye. In the kitchen, the blue tiles above the stove stand out against the surrounding greens and become a focal point that provides a visual anchor to the room. However, the synergy between the blues and greens ensures that the contrast is not too severe.

[4] TEXTURAL SHIFTS In addition to the subtle shifts in colour, Emery's interiors are also enriched by a variety of different textures. Here, there is the rugged bare beauty of the wooden floors against which the green woodwork and walls stand out all the more. Equally importantly, the tilework adds a new dimension to the space with the reflective glaze of the tiles helping to circulate light and adding a more dynamic quality to the space.

Character

Fifties Revival

DESIGNER	BADE STAGEBERG COX
COMPLETED	2011
LOCATION	LONG ISLAND, NEW YORK, USA

MID-CENTURY DESIGN is a particular passion for Jesse Gordon. Over the years he has acquired an impressive and carefully assembled collection of 1950s furniture, glass and ceramics, as well as an almost encyclopaedic knowledge of the subject. If he were not an attorney then surely Gordon would be a designer, architect or gallerist. When it came to finding the perfect home for his collection, naturally a seaside home on Long Island, dating from 1958, offered the ideal solution.

The family has kept a weekend and vacation home at Orient Point for many years as an alternative to everyday living in New York City. Here, at the tip of Long Island's North Fork, the coastline is enticing and the community is family-orientated. When the house came on the market, the family was tempted by both the mid-century feel of the architecture and the clifftop location. The building faces the sea to one side and looks out into verdant forestry to the other, giving the home both privacy and an extraordinary panorama.

The only drawback was that the house needed a lot of work. The bones of the building were strong, but the timber siding was rotting away and an update was long overdue. To help with the renovation and the reordering of a number of spaces, the Gordons turned to architect Jane Stageberg, of Bade Stageberg Cox. In addition to re-cladding the outside of the building in grey-stained cedar, Stageberg created a new roof terrace, adding to the two existing decks overlooking the sea. The master bedroom was also extended in size and scale, while a former garage was turned into a brand new guest bedroom. At the heart of the home is the open-plan living area, arranged around the original stone fireplace. Here, too, there was a good deal of work to be done. The interior timber panelling had to be replaced, while new oak floorboards were used to tie the space together. The old kitchen was replaced with a custom design – with ply-faced units and slate worktops – that is more open to the rest of the living space.

There was close collaboration between client and architect throughout, and Gordon sourced many fitted pieces for the house himself, including the vintage lighting and the tiles around the fireplace in the master suite. The house became the perfect backdrop to his collection of furniture, ceramics, books and other period treasures.

DESIGN INGREDIENTS

· Complementary tones

· Contrasting textures

· Eclectic sources

· Mid-century furniture

· Organic materials

[1] MEZZANINE STUDY A small landing or modest mezzanine level to one side of the main living space has been put to good use as a compact study area. The desk here is by French interior designer Christian Liaigre and the desk chair is by Charles and Ray Eames. The side window offers a view of the woodland, which shelters one side of the house, forming a strong connection with the outdoors. There is also a glimpse of the horizontal timber siding that clads the building and links visually with the wall panelling used inside.

[2] RETRO FURNITURE As a well-informed collector of furniture, Jesse Gordon has sourced a number of standout vintage pieces for the house. These include the mid-century Dutch sofa and two armchairs by Danish design great Ib Kofod-Larsen. The stereo console by the fireplace is an original Braun design by Hans Gugelot and Dieter Rams. Legendary Braun designs by Rams transformed the look and functionality of stereo systems in the post-war period and can be compared with Jacob Jensen's pioneering work for Danish electronics firm Bang & Olufsen.

[3] STONE AND TIMBER In the main living area the organic materials lend warmth and texture. The floors are oak while the stone fire surround is an original character feature. The timber wall panelling had been painted a rather dark and oppressive colour, so it was replaced with clear cedar fixed in position horizontally.

FLEXIBLE KITCHEN

Inspired by the mid-century character of the house itself, the new kitchen serves as the social hub of the home. It is a tailor-made design by Bade Stageberg Cox, and the fitted plywood units include splashes of colour. An extending, pull-out table serves as a neat breakfast bar; the stools are by Alvar Aalto for Artek.

[4] ACCENT COLOURS The use of colour in the living area is subtle but extremely effective. The organic tones of the timber panelling and flooring create a strong foundation to the space, against which the accent greens of the compact sofa and thick-piled rug – from Stark Carpet – stand out, but in a quiet fashion. The employment of such reassuring and natural tones forms an engaging echo of the woodland that surrounds the house, while the rug also helps to ground the composition of mid-century furniture pieces around the fireplace and hearth.

Peacock Pavilion

DESIGNERS	CHRIS REDECKE AND MARYAM MONTAGUE
COMPLETED	2010
LOCATION	MARRAKECH, MOROCCO

ARCHITECT <u>CHRIS REDECKE</u> had long dreamed of building a house for his family. He seized the opportunity to design not one house but three after buying an olive grove on the edge of a village outside Marrakech. In addition to the family home, Redecke created two 'Peacock Pavilions' in an individual style arranged around a communal pool and gardens. The interiors were created in close collaboration with his partner <u>Maryam Montague</u>, and these richly layered spaces feature her collections of art, ceramics and other treasures.

The site and setting are seductive, with views of the Atlas Mountains floating in the distance. Redecke's architectural approach mixes traditional Moroccan and North African influences – such as the horseshoe arches – with contemporary elements and comforts. The 'medina' pavilion, designed for guests, features a Western-style kitchen and modern services but also has a crafted, hand-made quality and an in-built sensitivity to the context and setting. 'There was conscious thought in the planning of the landscaping and the placement of the buildings,' said Redecke. 'The Moroccan imagery is not so much to do with the details but the forms – the arches, the towers and terraces.'

At the heart of the three-bedroom pavilion there is a double-height sitting room, topped by a domed roof. It is arranged around the fireplace, and a sequence of open arches partially divides the area from the entrance hall nearby. Brick floors laid in a parquet formation unite the spaces, while architectural detailing throughout reinforces the individuality of the interiors. Montague has layered the room with accent pattern and colour against a backdrop of crisp white walls. 'We wanted the pavilions to be places that you would like to stay where guests feel they have their own privacy and space,' she said. 'I really like the idea of having a house that feels like a curate collection of lovely and interesting things picked up in a souk or a bazaar.'

DESIGN INGREDIENTS

· Architectural features

· Emphasis on individuality

· Layers of art and ethnic treasures

· Moroccan traditions

· Romantic ambience

[1] ARCHITECTURAL DETAILING In addition to the Moroccan-inspired forms of the horseshoe arches – which are traditionally thought to keep away evil spirits – Redecke has employed a number of other architectural details that add character to the space. These include the small repeated wall niches and high miniature windows, as well as the low-relief arches and patterns integrated into the wall surfaces.

[2] STENCILLED FIREPLACE The fireplace is an important feature both architecturally and decoratively. The fire surround pattern was created by stencilling timber, while the indented arch above the mantelpiece frames the vintage poster perfectly.

[4] **ETHNIC TREASURES** As a seasoned traveller, Montague is continually bringing back pieces from her trips throughout Africa, India and Asia. Her treasures include an antique Persian chandelier (below), a colourful hand-beaded chair from Nigeria, crewel pillows from Kashmir and Yemeni sari fabric repurposed as curtains. Each element adds to the richly layered character and personality of the interiors.

[3] **PICTURE PYRAMIDS** The evocative covers of vintage French newspapers have been framed and arranged in pyramid formation within the outline of the indented arches on the plastered walls. A recurrent motif, the arch creates a vivid collage, the repetition of which in different parts of the room helps to tie the space together visually and thematically.

BEDROOM BLUES

This downstairs bedroom offers a peaceful sanctuary, lifted by the repeated blue notes against the white walls and timber floor. These colourful accents include the vintage bedspread from Rajasthan, the cushions made with a geometric patterned fabric sourced from Egypt and the stencilled ceiling, based on a patterned textile brought home from Bukhara in Uzbekistan. Despite variations in pattern, texture and provenance, the colour theme ties all of these elements together in a cohesive way.

Brooklyn Row House

DESIGNER	MARK DIXON ARCHITECT
COMPLETED	2009
LOCATION	BROOKLYN, NEW YORK, USA

THE RENOVATION AND REINVENTION of <u>Mark Dixon</u> and Alexandra Lange's terraced home in Brooklyn was a game of two halves. When they first bought the four-storey, 19th-century house, it came with sitting tenants on the upper two floors. Dixon, an architect, began work on the lower two floors initially, while trying to keep in mind what he might do with the upper levels when the tenants finally moved on. The whole project took about three years to complete and the greatest challenge – once Dixon and Lange had the whole place to themselves – was to make sure that the two halves met neatly in the middle.

Looking around the house, which sits on a quiet and leafy street in the Cobble Hill neighbourhood, it is actually difficult to see any of the joins at all. The space is united by the use of organic, light materials such as the plaster, the timber finishes and the wall panels coated in burlap sacking. It has a fresh, almost Scandinavian feel and mixes many custom-built elements with mid-century furniture and contemporary pieces.

When Dixon and Lange found the house, it had already had most of its period features ripped out, and for many years it had been divided into multiple apartments, before being turned into two separate duplexes. 'The period detail had all gone,' said writer, journalist and academic Lange, 'but we were excited about it, because Mark is a modern architect and did not want to have to deal with historical detail or feel bad about tearing it out.'

Dixon decided to give each floor a very clear identity. The lower-ground floor is a largely open-plan space, with a custom kitchen, dining area and family den – shared with the couple's two young children – that opens out to a rear garden and patio. The raised ground floor was opened up completely and transformed from two dark rooms into one generous salon with light feeding in from windows front and back. Tall bookcases designed by Dixon create a library that lightly separates the space from the entrance hall alongside. 'We decided to create this big, open space that we could use for more formal things,' said Dixon. 'We don't use it that much at the moment, with the children still so young, but we'd like to use it more. We wanted to clarify each element of the building and then make divisions between the spaces with cabinetry, like the bookshelves, so there are no solid partition walls.'

DESIGN INGREDIENTS

· Geometry
· Industrial qualities
· Limited palette
· Scandinavian influences
· Sedate atmosphere

[1] BOOKCASE WALLS The tall bookcases separate the room from the hallway and staircase nearby. However, this library wall is not full height, which allows light to pass between the spaces. In addition, openings in the wall, front and back, ensure easy circulation. The library lends a great deal of interest and personality to the room.

[2] RESTORED FLOORS Although many period elements had already been lost over the years, Dixon was able to preserve and restore the original floors in this part of the house. The wide timber boards are rich in patina and character and sit well with the new timber ceilings, creating an organic, cabin-like quality in the space.

[3] EXPOSED STEEL The timber features lend the space an organic feel, but this contrasts with the more industrial elements, such as the exposed steel beam and supporting columns. The raw quality of the steel and the open proportions of the space are reminiscent of loft living. At the same time, the exposed steelwork fits with the philosophy of trying to avoid solid walls and partitions, as far as possible, in order to facilitate the free circulation of light through the house.

GUEST QUARTERS

The upper floor of the house is devoted to an open-plan work studio, complete with Lange's old oak desk bought at a salvage store when she was a child. Dixon and Lange carved out a modest guest bedroom to one side of the studio using a partial partition wall for privacy. It offers a valuable resource for friends and family without giving up valuable space elsewhere in the house or compromising the studio.

[4] VINTAGE FURNITURE
The living room features a number of pieces of characterful vintage and antique furniture, anchored by a Knoll-style sofa and a 1950s abstract rusty red painting by Julian Stanczak. The striped armchair was purchased with the house itself and the vintage Charles and Ray Eames plywood chair came from Lange's grandparents. Within this mix, the circular antique library/dining table at the far end of the room adds a welcome note of contrast, while the repeated use of red accents for cushions and upholstery creates additional warmth.

Saint-Germain Courtyard

DESIGNERS	ELODIE SIRE/D.MESURE
COMPLETED	2011
LOCATION	PARIS, FRANCE

THE COMBINATION OF an eclectic, sophisticated design aesthetic and a period courtyard house dating back to the 19th century lends this five-storey home in the Saint-Germain district a seductive sense of character and depth. A blend of flea market finds, vintage pieces, architectural salvage and contemporary touches defines the spaces, including the dramatic and generously scaled master bathroom.

Arranged around a courtyard and a secret garden, the house – referred to as a 'golden cage' by its owner – is an oasis in central Paris: a place where the family can enjoy a sense of calm yet still be within the bustling streets around the Musée d'Orsay or the Jardin du Luxembourg in only a few minutes. The owners had hunted for a house in the area for many years without success. But then they got a call telling them that a period residence, which had once belonged to an ambassador, was now on the market; they decided to take the house five minutes after visiting for the first time. However, the building was in poor condition and needed a substantial amount of work and renovation. The owners turned to interior designer Elodie Sire and her design studio D.mesure, who stripped the house back to its bones and reinvented the interiors.

The master suite at the top of the house typically fuses many different elements into a cohesive whole. White walls and ceilings as well as large windows create a light and airy backdrop in the bathroom, while the dark timber floors offer a point of contrast and add texture. In addition to a number of vintage pieces, a salvaged stone fountain serves as a vast sink – and a focal point – while the bath is placed in the middle of this beautifully proportioned space, with room enough for a sofa to one side. 'I love the rich mixture of furniture, pictures, periods and materials,' said Sire. 'The master bathroom represents it very well for me: an open space without technology, a room where every item is beautiful and unexpected.'

DESIGN INGREDIENTS

· Architectural salvage

· Contrast of textures and tones

· Lighting options

· Scale

· Sophistication

[1] DRAMATIC RESONANCE The sink is a repurposed Spanish marble fountain, which creates a moment of surprise given its grand scale and particular individuality. Its unexpected quality adds to the delight of the room as a whole, as does the texture of the stone, which ties in with the pale walls but contrasts with the rich, dark parquet floors. The vintage lighting was sourced at the Paris flea markets and adds another layer of interest.

[2] BEYOND THE ORDINARY Visitors might expect the bathtub to be centred at right angles to the walls of the room, but placing the bath on a diagonal strikes an unexpected and intriguing note that makes it stand out all the more. On a practical level, the positioning of the bath also allows for more circulation space around it. Placing the ceiling light directly above the bathtub creates an intriguing and exciting composition.

[3] <u>**COMFORTABLE ELEGANCE**</u> The proportions of the room are generous enough to accommodate an upholstered sofa, by the metal balustrade that borders the stairwell. The settee brings colour and texture, but more importantly adds a layer of comfort that steers the space away from the purely functional and allows it to be warm, welcoming and indulgent, splicing together the rituals of bathing and the elegance of a sitting room.

[4] <u>**MIRRORED CHARM**</u> The adjoining dressing room and shower room are lifted by the use of vintage mirrored glass, sourced from the Clignancourt flea markets. The glass is used instead of tiles in the shower and also to face the cupboard doors in this annex to the master bathroom. It helps to circulate light and lends a greater sense of space and proportion, as well as serving a useful purpose to help with dressing.

BEDROOM IN SYMPATHY

The master bedroom and bathroom read as a cohesive suite of rooms, tied together by similar principles, textures and materials, with heavy double doors connecting the two. In this way, the spaces serve as equal and complementary partners with an easy and free-flowing relationship between the two. It is a refreshing ideal and one that provides an attractive alternative to the typical purely functional bathroom, tucked out of sight of the bedroom in almost apologetic fashion.

Estuary House

DESIGNER	JOHN PARDEY ARCHITECTS
COMPLETED	2011
LOCATION	NEWPORT ESTUARY, WALES, UK

THIS CONTEMPORARY HOME designed by architect <u>John Pardey</u> makes the most of an extraordinary location. Sitting upon the Newport Estuary in Wales, looking out to sea, the house is tucked into a gentle, green hillside with a boat shed and beach below. The design of the building maximizes the sense of connection with a mesmerizing vista of the estuary, particularly from the upper level, which hosts an open-plan living space full of character and natural warmth.

The owners of the house have known the area for many years. They come to Wales for most of the school holidays, and they are often joined by friends and extended family, some of whom live nearby. They bought an existing building on the northern shore of the estuary, within the Pembrokeshire Coast National Park, with the intention of replacing it with a more contemporary and contextual design that made the most of the site. 'The view is spectacular and constantly changing,' said Pardey's client. 'I can sit and watch the view indefinitely with the wildlife, the dog walkers, the fishermen, the kayaks and the boats swinging on their moorings. The view is so transfixing that we wanted every room to enjoy it.'

Pushed gently into the hill, the building has a masonry retaining wall to the rear anchoring it to the site and creating a 'container' for service and ancillary spaces. The front section of the house was designed with a much lighter touch, providing a pavilion of timber and glass looking out across the water. The lower level holds the majority of the bedrooms, while the upper storey contains an open-plan living and kitchen area plus a separate family room and the master suite. These spaces enjoy the best of the views and the light, sheltered by a soaring roof line with high clerestory windows towards the northern side of the building and long expanses of glazing connecting with the balcony facing south. There are also elevated decks at either end of the house, projecting outwards over more sheltered terraces below. 'We wanted to be able to open the house so that inside felt like outside,' said the owner. 'But even in winter the open-plan living room and kitchen is a light, bright space where you can watch the weather coming in. We like the informality of this space, where one person can be reading a book, while another is cooking and a third drawing at the table – all in their own worlds but sharing each other's company and absorbing the view.'

DESIGN INGREDIENTS

- Context
- Exposed timber
- Inside–outside living
- Natural materials
- Proportion

[1] EXPOSED BEAMS The timber frame was made with iroko, a hardwood with a fine grain and a warm, expressive quality. The exposed frame lends a semi-vernacular, almost barn-like quality to the house, which retains an airy lightness thanks to the expanses of glazing and crisp white walls. The height of the ceiling, particularly where it meets the run of clerestory windows towards the rear of the building, also adds to the refined airy quality.

[2] SERVICE SPACES An integrated fridge, pantry and other service spaces are tucked away against the spine wall that runs along the back of the house. The neat positioning of these ancillary spaces frees up the floor plan at the front of the building for more open, social zones that enjoy the best of the light. The generously sized fridge is a welcome amenity in a holiday home for a large family.

[3] CUSTOM ELEMENTS

The tailored timber kitchen and dining table add individuality and personality to the living space, while also ensuring that each element sits well within the proportions of the room as a whole. The kitchen features plenty of integrated storage, to keep the surfaces clutter free, as well as a useful breakfast bar at one end. Importantly, the U-shaped design offers the sense of being in a room within a room, while still feeling part of a larger social space. The positioning of the structural timber supports helps to define each area.

[4] ORGANIC MATERIALS

The use of so many natural materials – including the timber frame of the building – adds both warmth and character to the interiors. The pale wood dining table is fashioned from Douglas Fir boards supplied by Danish flooring experts Dinesen, who also provided the floorboards. Sussex-based furniture designer John Hollis manufactured the custom kitchen using a richly veined timber called Tigerwood. The combination of different but complementary timbers adds great variety and contrast.

INTEGRATED DECKS

In addition to the balcony running along the front of the house, there are also elevated decks at either end of the building. One of these is used as an outdoor sitting room, with a fluid and easy sense of connection to the main living area within. It also serves as an ideal vantage point and viewing platform for appreciating the surroundings. These outdoor rooms make particular sense when used in close conjunction with the key living spaces on the upper level.

Ochre Barn

DESIGNER	CARL TURNER ARCHITECTS
COMPLETED	2011
LOCATION	NORFOLK, UK

EVEN FOR ARCHITECT and serial renovator Carl Turner the sheer scale of this project was daunting. The challenge was how to preserve the volume and character of the vast and open Victorian threshing barn while turning it into a practical home. For Turner, the solution was to create a series of sculpted pieces of furniture within the building that allow the dramatic outline of the space to shine through. The kitchen and utility block, topped with a mezzanine study, read like sculptures in an open gallery, while the bedrooms are contained neatly within the more intimate proportions of a former animal shed alongside.

Turner and his partner, Mary Martin, have worked on a whole series of projects for themselves since they first met and wanted a place in the country for weekends and holidays. Having bought the barn – in the rural lands bordering Norfolk, Cambridgeshire and Lincolnshire – Turner decided to manage the work himself, trying to accommodate site visits during weekends, holidays and free moments from his work schedule. 'The only way to really understand how a building is put together is to do it yourself,' he said. 'Here, I was really taken by the building more than anything, although it does also have a great outlook onto the fields. We met the tenant farmer who was here in the 1950s and he said that Ochre was revered as the best barn in the area.'

Turner designed nearly all of the furniture and internal elements himself, after finding that conventional, shop-bought designs looked completely out of place within the raw interiors of the barn. Many pieces, such as the beds, shelves and seating units, are made out of oriented strand board, or OSB, which complements the rustic barn in colour and texture. 'We could have divided up the space and crammed in as much living space as possible, but for us that was not what it was all about,' said Turner. 'We treated it almost like an important ruin, stripping everything back so that internally the barn is still intact. Then we designed the furniture and functional pieces as objects floating in the space.'

The master bedroom and bathroom are part of one large area, sitting within the adjoining stables to the barn, which offered space enough for four generous bedrooms. Here, there are also a wood burning stove and reclaimed timber floors, creating a warmer, softer and more intimate retreat.

DESIGN INGREDIENTS

· Custom-made furniture

· Limited palette of materials

· Minimalism

· Raw edges

· Vernacular

[1] INCONGRUOUS TOUCHES In addition to its obvious organic materials, the barn features a number of surprising elements and unexpected touches that are both playful and imaginative. One of these is the inclusion of two deck chairs (from Designers Guild) positioned in front of the fireplace – pieces that would normally be seen outdoors. Turner is an enthusiastic collector of salvaged and flea market treasures and the vintage doll's house is another unusual addition to a relatively sparsely furnished bedroom space.

[2] HEADBOARD WALL
Turner wanted the generous proportions and roof trusses of this bedroom suite to remain visible, because together they create the feel of a rustic loft. The half-height headboard wall anchors the bed, flanked by bedside tables, without interfering with the perception of the overall space. The bed itself features a series of hidden floor supports, which creates the illusion of a floating platform cantilevered from the headboard. An en-suite bathroom is tucked away neatly behind the partial partition.

FLOATING FURNITURE

Turner's philosophy throughout the design
of the barn interiors was to preserve the open
proportions of the agricultural building, while
areas such as the kitchen and home office
become free-floating elements within the space.
The same is true of the custom-made furniture
designed by Turner, including the display shelves
in the living area, used to exhibit an assembly of
photography and artworks. Turner also designed
the seating for this space, while the red chair by
Charles and Ray Eames throws in some vivid
accent colour.

[3] RECLAIMED FLOORS

Salvaged timber was sourced from
a former factory in Manchester for the
flooring. The vintage floorboards fit
well both with the rustic industrial
look of the barn and the new elements
made with oriented strand board,
such as the shelving units and bed
surround. Reclaimed and salvaged
materials sit smoothly within
conversions and remodels of period
buildings, such as Ochre Barn, where
spotless new floorboards might look
out of place. At the same time, the old
timber adds character and texture to
the space itself.

[4] PERISCOPE BATHROOM

The bathroom is not only defined
by the headboard wall but also by a
shift in floor material, with polished
concrete used in the 'wet' area rather
than timber. The bath surround is
made of oriented strand board, which
affords a mottled, sandy woodchip
texture that reminds Turner of the
colour and tone of straw bales. Next to
the bath is a toilet contained within a
periscope cubicle, whose snout reaches
towards the ceiling where it grabs
natural light via a high internal window.
The chair is a classic mid-century
design by Harry Bertoia for Knoll.

Hidden House

DESIGNER	STANDARD
COMPLETED	2006
LOCATION	LOS ANGELES, CALIFORNIA, USA

DEEP IN THE HEART of a secluded and leafy neighbourhood, Laura Gabbert and Andrew Avery have conjured up a California haven open to the sun and the land. The Hidden House is a beautifully crafted, low-slung, single-storey retreat – designed by Los Angeles-based firm Standard – tucked away in the rolling hills of Glassell Park, a quiet enclave of the city. The heart of the house is a big and open family lounge plus kitchen, with a separate space devoted to a sitting room and dining area.

When Laura Gabbert and her husband, Andrew Avery, first drove down a dirt track at the heart of a hidden canyon, they soon realized that they had discovered something very special. They had been looking for somewhere to build a new family house, and out in this unusually peaceful and leafy part of Los Angeles they found plenty of land and a great opportunity to design a tailored home with an enticing sense of both space and privacy.

Creating a home from scratch came naturally to them: Laura's father has a passion for design and founded the stylish US furniture chain Room & Board, and Andrew's parents had built a family house when he was a child. They teamed up with architects Silvia Kuhle and Jeffrey Allsbrook of Standard and began to collaborate on a home that would celebrate the unique landscape and setting. The site came with a run-down ranch house and a mess of outbuildings and scrub, which were replaced by a pavilion-style home that maximizes connections to the terraces and landscape, allowing light and breeze to pass straight through.

The Hidden House is dominated by two generously scaled open spaces, both rich in character and texture. One holds the family room and kitchen area, with huge sliding glass doors to one side that open directly onto the courtyard terrace outside, complete with a summer dining table. There is also a combined sitting room and dining room that has pivoting glass doors to both sides, which connect the whole space seamlessly to the outside. With two young children, Laura and Andrew wanted to create living areas that were flexible and fluid, with hard-wearing surfaces, furniture and finishes. Nothing in their home is too fine or precious that it cannot easily survive family wear and tear.

· Cohesion

· Durable materials

· Easy flow inside to out

· Mid-century furniture

· Warm textures

[1] VINTAGE MODERN

Although this house is newly built, it is imbued with character through the materials and furniture selected, which provide both texture and warmth. A mid-century Scandinavian influence is expressed strongly in the living area, with a set of Wishbone chairs by Hans J. Wegner and a vintage Danish sideboard in rosewood. The dining table was made using reclaimed timber and it has a warm, organic flavour, while the Akari pendant ceiling light was designed by Isamu Noguchi and sourced from Room & Board.

[2] WOOD BLOCK FLOORS

Laura's father had used wood block flooring throughout his furniture stores, which inspired the family to use a similar idea in the Hidden House. The wood block floors were made using offcuts of timber and they offer a more rustic and informal take on traditional parquet. The floors were then sanded and stained, thus creating a more irregular and textured surface than standard floorboards. 'We wanted to use quite a bit of wood because we didn't want a cold, cavernous modernist house,' said Laura.

[3] HEARTLAND KITCHEN The kitchen, made with Baltic birch, is perfectly positioned within the floor plan of the house. It is easily accessible from the dining room but also offers instant access to the outdoor dining table on the deck via the sliding walls of glass. At the same time, part of the kitchen island can be used as a breakfast bar; the bar stools – with chrome legs and gently contoured leather seats and backs – are Radius models from Room & Board.

[4] FLUID CIRCULATION The informal plan of the house allows for an easy flow between inside and outside spaces and also between the two main living areas that sit in an L-shaped formation. Both are interconnected, yet each has its own distinct identity and offers individual spatial experiences. One is slightly more formal and sees more use in the evenings (dining/sitting room) and the other is more casual and suited to daytime and family use (kitchen/lounge).

OUTDOOR LOUNGE

The house features a number of outdoor rooms and terraces, which make the most of the picturesque and private setting. This fresh air lounge to one side of the dining room is framed by lush grasses and greenery, anchored by the textured grey side wall. It makes for a partially sheltered and inviting space with easy access to the interiors via the wall of pivoting doors.

Green Manor

DESIGNER   SPRATLEY STUDIOS

COMPLETED   2009

LOCATION   OXFORDSHIRE, UK

THE IDEA OF TRANSFORMING a chilly manor house into a green and sustainable family home might sound a little daunting. However, this is exactly what has been achieved with this 17th-century Oxfordshire home. At the same time, a striking contemporary extension was built to fill a former courtyard at the heart of the house. This new kitchen and central living space now form the hub of the manor, which has swapped its old kitchen range and oil-fired boiler for eco-friendly living and its own sources of sustainable energy.

Architect Jeremy Spratley of Spratley Studios was commissioned to bring together the building in an effective and practical way while also investigating ways of making the house more eco-conscious. The original kitchen looked into an internal courtyard with no sense of connection to the impressive gardens, and moving around the house was complex. 'With a lot of old houses that have been added to over time you do end up going on these little trips all over the place,' said Spratley's client. 'Now you come into the house and straight into the centre of it. The kitchen is really a hub and everything circulates off this space so you are not forever walking down corridors. We really wanted to create a sense of surprise. You see this lovely period house and you come inside and suddenly you are in this amazingly light and fresh open space.'

This pivotal area is large enough for a generous bulthaup kitchen to one side and also a dining space. It feeds into other key living areas, such as the sitting room and family room; it also flows into the entrance hall and connects to the rear gardens. The glass roof brings in a welcome flood of natural sunlight, while the glass staircase provides easy access to the bedrooms upstairs. 'It also means that we use the original part of the house much more than we did before, because the layout is so much more practical,' said the owner. 'And we found ourselves drawn into a more contemporary look and feel for the extension. We had great fun choosing the furniture, especially the Danish chairs and stools, and trying to use the best possible materials.'

The manor house also employs a solar thermal system to supply hot water, while an array of solar photovoltaic panels on the south-facing roof of one of the new oak-framed outbuildings provides electricity. This combination of eco-friendly sources of power has cut down energy bills drastically.

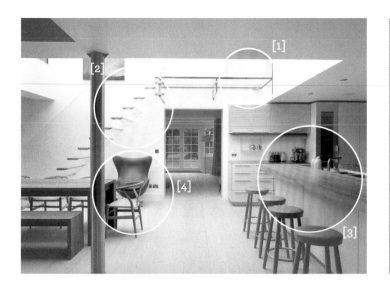

DESIGN INGREDIENTS

· Contrast of timber and glass
· Elements of surprise
· Flexible living
· Flow of light
· Narrative

[1] ATRIUM LIGHT WELL

Integrating the former courtyard into the layout of the manor not only creates a new family-friendly living space, but also provides an atrium that draws natural light deep into the heart of the building. A substantial skylight brings sunlight down into the kitchen and dining area, and enlivens the sitting room and other adjoining spaces. 'We knew that we didn't want to treat this new space in a conventional way,' said the owner. 'We wanted something more unusual, hence the curved glass roof and making the new glass stairs a feature.'

[2] GLASS STAIRCASE

The glass staircase and landing provide a new circulation route to the upper storey and offer more direct access to the children's bedrooms in particular. The use of structural glass steps and a glass balustrade means that the flow of light through the space is uninterrupted, while its contemporary spirit offers a foil to the more traditional parts of the house, including the original staircase. Atmospheric lighting has been integrated into the ends of the glass stair treads, and this becomes apparent in the evenings.

[3] FAMILY KITCHEN The well-proportioned bulthaup kitchen provides a good range of surfaces and storage ideally suited to family life. There are two islands, positioned alongside one another and offering a great deal of flexibility as to how the kitchen is used, as well as a wall of side units. The timber topped island, closest to the dining area, also serves as an additional eating area, with bar stools by Hans J. Wegner.

WELCOMING ENTRANCE

The entrance hall is a seductive and welcoming blend of old and new, with a number of period elements – the exposed timber frame and the integrated coat cupboard by the door, as well as the front door itself and the clerestory window – combined with freshly laid floors and contemporary lighting. The neutral colours and a minimalist design approach allow each of these elements to make an impact.

[4] SCANDINAVIAN FLAVOURS In addition to the Wegner bar stools, this reinvented section of the house features other Scandinavian pieces with a warm, organic and sculptural quality. They include the leather Egg chair by Arne Jacobsen and dining chairs by Wegner, which sit well with the Dinesen floorboards that flow into the sitting room and hallway. Scandinavian mid-century designs by Wegner, Jacobsen and others are characterized by their engaging, soft, modernist aesthetic and they work well within contemporary spaces.

Storefront House

DESIGNER	DIANA KELLOGG ARCHITECTS
COMPLETED	2005
LOCATION	TRIBECA, NEW YORK, USA

IN TRIBECA THERE ARE STILL a few areas that recall Manhattan as it was one hundred years ago. Architect Diana Kellogg and her family live in one of these types of streets, full of vintage character. The first thing that greets visitors as they walk down the road towards the discreet front door is an extraordinary enclosed bridge, which once tied together two sections of the long-gone New York Hospital. Kellogg lives in a neighbouring building: a former Victorian cold storage warehouse with a shop at the front that was used for selling butter and cheese.

Once inside the front door, it is obvious that the building has been radically reinvented from within. It now serves as a unique family home for the architect, her husband and their two children. 'It was clear that this was something different from the other buildings around it, which were mostly used as warehouses,' said Kellogg. 'It was a storefront with windows to the street, which gives us more light. I liked the elements that were here – the traces of history that give the building authenticity. That was really the starting point for me.'

The family used to live just around the corner but were on the lookout for a bigger home. The architect had known about the old warehouse for years and had kept a close eye on it, so when it came up for sale she stepped in straight away. Although the building had already been converted into a house, over three main levels, Kellogg was unhappy with the layout and partitioning of rooms, which positioned the main living area down on the lower-ground floor, where there is now a large den for the children. She was also determined to make the most of the ground floor with its shop windows, chestnut ceiling beams and characterful bare brick walls. Her redesign created a large open-plan living space with a seating area at one end and a dining zone towards the other, plus a galley-style kitchen neatly tucked away in an adjoining alcove.

Kellogg stripped back the paint on the chestnut beams to expose the grain of the wood, while the floors are laid with reclaimed timber. She designed a simple brick fireplace at the far end of the room, which looks as though it has always been there, and painted the surrounding brickwork here and at the opposite end of the room with crisp white paint to help bounce natural light throughout the space.

DESIGN INGREDIENTS

· Arrangement of artworks

· Authenticity

· Circulation of light

· Industrial qualities

· Organic texture

[1] LIGHT FANTASTIC The expansive storefront window introduces a rich quality of natural light into the key living spaces, while also lending character to the building. Kellogg custom designed a window seat made from reclaimed timber; it makes a perfect spot for reading and provides additional seating near the fireplace when entertaining friends.

[2] REFLECTIVE WALLS The exposed brick walls at both ends of the living area were painted white to keep the natural light circulating through the space. The earthy colours of the brick itself would have had the opposite effect. Mirrors and internal windows are some of the other devices used to keep sunlight moving through the house.

[3] GROUPED ARTWORKS A number of paintings and artworks are grouped together between the window and the new, painted brick fireplace and chimney breast, creating an irregular collage. The most colourful of these pieces is placed at the top of the composition and stands out all the more against the bright white wall. The eye is inevitably drawn to this painting and to a high point in the living space, which reinforces the sense of height within the room and draws attention to the organic beauty of the exposed ceiling beams.

[4] NOGUCHI LIGHTS Two large pendant lanterns by Isamu Noguchi float over the dining table and the seating zone. They help to define these two key areas, and the paper globes also disrupt the linear character of this part of the house. Noguchi was a celebrated Japanese American designer and artist, who began working on his range of Akari lanterns on a visit to Gifu in Japan during the 1950s, when he was invited to create new designs that would help revive one of the city's traditional industries. He also designed furniture for Herman Miller and Knoll.

GALLEY KITCHEN

The majority of the kitchen is tucked away neatly within a galley-style alcove to one side of the living space, effectively clearing away kitchen and pantry clutter. The kitchen units are designed by Kellogg, made with recycled timber from old lockers found on Coney Island. The cooking range is one of the few pieces within a secondary kitchenette on the other side of the room by the dining table, so that the act of cooking becomes a more social experience.

Station Chalet

DESIGNER	ANTONIE KIOES
COMPLETED	2008
LOCATION	GSTAAD, SWITZERLAND

THIS MOUNTAIN HOME has an extraordinary provenance. For much of its history, the building was a transformer station and station master's house for the Montreux–Oberland Bernois railway, whose trains still stop at the platform outside, serving skiers and commuters. Architect Antonie Kioes has transformed the building into a warm and characterful home for herself and her family. One of the key spaces in the house is the spacious sitting room, with a large picture window looking across to the mountains and down the valley towards Gstaad.

Antonie and her husband, and their four daughters, share a love of the mountains and winter sports. The family used to own a chalet near Zermatt but were increasingly drawn to Gstaad by its natural beauty. They began hunting for a small farm or similar building that they could convert into a home, but then stumbled across the station house in a small hamlet just outside Gstaad, surrounded by fields and pasture and well positioned for the mountain vista.

Converting the station into a welcoming chalet represented a considerable challenge. The portion of the building that hosted the 8000-volt generators was taken out of use in 1987, but there was significant oil pollution in both the house and the garden, as well as other industrial mess that had to be cleared away before work could begin. The owners preserved two of the generators and the control panel in the triple-height transformer hall and slotted a kitchen and dining area around them.

With high ceilings and a striking sense of scale and volume, the sitting room is another converted industrial space. This inviting retreat adjoins the transformer hall but is positioned at a higher level, with the master suite situated directly below it. Antonie installed a large picture window at the far end of the sitting room to frame one of the best views in the house. This open vista serves as a focal point in the room. Although the living space is large and open, the architect ensured that it also feels warm, welcoming and comfortable. One seating area has been arranged around a fireplace at one end of the room, while another seating zone collects around a library wall at the opposite end. Many custom elements – including the red check fabric coating the walls – are mixed with contemporary furniture and mid-century pieces within a characterful composition.

DESIGN INGREDIENTS

· Dramatic proportions

· Fabric walls

· Framing the view

· Incongruity

· Large-scale artworks

[1] PICTURE WINDOW

The large new picture window frames a mesmerizing view of the mountains and the snow-capped trees in the distance. It not only becomes a key element in the room, tying the interiors to the powerful natural setting, but also has the dramatic quality of a living painting or panoramic photograph. In the evenings, a crimson curtain pulls across the window, thus creating a more intimate atmosphere, even within such a generously scaled room. 'The landscape is beautiful here,' said Antonie. 'I like it very much.'

[2] COMFORTABLE SEATING

In addition to a sense of drama and scale, another essential ingredient for this cosy chalet-style sitting room is comfort. The large patterned Scandinavian rug on the rustic timber floor hosts a neutral L-shaped sofa, created by Paris-based architect and designer India Mahdavi, which faces both the picture window and the timber-clad custom fireplace. The low-level daybed in front of the window is a made-to-order design, whereas the vintage bowl-shaped armchair is by French designer Jean Royère.

INDUSTRIAL CHIC

The transformer hall is a dramatic industrial space with a soaring roof line and tall windows. The owner investigated the idea of donating the vintage generators to a museum but could not find an interested party, so decided to keep them both and the control panel nearby. Only one piece of machinery had to be removed to make space for the kitchen. These giant machines may appear incongruous in a home, but they have a personality of their own and the domestic interiors have been woven around them with great success.

[3] <u>CUSTOM FABRIC</u> The walls are coated in a vibrant custom check, designed by the owner with textile manufacturers Arpin. These textured walls soften the space so that it feels more intimate than the scale and proportions of the room would suggest. Painting the ceiling boards white adds a lighter note and echoes the snow-capped roof lines in the valley below. The colourful, triple-headed standing lamp is a vintage piece from ArteLuce.

[4] <u>EPIC ART</u> Within spaces of such height and volume, small paintings and photographs appear lost. The family sourced a number of large-scale artworks for the house, which add another dimension to the interiors and lend an additional layer of character and drama. These include a large framed photograph (above) by the window by Canadian artist Rodney Graham and a black and white drawing by Swiss-born artist Ugo Rondinone.

Rural

Tower House

DESIGNER	GLUCK+
COMPLETED	2012
LOCATION	ULSTER COUNTY, NEW YORK, USA

WHEN ARCHITECT THOMAS GLUCK decided to build a vacation house for his family, it helped that he already knew the site intimately. He had spent part of his childhood growing up on this 19-acre (7.7-ha) parcel in Ulster County, about two hours' drive north of New York City, and wanted his own children to be able to enjoy the freedoms offered by this rural enclave as much as he had. Having picked out a particular spot on an elevated and forested plateau, Gluck came up with the idea of a tower house among the trees that would make the most of a panoramic view northwards to the Catskill Mountains.

'Accessing the view and creating a living experience up in the treetops became the generator for the whole project,' said Gluck, who shares the house with his wife, Anne Langston, and their two children. 'It's really the experience of being in a tree house. Looking northwards to the mountains I would say that you can see 20 or 25 miles on a clear day and the money shot is the big view. But the trees are around you on the other three sides so when you look out you see them swaying in the wind.'

The Tower House is a striking and unexpected sculpture sitting in the forest, with a tall, vertical shaft climbing upwards. This is intersected at the fourth storey by an elevated, horizontal, cantilevered box – looking out towards the mountains – which holds the main living spaces. The house is one of a number of buildings on the site, which has been in the family for many years. Gluck's father, and founding partner at their architectural firm, Gluck+, started out with an 1820s cottage that he extended in the 1980s, followed by a guest house and library. The Tower House, which was co-designed by father and son, represents the latest addition to the site.

The house is accessed via a woodland path that leads through the trees to the base of the tower. On the ground floor is the children's bedroom, with custom-built beds and storage units painted vibrant yellow. The next two storeys hold the master bedroom and guest rooms on an identical floor plan, with bathrooms alongside within a central core that contains all the plumbing and services. Climbing upwards to level four, the house opens out into a horizontal living area: the elevated hub of the home. This is a largely open-plan space, featuring the family seating area arranged around a wood burning stove.

DESIGN INGREDIENTS

· Accents of colour

· Distinct zones

· Framing the view

· Geometry

· Living in the trees

[1] WINDOW SEATS

Custom-made window seats run down one side of the elevated, open-plan living and dining room, forming a comfortable spot for appreciating the views and the verdant greenery of the tree canopy. The green cushions add colour and echo the natural hues of the trees that surround the house. 'It is amazing being up in the living room because you really are up among the trees and in it all,' said Gluck. 'It's constantly changing – at dawn, at dusk, when it rains, when there's a snow storm. You never tire of it.'

[2] DISTINCTIVE DINING

The dining table and chairs sit within an area that is lightly defined within the overall proportions of the room by subtle touches. The floor is painted light grey here rather than white, whereas the ceiling is slightly indented and also painted grey. These devices continue into the adjoining kitchen and serve to demarcate the portion of the fourth floor that is attached to the supporting body of the tower below. The rest of the room – painted white – is the section that forms the cantilevered box floating in space.

[3] **SCULPTED STOVE** The wood burning stove forms a warm focal point within the room and enhances the enjoyment of the space. Modern stoves also offer an opportunity to introduce pleasing sculptural shapes, which can be eye-catching and sometimes unexpected. This Shaker stove, manufactured in Germany by Wittus, was designed by Antonio Citterio with Toan Nguyen.

TOWER HOUSES

Elevated homes and tower houses offer a vivid connection with their surroundings, particularly in open, rural settings. Large expanses of glass and picture windows frame these mesmerizing views, which become a key part of everyday living. Contemporary tower houses draw inspiration from many sources, including water towers, forest fire lookouts and observation platforms, as well as from agricultural structures such as grain silos.

[4] **RUG ZONES** The rug helps to define the main seating zone and also provides texture, colour and warmth. The citrus hue stands out all the more against the backdrop of the white floorboards and walls. Near the window a small and colourful jigsaw piece rug frames a play table and stools for the children. The two sculptural plywood chairs are designed by Hans J. Wegner and the slatted, bench-style coffee table is by George Nelson, produced by Herman Miller. Bookcases and storage units are set underneath the tailor-made window bench.

Landscape Living

DESIGNER   VICKY THORNTON

COMPLETED   2008

LOCATION   TARN-ET-GARONNE, FRANCE

ARCHITECT <u>VICKY THORNTON</u> created this fresh French retreat within a sublime setting that she has known well for many years. Her parents had a farmhouse nearby for two decades, and when they decided to sell up, they gave their daughter a piece of land on which to build a new house of her own. The building is a contemporary escape, set within a landscape of rolling hills and woodland, as well as winding lanes and small hamlets. Sitting on the brow of a hill, Thornton's home opens itself up to the vista, with the main living spaces leading onto an elevated terrace that overlooks the valley below.

The two-storey house in Tarn-et-Garonne in south-west France was designed around the natural vantage point offered by the sloping site, tucked gently into the hillside and pushing out towards the vista like a camera lens or viewfinder. 'It was always the idea that the house would project out into the landscape,' said Thornton, who designed the building in conjunction with Jef Smith of Meld Architecture, based in London. 'But we were also really interested in using local materials that would sit well with the surroundings.'

The building was constructed using a base level of recycled local limestone, plus a timber frame clad

in chestnut wood. The approach is accessed via a pine plantation at the back of the house, which provides a reassuring green boundary to the site. The main entrance is to the rear of the upper storey, and this level is devoted to the master bedroom and a large, open-plan living, dining and kitchen area that leads out to the elevated terrace. The interiors are dominated by walls and ceilings made of oriented strand board (OSB) – formed from compacted woodchip – which gives a simple and rustic look to the space, contrasting with the crisp white dining table and other furniture. Downstairs, the interiors are rather different,

because here the thick stone walls are coated in lime render. There are two further bedrooms, one of which is a large studio room that could be easily adapted into a pottery studio should Thornton find more time to indulge her second career as an accomplished potter.

There is also a utility room, complete with two large tanks to hold harvested rainwater for irrigation and for flushing the toilets. This eco-friendly home has a sedum roof and natural cross ventilation, which eliminates the need for air conditioning even in the summer months, and there are also solar panels to heat the supply of water.

DESIGN INGREDIENTS

· Maximizing the views

· Raw textural finishes

· Rustic qualities

· Sense of freedom

· Tranquillity

[1] ORGANIC TEXTURES In contrast to
the polished concrete floors, the straw-coloured
oriented strand board used for the walls and
ceilings adds texture and warmth to the space.
The raw and informal character of these materials
sits well with the rural French setting and offers
echoes of barns and hay bales. The straw-coloured
sofa also complements the natural surroundings
and ties in well with the sunshine yellow splashback
in the kitchen.

[2] OPEN CHOICES The combined dining and
relaxation space – complete with a wood burning
stove and a library wall to one side – offers a choice
of seating and dining areas. In addition to the sofa
– from Ikea – and the formal dining table by the
kitchen, there is a round table and chairs next to the
open windows to the front of the space and another
set on the cantilevered terrace. These elements offer
a series of options as to how the space is used and
enjoyed, thereby enhancing the sense of freedom.

PROTECTIVE SHUTTERS

A sequence of timber and steel shutters allows the house to be shut down and closed up easily when not in use. The shutters protect the building and the interiors from the elements and form a key part of the low-maintenance design philosophy. For a weekend or holiday house, in particular, such elements are practical and reassuring. Finishes within and without the building are purposefully rugged and hard wearing, which suits the informal nature of the house and avoids the need for constant maintenance and repair.

[3] CLERESTORY WINDOWS

A sequence of high clerestory windows complements the folding glass doors at the front of the house. These additional windows introduce a rich quality of light into the home and add to the sense of openness to the land and sky. They also help to provide natural ventilation in the summer months by venting hot air and allowing a natural breeze to flow throughout the building. When natural light is sourced from several different directions, it will always create vivid illumination for interior living spaces.

[4] ELEVATED TERRACE

The multifunctional living area flows out seamlessly to the expansive elevated terrace via a series of folding glass doors. This combination of indoor and outdoor rooms generates a welcome impression of liberated open space. Furthermore, the design of this key aperture creates a powerful picture frame for the open views of the valley, hills and woodland beyond. 'I always gravitate to the front terrace, which is where I choose to eat all my meals,' said Thornton. 'You can also look out from there and watch the sun set.'

Scenic Sanctuary

DESIGNERS ARABELLA RAMSAY/ZEN ARCHITECTS

COMPLETED 2012

LOCATION JAN JUC, VICTORIA, AUSTRALIA

HAVING GROWN UP on a sheep farm in Victoria, fashion designer Arabella Ramsay has always loved being in the countryside. After a period living in Melbourne, with three of her own stores and a hectic schedule, she decided that she needed to take a step back towards her 'country girl' roots. With her husband, Chris, and their two daughters, she moved to Jan Juc and a new home within 6 acres (2.4 ha) of woodland. Here, Ramsay redesigned the main living spaces to forge a strong indoor–outdoor relationship and a constant sense of connection with the natural surroundings.

For Ramsay, Jan Juc represents a beautiful compromise. Her husband runs yoga studios in Melbourne, where he also teaches, and has a great love of surfing. The fact that nearby Bells Beach is one of the best surf spots in Australia was enough to tempt him out of Melbourne, while the tranquillity and quiet, rural surroundings of the house were big attractions for Ramsay. 'I grew up with open spaces, paddocks and green grass and was missing it all when I was in Melbourne,' she said. 'Living down here and having the lifestyle of growing our own food and having our own eggs in the morning fits with our philosophy. And there's a lot more freedom for the children here and the chance to grow up a bit more humble and connected to nature.'

Designed by Melbourne-based Zen Architects, the house places a strong emphasis upon sustainability. The building features solar panels on the roof, a system for harvesting rainwater and a worm farm for dealing with natural waste. The fabric of the building was made with straw bales, coated with a mud and cement render, and supported with heavy-duty timbers recycled from Geelong pier.

Ramsay embraced the house and the ideas behind it, but wanted the interiors to be more family friendly and inviting. The main living space at the front of the building was reinvented with light and bright whites and creams as well as larch floorboards, while the old kitchen was replaced by a tailored design complete with an Aga. Ramsay also extended the deck at the front of the house, creating a natural flow from inside to out. This terrace makes an ideal playroom and a great venue for eating outside. In addition, the outdoor zone provides a perfect stage for appreciating the woods and nature itself, from the black cockatoos to the kookaburras and white hawks.

DESIGN INGREDIENTS

· Abundance of texture

· Eco-friendly materials

· Homely feel

· Inside–outside living

· Playfulness

[1] RUSTIC TABLE The circular table by Mark Tuckey sits well within the living space, positioned between the kitchen and the sitting area. With their natural bark finish, the tree trunk legs of the table provide a modern rustic note and also complement the timbers inside and outside the house. The hefty recycled supporting pillars were reclaimed from Geelong pier.

[2] COLOURFUL KITCHEN The designer created a new kitchen in conjunction with Scott's Country Look Kitchens based in Geelong. Pride of place goes to Ramsay's beloved Aga – the stove she grew up with on her parents' farm – in a powder-blue colour. A similar shade was used for the kitchen units, thus adding warmth and contrasting with the textured white walls and timber floors.

OUTDOOR LOUNGE

For Ramsay and her family, the fresh air lounge is a favourite spot, with its open views into the woods. This outdoor sitting room was designed around the wood burning pizza oven, which also serves as an outdoor fireplace. The integrated timber seating and planters complement the organic character of the house.

[3] LARCH FLOORS Ramsay reinvented the main living spaces with a focus on bright, warm colours and welcoming natural textures. The transformation included replacing the old concrete floors with larch floorboards, which tie together the combined kitchen, dining area and sitting room. Layers of lye treatment and brushed white oil were used to seal and protect the Mafi floor.

[4] STATEMENT LIGHTING
The Chimbarongo chandelier from the PET Lamp workshop hangs over the dining table. It is a hand-made lighting feature from Chile, manufactured using recycled wicker and repurposed glass bottles. The light makes a standout statement within the space, whereas its textures and provenance sit well with the green design ideas contained within the home as a whole. The architecture of the house features a number of other recycled materials, while water and other resources are also recycled as much as possible.

Farmstead Modern

DESIGNER	LUCY MARSTON
COMPLETED	2012
LOCATION	SOUTHWOLD, SUFFOLK, UK

CREATING A MODERN HOME with the depth of character and warmth that you might expect of a period house can be quite a challenge. However, this was exactly architect <u>Lucy Marston</u>'s ambition when she set out to create a new family home on a former farmstead not far from the seaside town of Southwold. Instead of making a radical statement, Marston was more concerned about designing a contemporary farmhouse that connected with the former farm buildings nearby and the open landscape that surrounds the building.

'Originally we were looking for a period property to extend or refurbish rather than building a new house,' said Marston. 'My husband didn't really want to build a modern house to begin with, but the site we finally found was so unique that we decided to go for it. Part of the brief, though, was to make a modern house with the depth of a period property and that meant having things like an inglenook fireplace, exposed ceiling beams, wide landings and slightly quirky spaces.' The couple spent a number of years looking for the right location in Suffolk. The site they found ticked all the right boxes, as it is surrounded by verdant pasture but within easy reach of the coast. The old farm buildings consisted of two single-storey, red-brick Victorian barns and a derelict row of three small former farm labourers' cottages where the farmhouse now stands.

The new house is built with a timber frame and a coat of red brick, which helps tie in the building with the barns alongside. Marston was partly inspired by traditional Suffolk long houses and planned a home that is only one room deep. She created a combined kitchen, dining and family room at one end of the house and a more intimate sitting room, complete with an inglenook fireplace, at the other. Between the two lie a reading room and a playroom, looking out across the fields. These four spaces are connected not only by a long hallway at one side of the house but also by a sequence of sliding pocket doors at the other, allowing the individual rooms to be open to one another or closed off for privacy.

Many elements throughout, including the kitchen and staircase, are custom designs, mixed with antique shop finds and vintage eBay treasures. The crafted, detailed approach to the interiors and the organic patina of the materials carry echoes of Shaker style and the Arts and Crafts Movement, but put through a contemporary filter.

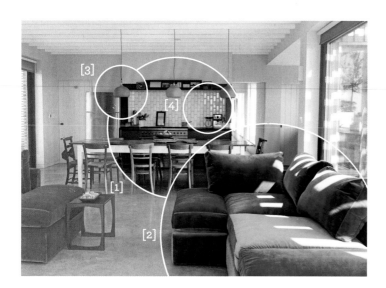

[3]
[4]
[1]
[2]

DESIGN INGREDIENTS

· Clarity

· Comfortable proportions

· Juxtaposition of colour

· Linear contrasts

· Vernacular

[1] FARMHOUSE KITCHEN The space is a contemporary take on the big, open farmhouse kitchen, with room enough for a family dining table plus – in this case – comfortable seating. Marston's design updates the theme for today, with a contemporary Smeg range and modern services and appliances blended with vintage touches, such as the antique dining table and chairs.

[2] MODULAR SOFA The modular sofa can be rearranged within a number of different permutations, creating some flexibility as to how the living space is used. Here, the sofa is arranged in an L-shaped formation around the corner fireplace, with its wood burning stove, and it also introduces a vibrant splash of colour and a soft texture that enrich this family space.

SKY-BLUE BEDROOM

Marston employed a subtle range of light and earthy colours for the interiors on the ground floor of the house, but on the upper storey she opted for a selection of brighter skyline tones. Here, in the master bedroom, the walls are painted a sumptuous teal blue, complemented by notes of vibrant green in the tiles surrounding the fireplace and the curtains. Large picture windows, with inset blinds, offer views out across the farmland.

[3] **PENDANT LIGHTING** The ceramic ceiling lights – by Hand & Eye Studio in London – have a rounded, sculptural quality that adds a fresh dimension. Their contemporary character reasserts the essential modernity of the space, despite the traditional, vernacular influences. The terracotta colour creates a vivid juxtaposition with the blues, whites and creams seen elsewhere in the room.

[4] **VERTICAL TILING** The open-plan room is inevitably defined by a series of horizontal lines and planes, as seen in the ceiling beams and the parallel orientation of the dining table and kitchen worktop. However, the use of kitchen splashback tiling arranged in a vertical formation provides a welcome note of contrast and offers a more pleasing and unexpected pattern than a traditional format.

Seaview Surf House

DESIGNER	CHRIS CONNELL
COMPLETED	2008
LOCATION	LORNE, VICTORIA, AUSTRALIA

WHEN DESIGNER <u>CHRIS CONNELL</u> set about creating a beach house for himself, he wanted to make sure that it would be a home he could really enjoy. Thinking ahead, he designed a modest retreat that could be used summer and winter, and that required a minimum amount of maintenance and upkeep. The materials are heavy duty and the interiors are robust with nothing precious or pretentious. However, Connell's contemporary beach house still manages to be sophisticated and inviting. It is the ultimate reinterpretation of the great Australian beach shack.

Connell and his partner, stylist Wendy Bannister, looked at a few properties – mostly beach cabins – but were beaten to the post every time. Then one day they came across a piece of land for sale on a steep slope facing Loutit Bay in Lorne, Victoria. Initially they were put off by the gradient of the hill, but when they walked up to the site they realized that the views were extraordinary. They decided to buy and build. 'It's a place where you should be able to relax and not worry about things,' said Connell. 'There are people who come down here and spend their whole weekend looking after their house and painting and doing this and that. We wanted to be able to spend the weekend here and really relax. The only manual thing I do is chopping up timber for the wood burning stove and that's something I enjoy doing.'

The house cantilevers out from the hillside in dramatic fashion, supported by steel legs, and is highly insulated – including the exposed underside – for year-round use. The exteriors are coated in spruce, while French oak was used for the floors, kitchen and cabinetwork inside. The main living space is open plan, leading towards sliding glass doors at the front of the building that retract to form an open balcony connected to the landscape and the views of the sea. A studio sits just behind the main living zone, where Connell has set up his easel and likes to paint.

The interiors of the house are intended to be hard wearing, as well as inviting. The leather sofa, the dining table and a number of other pieces were designed by Connell himself. The vintage leather chairs were nicely worn long before they arrived here, and the Artek stools were salvaged from the trash when Connell came across a restaurateur clearing out his old seating.

195

DESIGN INGREDIENTS

· Balance of old and new

· Hard-wearing materials

· Informality

· Movable walls

· Unity

[1] FLEXIBLE LIVING A series of sliding walls allows for a great deal of flexibility as to how the house is used. When Chris and Wendy are home alone, the sliding walls between the bedroom and studio at the rear of the house, and between the studio and living room, remain fully or partially open, with a free-flowing connection between all of these interlinked spaces. When drawn shut, these doors transform the studio into an enclosed guest bedroom with full privacy for visitors.

[2] BLACKBOARD WALL The blackboard wall by the kitchen offers a distinctive colour contrast with the organic tones of the rest of the living space, but it also doubles as an improvised noticeboard and drawing surface. Integrated blackboards have become increasingly common in kitchens – and playrooms – as a 'canvas' for memos and spur of the moment art. They lend the space a more personal element that can be adapted and updated over time.

[3] VINTAGE MODERN

A number of vintage and mid-century pieces bring welcome texture and character to the open-plan living, dining and kitchen space, which forms the heart of the home. These include leather chairs by Danish designer Børge Mogensen, which sit well with the leather sofa designed by Chris Connell for his own furniture company, MAP. 'There's nothing too precious here, nothing we need worry about. And the house is designed so that we don't see any neighbouring houses,' said Connell. 'All we see is green and blue and the sky.'

[4] LOW MAINTENANCE

Contemporary beach houses, like Chris and Wendy's home, are defined by a strong sense of connection to their surroundings and a welcome degree of informality. Hard-wearing and low-maintenance materials and finishes have been used for the flooring and movable walls, whereas the dining table, stools and leather sofa are all able to withstand a good amount of wear and tear. In addition, these elements are not adversely affected by the salt air and sea breezes that blow in frequently from the ocean.

OUTDOOR ROOMS

As expected of a beach house, the main living spaces flow freely to an outdoor room alongside. This relaxation deck leads in turn, via a wooden walkway, to an outdoor dining room, sheltered by an awning. Both areas offer welcome glimpses of the sea and a strong sense of connection with the surrounding bushlands.

Valley Farm

DESIGNER	PIERS TAYLOR
COMPLETED	2011
LOCATION	BATH, SOMERSET, UK

NESTLING WITHIN A QUIET, green English valley, Starfall Farm has a very special feel to it. Finding the house, after a journey down the narrow, winding lanes with fields on either side, is to make a discovery. Owners Anna Benn and Xa Sturgis were certainly seduced by Starfall and its magical location when they first came across it. For Anna – a garden designer and writer – it was the opportunity to create a garden, as well as a fresh and welcoming home, that was so enticing.

The family lived in the Georgian farmhouse, much as it was, for a year before getting planning permission to replace the old barn alongside the house with a new addition that would afford an open family living space, combining a kitchen, dining room and seating area, with a direct connection to the garden. 'We decided that we really wanted to do something – to have a project and a garden,' said Anna. 'This was a run-down farm that had been used as a dog breeding centre for Jack Russells. I thought it was just the kind of thing I wanted – a small farm, nothing big, in a good location and with a south-west facing garden.'

Architect Piers Taylor was recommended to them, and once Anna and Xa had seen Taylor's own home nearby – a vintage gamekeeper's cottage with a contemporary wing – they knew that they had found the right man for the job. 'Xa and Anna really wanted a raw, new building that would patina and age well and settle into the landscape,' said Taylor. 'We wanted something that could take everything that is thrown at it – all the chaos of family life.' He designed a single-storey addition clad in Siberian larch, which was also used to coat the old 1970s extension alongside, tying the two elements together while contrasting nicely with the rugged Bath stone of the original farmhouse. The materials are as organic in feel and tone as the wood that coats the building, with a mix of raw plaster walls and plywood for the kitchen units. The kitchen island was created with poured concrete, made by the contractors and trowelled smooth by Taylor.

The new building also includes a utility room, a shower room and a master bedroom, offering a view out onto the wild flower meadow. This addition connects neatly to the main house, which has been simply but sensitively reordered to create four bedrooms upstairs, as well as a study and L-shaped sitting room downstairs.

[1] TAILOR-MADE KITCHEN The kitchen was designed by the architect with plywood units and an island made with poured concrete. The fitted units reach up to the ceiling, making good use of the available space and creating a pleasing junction between the two planes. The plywood adds warmth to the interiors, contrasting with some of the more industrial finishes.

[2] RAW FINISHES Concrete was used for the poured floors and to make fitted benches and window seats to one side of the room. The walls are finished only in waxed plaster, which has a raw informality and an organic quality that sits well with the rustic nature of the setting. This treatment of the space carries echoes of the original barns and outbuildings on the site.

[3] VINTAGE FURNITURE

The dining table and chairs are vintage mid-century pieces by British furniture manufacturer Ercol, sourced from an antique shop in Bath, and the light above the table is another 1950s piece. They complement the contemporary interiors and add a layer of depth and character to the space. Mid-century pieces have real flexibility to them and usually suit both contemporary and traditional contexts. The organic warmth of the timber furniture sits well with the raw plaster and the plywood used for the custom kitchen.

[4] BEDROOM BATHTIME

The master bedroom can be glimpsed along the circulation corridor, sitting at the far end of the new building. As the only bedroom in this part of the house, with the other bedrooms situated in the adjoining farmhouse, it enjoys a welcome degree of privacy. A claw-foot bath positioned in front of the picture window, within the bedroom itself, is an inviting and imaginative touch, connecting the ritual of bathing with an open vista of the private landscape, complete with its colourful meadow flowers.

OLD AND NEW

The design of the new building, with its timber cladding and pan-tiled roof, carries many echoes of barns and traditional farm buildings, which ties it to the history and context of the setting. At the same time, the new addition is distinctly contemporary in outline and form, with a flexible, open layout that brings a fresh dimension to everyday living at Starfall and offers a new hub for the family. 'The idea was not to create a precious building but to design something that could accommodate the way that the family wanted to live in it,' said Taylor.

Byron Cottage

DESIGNER	MIV WATTS
COMPLETED	2002
LOCATION	BYRON BAY, NEW SOUTH WALES, AUSTRALIA

BRITISH INTERIOR DESIGNER <u>MIV WATTS</u> has a long-held love of Australia. She lived in Sydney for a decade and has been returning ever since, with the trips becoming annual after discovering Byron Bay. She now spends the first three months of the year here with her partner, Mike Gurney, enjoying the many delights of their countryside cottage, surrounded by nature. Chief among them is the sequence of outdoor rooms that Watts has created on the verandas that wrap their way around the house. These rooms provide ideal relaxation points connected to the surrounding greenery and wildlife.

Watts and Gurney bought the cottage in the same year that they first discovered Byron Bay. Right up on the easternmost point of New South Wales, between Sydney and Brisbane, the bay has become a focal point for artists and creative spirits as well as for surfers and fishermen. It combines the natural beauty of coast and countryside with a fine collection of restaurants, stores and cafés. 'I love the fact that we are in the middle of unending natural beauty but just a few miles from absolute sophistication and the best coffee,' said Watts, who now divides her time between England, France and Byron Bay. 'For Mike, it's the wildlife, the parrots that gather each day in the native bushes and the eagles and herons that soar over the creek. For me it's much the same – we love the gorgeous rainforest that the house stands within and the creek that runs through the property.'

The timber house with a tin roof was constructed in the 1980s by a master carpenter and craftsman in Federation-era style using reclaimed and salvaged timber. Watts and Gurney respected the eco-sensitive philosophy behind the design of both the house and the garden, also using recycled wood for a new bathroom extension and the reinvention of a nearby shed, which is now used as a guest house for visiting family and friends.

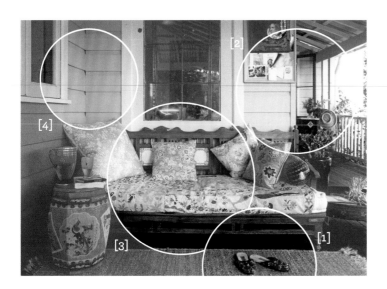

DESIGN INGREDIENTS

· Indian influences

· Layering of pattern and texture

· Nature in the home

· Outdoor rooms

· Soothing atmosphere

[1] OUTDOOR RUG The use of carpets and rugs on the veranda, laid over the timber deck, helps to further reinforce the notion of an inviting space layered with texture and warmth. Given the intimate sense of connection to nature, with its bird- and wildlife, such elements need to be hard wearing and not too precious. Watts and Gurney often find 'house sitters', some welcome and some not so welcome, even inside the cottage. 'We wake up, make coffee and sit out on the veranda, looking down at the creek, watching the white tailed eagle, or the wallabies preparing their day.'

[2] PERSONAL TOUCHES There are a large number of personal touches that reinforce the idea of a rounded outdoor room, including cushions, pictures, photographs and books. In the subtropical climate of Byron Bay, particularly in summer, many waking hours are spent outside and such fresh air spaces become an essential part of daily life. 'In the evening we move to the charpoy on the front veranda with a glass of wine and watch the sun go down. That's my favourite spot for reading and snoozing,' said Watts.

[3] INDIAN FURNITURE

Watts sourced and shipped much of the furniture for the interiors, decks and verandas from India shortly after buying the house. The country is one of a number of important influences upon her work as a designer. Here, the hand-carved Indian sofa becomes the characterful anchor for the restful fresh air sitting room, protected by the overhanging corrugated tin roof that borders the house. 'The whole building is about outside-in,' said Watts. 'We have none of those silly fly screens shutting us off from nature.'

[4] CLAPBOARD CHARACTER

Watts painted the clapboard walls with a soothing pale grey-blue paint, with a touch of French inspiration. The colour was mixed specially by a local supplier in Byron Bay, using recycled sump oil. This hard-wearing, practical finish makes for a soothing backdrop and lends fresh character to the house as a whole.

OUTDOOR DINING

The designer created an outdoor dining room on the deck alongside the kitchen, with the surrounding greenery providing a welcome degree of shade and shelter, as well as an enticing, verdant setting. Paper lanterns hang from the trees, adding colour and interest, while the simple trestle table and garden chairs are complemented by an imaginative and colourful choice of glassware and china.

Farmhouse Modern

DESIGNER	UXUS
COMPLETED	2011
LOCATION	WILTON, CONNECTICUT, USA

THIS FORMER HUNTING LODGE, dating back to the 1930s, is full of surprises. From the outside, the house has a traditional look – with an open porch and clapboard finish painted in a crisp white – while the surrounding woodland offers a gentle, green cushion between the house and the outside world. Once inside the front door, the spider-like Moooi chandelier and walls of periwinkle blue confirm that this is a farmhouse with a twist.

After living in Amsterdam for many years, the owners and their children moved back to the United States and decided that they wanted to live in the countryside. They settled upon Connecticut, where they found an idyllic and secluded spot, surrounded by trees and wildlife. They then turned to George Gottl and Oliver Michell of the design practice UXUS. 'The white family room at the centre was the original part of the house,' said Gottl. 'But then the kitchen and living room area were grafted on later, in the 1950s. Some original details remained – the stone fireplace, the flag floors in the hallway – and the floor in the main room was beautiful, even though we painted it white.'

Structurally, the house was in good shape, but the previous owners had gone for a dated, rustic Americana look. Gottl's client wanted something much more sophisticated, with a modern edge and a European sensibility as well as a selection of pieces by designers such as Piet Hein Eek and Hella Jongerius. 'We wanted to make the space contemporary but we also wanted it to be comfortable and to unify the house,' said Gottl. 'The owners have a large extended family, so we wanted to create a home where everyone can come together but where you can still have different activities happening in various parts of the house.'

This ambition is achieved with a fluid, welcoming layout for the main living spaces and little in the way of solid dividing walls. A wooden balustrade separating the sitting room and the white family room was replaced by a custom-built lattice of white bookshelves. The family room is the hub of the house, with high ceilings and exposed beams. UXUS added windows to either side of the stone fireplace and created a seating area around the fire. However, the room is still big enough for a generous dining table with colourful dining chairs by Leslie Oschmann, which stand out all the more against the neutral backdrop.

DESIGN INGREDIENTS

· Bright white backdrop

· Informality

· Playful elements

· Repurposing

· Rugged textures

[1] WHITE ON WHITE The white family living room sits at the heart of the home, with open access to the kitchen to one side and a more formal sitting room to the other. Walls, floorboards, beams and ceilings are all painted white in this particular part of the house, creating a bright and inviting centre point for the home and a vibrant backdrop against which touches of colour and texture stand out. The high ceilings and large windows also promote a feeling of space and openness.

[2] BOOK STACKS The custom-designed vertical book shelves in front of the windows by the fireplace add a surprising and playful note to the room. The tall irregular towers also turn the books themselves into an eye-catching feature, promoting the idea of a library turned upon its head. Inventive gestures such as this can make a marked impact and introduce personality and individuality to a space.

[3] <u>REPURPOSED FURNITURE</u> The house features a number of pieces of repurposed and reinvented furniture by UXUS and other designers. These include the dining chairs by Leslie Oschmann of Swarm in Amsterdam, who finds vintage furniture in flea markets and paints or embellishes it to create something new. Each of these chairs tells a story, through the murals painted upon them, adding colour and conversation to the space.

[4] <u>FIREPLACE WALL</u> The wall of stone around the fireplace stands out against the neutral colour scheme and provides a focal point for the living space. The rugged texture of the stone is brought alive by the placement of two extra windows either side of the fireplace, which provide additional natural light that amplifies the natural beauty of the stone. In the evening, the fireplace becomes the centre of gravity for the house as a whole.

COUNTRY KITCHEN

The living room leads into a generously scaled family kitchen. This is a contemporary take on the farmhouse kitchen, with timber floors, exposed beams and kitchen units painted a soothing grey. There is room enough for a breakfast area with a dining table by Dutch designer Piet Hein Eek, TOLIX® chairs by French metalworker Xavier Pauchard and a Skygarden ceiling light by another Dutch designer, Marcel Wanders, for Flos.

Forest Escape

DESIGNER	ADAM ROLSTON
COMPLETED	2005
LOCATION	COLUMBIA COUNTY, NEW YORK, USA

FOR ARCHITECT <u>ADAM ROLSTON</u> this rural retreat in upstate New York represents a dream fulfilled. He had partly designed the building before he found the site and then refined his ideas further once he discovered a perfect spot in Columbia County, with the Berkshire Mountains to the east and the Catskills to the west. Set within a clearing in the midst of woodland, the house makes the most of the surroundings with an intimate sense of connection provided by a sequence of sixteen pairs of glass doors positioned front and back. The interiors have a warm, restful and organic character, well suited to the setting.

Rolston searched for many months for a site for his dream home, hoping to find a suitable piece of land to create a weekend and holiday escape for himself and his partner, research psychologist Martin McElhiney. The parcel that they finally secured is on the brow of a steep slope, an awkward location that necessitated careful consideration over the orientation and positioning of the single-storey building.

The design of the house fuses vernacular sources of inspiration – particularly the form, shape and roof line of local barns and agricultural buildings – with Scandinavian and Japanese influences. The trees surrounding the house were preserved and form a natural sun screen in the summer months and a protective sense of enclosure during the winter. Key to the design are the sequences of glass apertures either side of the building, which frame the views of the landscape and create a degree of transparency that contrasts with the pure black outline of the building and its coat of stained black pine. 'It was all about finding the perfect and minimum scale for the house that we were happy with,' said Rolston. 'In a way, the whole house becomes our front door and the fact that we have no distinct entrance takes away some of the formality about the way that the house works.'

The layout is simple but effective, with bedrooms at each end and an open-plan and multifaceted living space at the centre. Service cores holding bathrooms and utility spaces separate the bedrooms from the living space, with pocket doors to either side of the cores that can be drawn across for privacy if required. The interiors are enriched by fine craftsmanship, custom elements and many personal touches by Rolston and McElhiney.

DESIGN INGREDIENTS

· Countryside view on both sides

· Craftsmanship

· Equilibrium

· Focal point stove

· Linear layout

[1] CRAFTED KITCHEN The custom kitchen, made with the same American black walnut as the floors, has the look and feel of a crafted, single piece of furniture, and it floats within the space as such. A cooktop and sink are integrated into the timber worktop, but plenty of room remains on the surface, which can be used for eating breakfast or lunch as well as for preparing food. The stools were found in a dumpster at a New York university.

[2] FOCAL STOVE A wood burning stove, produced by Danish company Scan Design, has been slotted in between the double doors at the front of the house. This type of stove, with its slimline pipe flue, is not only more efficient and much safer than an open fire but it also takes up less space, while still providing a welcome focal point within the room.

[3] CUSTOM CONSOLE A custom console table is positioned just behind the vintage 1970s reupholstered sofa. These two large, linear pieces create a strong combination right at the heart of the home, with the console – designed by Martin McElhiney – offering a surface on which to display plants, vases and personal treasures that bring the space to life.

[4] TEXTURED RUG The patchwork cowhide rug from Sacco Carpet in New York provides texture and subtle geometric pattern while helping to anchor the seating area around the stove. It is part of a composition that sits at the heart of the house, with the kitchen area to one side and the dining table to the other. Quirky touches such as the burl and stump side table and the custom birch twig floor lamp (made by McElhiney) add elements of contemporary rusticity.

CUSTOM ARTWORKS

The colour photograph mounted on the wall by the dining table was taken by Adam Rolston. It depicts a blurred view of sunlight streaming through the trees on the drive from New York City – where Rolston and McElhiney live and work during the week – to Columbia County via the Taconic State Parkway, a scenic route lined with forestry. The photograph sits very naturally within the context of the interiors and the woodland setting, adding another personal layer of interest and narrative to Rolston and McElhiney's home.

Hilltop Farmhouse

DESIGNERS FIONA LYNCH/JACKSON
CLEMENTS BURROWS

COMPLETED 2011

LOCATION HEALESVILLE, VICTORIA,
AUSTRALIA

THE ROUTE TO <u>FIONA LYNCH</u>'S FAMILY FARM runs east of Melbourne through the vineyard trail of the Yarra Valley. Just before the town of Healesville it heads north up into the hills and along a winding track that leads to a cattle farm, where the contemporary farmhouse sits, looking out across the pastures and woodlands. This striking hilltop home is a replacement for the family's original house here, lost to bushfires, and it makes the most of its prominent position. An open-plan living space at the heart of the building opens up to decks on either side and to the broad vista of the Victorian countryside.

The cattle farm has been in the Lynch family for many years and it is home to a healthy herd of Herefords. Fiona's parents built the original timber farmhouse, but it was lost in 2009 to the devastating bushfires that claimed about 2,000 houses across the region. Fortunately, no one on the farm was hurt and the house was well insured, which provided the opportunity to rebuild.

The family talked over plans for the property, which is used at various times by three generations. The new house had to be flexible enough to cope with different numbers of people and a variety of needs, as well as be well suited to the site and surroundings. Together, the family considered a number of designs, made available by leading Australian architects in the wake of the fires, before deciding on a house by <u>Jackson Clements Burrows</u>.

This single-storey building with a mono-pitched tin roof and tin shell exterior walls is positioned just over the brow of the hill that hosted the original farmhouse, but it still benefits from extraordinary open views. The interior layout and finishes were tailored by Fiona, who has her own interior design practice based in Melbourne, while one of her five brothers managed the financial aspects of the project.

An open-plan kitchen, dining and seating area sits at the centre of the building, with large sliding glass windows to either side that pull back to open onto adjoining decks. This creates a degree of transparency at the heart of the home, and occasionally swallows dart through from one side to the other, swooping over the dining table as they go. Two bedrooms are situated at one end of the house, with a third plus a large bunkroom for the children at the other.

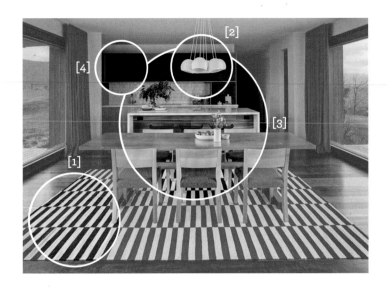

· Flexible living

· Geometric patterns

· Inside–outside

· Made-to-order furniture

· Transparency

[1] GEOMETRIC RUGS

The geometric black and white rugs, laid over the spotted gum floorboards, help to define both the dining zone and the seating area within the overall proportions of the space. They also add a graphic quality that enlivens the room and ties in well with the tartan check fabric used to upholster the sofa. This piece of furniture was sourced from Jardan in Melbourne, a family-run design company that crafts every item to order. The oval coffee table is by Temperature Design and the Archie armchairs are from Jardan, too.

[2] FEATURE LIGHTING

The sculptural Sphere 7 aluminium ceiling light suspended over the Mark Tuckey dining table creates a focal point in the living area. It also makes the large open space seem more intimate and welcoming. The design of the light fitting, by Alain Monnens for Belgian firm tossB, subtly subverts the linear character of the architecture and interiors and adds a fresh dimension to the room. It draws the eye upwards and then outwards, taking the focus away from the strong geometry of the interior architecture and thus softening the space.

[3] ISLAND BAR Given that the house is used by the extended family, which is blessed with a total of seventeen grandchildren, flexible living is a key part of the design philosophy. This includes the kitchen island, which can double as a breakfast bar or lunch counter, supplementing the formal dining table alongside.

[4] SUBTLE STORAGE A generous amount of built-in storage allows the house to remain uncluttered and welcoming. The kitchen features a range of storage units above and below the work counter, with a separate pantry tucked away at the beginning of the circulation corridor to one side. This corridor also features a sequence of large built-in cupboards.

TRANSPARENT SPACES

The idea of a transparent home, one that allows the eye to pass through the building, assumes particular importance in such a sublime setting. Sliding glass doors to the living area retract for a direct connection with the surroundings, while the decks are used as outdoor rooms for eating and entertaining. 'The layout does give the family a lot of flexibility to do with how we all use the house,' said Lynch. 'Usually there are two families or three, and sometimes, if we are lucky, we might get the house to ourselves. We tend to relax a lot up here – cooking, eating, making coffee.'

Urban

Living Patterns

DESIGNER   DAVID KOHN ARCHITECTS

COMPLETED   2011

LOCATION   BARCELONA, SPAIN

Having developed a particular passion for Barcelona, two brothers bought this apartment in the Gothic Quarter. It sits on the *piano nobile* of a five-storey building, dating from the late 19th century, which retains several period features such as ceiling mouldings and balconies. The siblings asked architect <u>David Kohn</u> – whom they had known since their school days – to update and reinvent the interiors, which he did with a great deal of ingenuity and originality. A key element is a new tiled floor, which is full of ideas and narrative as well as colour and pattern.

In the Gothic Quarter the building sits at a key junction, which lends the structure an unusual triangular shape comparable to that of the Flatiron Building (1902) in New York. The district is full of character and makes a perfect base for exploring the city. 'It's very picturesque with narrow streets, lots of nightlife and close to the beach,' said Kohn. 'The area was relatively inexpensive when the brothers bought the apartment and has gentrified a little, but retains a certain urban huskiness. One of its claims to fame is that Picasso had his studio here.'

The brothers – one of whom lives in the United Kingdom and the other in Hong Kong – had owned the property for many years before they commissioned Kohn. The apartment was in poor condition, with cracked floors and basic service spaces, and it had been subdivided into several separate rooms. Kohn stripped out three partition walls to open up the space and reveal its full volume, with high ceilings and a rich quality of natural light. The new layout is essentially loft-like and open plan, with the seating area, kitchen and dining zone contained within one multifunctional space. However, there are other distinct elements that read more like pieces of furniture or installations than separate rooms. These include a vestibule with glass doors that marks the transition from the public to the private realm. A timber tower at one end holds two bedrooms, while another is contained within a modest mezzanine that borders one internal wall, without upsetting the sense of space and volume. Character and personality come from the many tailored and narrative elements within the space, from the mezzanine library to the custom tiles. 'When you are in the apartment, it really is a place to raise your aspirations of being in Barcelona,' said Kohn. 'It is joyful and calm in equal measure.'

DESIGN INGREDIENTS

· Geometric pattern

· Mezzanine level

· Narrative

· Period features

· Public and private realms

[1] FLOOR PATTERN On one level, the tiles designed by Kohn introduce colour, pattern and dynamism. The shift in dominant colour across the apartment from green to red also metaphorically marks the realms of the two brothers. The geometrical tiles were made by Spanish firm Mosaics Martí, which supplied tiles for several Antoni Gaudí projects in Barcelona. They draw inspiration from a number of sources, including the historic patterns of the Middle Ages and floors designed by 20th-century Italian architect Piero Portaluppi.

[2] HIGH LIBRARY The library shelving is one of a number of elements within the apartment that read as installations and accessories to the main living space. Mounted high on one wall, the custom library forms a continuation of the slim mezzanine level and provides a bold visual connection between the brothers' bedrooms at either end of the apartment. The library ladder can be moved around the space to access the books and the mezzanine itself. At the same time, the book collection adds another layer of texture and character to the space.

INSTALLATION BEDROOM

The notion of pods and installations has been explored by a number of architects and designers as a way of providing private space within a more open-plan environment. Here, one bedroom sits upon the mezzanine while two are contained within a twin-storey structure at one end of the apartment. This crafted timber box has the feel of a custom-made piece of furniture rather than a separate, subdivided space. The use of the adjustable timber louvres for the pod offers the opportunity to control the available light with ease, while also maximizing privacy as required.

[3] **GALLEY KITCHEN** The kitchen is a somewhat enigmatic element within the living area. Its galley-style design, tucked away under the mezzanine bedroom, makes for a compact and unobtrusive component and allows the living space to feel open and unimpeded. A generous amount of integrated storage means that the area as a whole remains uncluttered, with cooking utensils, china and glassware tucked neatly away. At the same time, the tiled blue splashback sings out, echoing the hues of the Knoll sofa and chairs.

[4] **CUSTOM FURNITURE** The apartment features a number of Knoll furniture designs, but the dining table was created especially for the space. Designed by David Kohn, its unusual tapered form echoes the irregular shape of the apartment itself, and – together with the tall, wall-mounted mirror nearby – creates a kind of exclamation mark at the apex of the room. The webbed dining chairs are by Jens Risom for Knoll; he was one of the first designers to work for the company in the 1940s and one of the first to introduce Scandinavian-style furniture design to the United States.

Brooklyn Bakehouse

DESIGNERS	BEN BISCHOFF/MADE
COMPLETED	2011
LOCATION	BROOKLYN, NEW YORK, USA

For Dawn Casale and Dave Crofton, a generously sized, welcoming kitchen was a priority. The couple run two boutique bakeries in Brooklyn and also hold baking classes, so for them the kitchen was always going to be the heart of their home. Having outgrown their former apartment, Casale and Crofton spent some time looking for a family home within easy striking range of their stores. They were not keen on the traditional period brownstone row houses, for which Brooklyn is renowned, but leapt at the chance to buy a three-storey house that offered the opportunity to craft informal, open-plan living spaces while retaining the loft-like feel that they both love. The key area in the house is the light and generously scaled living room on the ground floor, with a new kitchen right at the centre.

Casale and Crofton turned to architect Ben Bischoff of MADE, who had worked on the design of their bakery cafés. Both client and designer shared the excitement offered by a clean slate, given that all the period features had already been stripped away. This left them with a real sense of freedom to shape the new interiors to the needs of the family, including the couple's two young children.

Bischoff moved the existing staircase away from the front door to create a more enticing entrance zone and to free up the plan of the ground floor. Here, he placed the seating area at one end and the main dining area at the other. Between the two sits the new kitchen, with a long galley against one wall complemented by a substantial island. 'We wanted the kitchen to be functional, warm yet industrial, welcoming and not overly precious,' said Casale. 'We wanted a kitchen that begged to be used, and use it we do.'

Some of the cabinet work was made from Douglas fir, but with inexpensive drawers and a marble sink surround salvaged from an earlier MADE project. Where possible the architect and client used reclaimed and repurposed materials to save on the budget. This enabled them to reserve some funds for decorative flourishes and character touches, such as the David Weeks ceiling light that hangs over the dining table. The new staircase to one side features an integrated display unit, while ducts and services are left partially exposed in keeping with the semi-industrial aesthetic favoured by Casale and Crofton.

[1] FOCUS RANGE The kitchen design revolves around the large Bluestar range and hood, which form an anchor to the room and a functional delight for a family of bakers and cooks. The cabinetry itself is a hybrid of affordable Ikea carcasses and tailored joinery made with salvaged Douglas fir. Adjacent to the island, a breakfast table doubles as a homework and study station.

[2] BLACK AND WHITE Most of the brick walls have been painted white, apart from those around the stairs. With the painted floorboards, these textured white surfaces bounce light through the space and form a bright backdrop for family life. Certain pieces stand out well against this neutral palette, particularly the black dining table and matching chairs, as well as the Cross Cable light above, designed by New York-based David Weeks.

[3] **DISPLAY SHELVES** The new staircase, designed by Ben Bischoff, has a custom-crafted quality. A floor-to-ceiling display unit integrates with the staircase and forms a striking feature in itself. With space for glass, ceramics and cookery books, it is both part of the kitchen and part of the stairway at one and the same time.

[4] **INDUSTRIAL CHIC** The heavy-duty refrigerator, powerful range and exposed ducts have echoes of a commercial kitchen. This semi-industrial aesthetic is associated particularly with open-plan loft living, which provided an aspirational model for Casale and Crofton as they designed their three-storey home.

MINIATURE GALLERY

Two simple shelves mounted on the whitewashed brick wall create a display area for photographs and artworks. These pieces become a gallery in miniature for treasured images; collectively they form a collage of shapes and colours that serves as a visual library for the family. The variety of the frames adds interest, while the colours of the pictures stand out effectively against the neutral backdrop.

Montmartre by Design

DESIGNER	ERIC ALLART
COMPLETED	2006
LOCATION	PARIS, FRANCE

ASK ERIC ALLART WHAT HE DOES for a living and he will reply in succinct style: designer, decorator and dealer. His apartment near Montmartre, not far from the Sacré-Cœur Basilica, is where all of these passions combine in one enticing retreat. On the fourth floor of an early 20th-century apartment building, Allart's home is a very personal response to the space and the character of the building itself, hosting a number of his own pieces and work by several of the designers that he represents. Within the blend, there is a particularly strong showing for design from the 1970s.

'I completely redesigned the apartment after I bought it,' Allart said. 'The building won an architecture prize from the city of Paris in 1901 and the apartments are quite large, although I have one of the smallest. There was a lot of work to be done but I tried to respect the spirit of the building and to respond to it. We redid everything.'

The heart of the apartment is a double sitting room, made up of two interconnecting spaces that can be subdivided easily by folding doors. With balconies to the street, this living space is rich in sunlight, while the walls are painted in a soft, soothing *eau de nil* and the floors are stained a warm walnut colour. Allart replaced the fireplace at one end with a period find and placed a circular Gothic-style mirror above it; bookcases to either side form a neat and ordered library. He then set about layering the room with pieces by designer Willy Rizzo, sculptor Fred Brouard and others.

Having opened up the apartment, Allart used large wall-mounted mirrors in the hallway as an effective way of bouncing light through the interiors. He also utilized half-glass internal doors to improve the flow of natural sunlight in transitional places. 'I have used two large mirrors with white frames in the hallway facing out to the windows,' said Allart. 'It's a very old idea to reflect light and make the apartment seem more spacious. The kitchen, though, has more of a country feel. We restored the tiled floor, which is original. There is enough space to cook and to have dinner.' In fact, the kitchen is large enough for a dining table – also designed by Allart – while a built-in display cabinet shows off a collection of china and glassware. In contrast, the bathroom is the most contemporary and minimal space in the apartment, enriched with dark-coloured wenge woodwork.

DESIGN INGREDIENTS

· 1970s influence

· Original features

· Statement lighting

· Symmetry

· Vintage furniture

[1] **MIRROR ART** The eye-catching mirror above the fireplace is a design by Eric Allart. Like the period fireplace, it becomes a key focal point in the room and introduces movement and dynamism through its reflective qualities. Mirrored glass is also used in other areas of the apartment to help circulate light.

[2] **FEATURE BOOKCASES** The two bookcases are 1970s designs by Willy Rizzo. They lend a pleasing symmetry to this part of the room and provide storage, library shelving and a place to display ceramics and other treasures. More than this, they form an elegant, crafted feature in themselves, with their lacquered black finish standing out against the grey walls. The leather armchair is a vintage 1940s piece by Danish furniture designer Børge Mogensen.

NEAT DESK

A slim, vintage, two-drawer desk occupies one side of the living room, set up as a small unobtrusive work station. When not in use as a desk, it doubles as a display table, slotting in neatly to a corner where two rooms have been conjoined to create one large open-plan living space. Folding doors can be used to separate the two sections as required, thereby offering a flexible way of living. The desk itself is a 1970s piece: 'The furniture in the apartment is 70 per cent from the 1970s,' said Allart. 'It's one of my favourite periods of design.'

[3] **LAMP LIGHTING** Instead of ceiling lights and spotlights, Allart has opted for a collection of sculptural wall lights and lamps throughout the apartment. These pieces are much more than functional task lights and add a fresh layer of interest to the living space. Among the collection are designs by Willy Rizzo and Allart himself.

[4] **PERIOD DETAILING** Ceiling mouldings, parquet floors and large windows with balconies add an engaging layer of character to the apartment and have been retained where possible. Allart was keen to preserve and restore the original features, and the old floors were repolished and stained a walnut colour. The fire surround that Allart inherited when he bought the apartment was not in keeping with the rest of the interiors and was replaced by another period piece.

Infill House

DESIGNER	TIM GLEDSTONE
COMPLETED	2010
LOCATION	LONDON, UK

ARCHITECT TIM GLEDSTONE adopted an inventive and original approach to the challenge of squeezing a family house onto a slim and unusual London site. Built on a stray piece of land at the end of a terraced street, the new building maximizes every inch of available living space. The internal courtyard is a crucial part of the plan, liberating the main living areas and providing a sense of connection with the outdoors. It also draws light and air deep into the heart of the building, which now provides an inviting family home for Gledstone, his wife and their two young children.

Only the narrow facade of the house, overlooking the street, connects with the urban landscape beyond, because the rest of the site is completely landlocked by neighbouring buildings and boundary walls. Gledstone drew inspiration from Japanese architecture, particularly the traditional timber merchants' houses of Kyoto, which were arranged around hidden gardens. Japanese innovations in space-saving modern urban architecture also proved a key reference point. 'The Japanese are really masters of tight spaces,' said Gledstone, who designed and built his Wandsworth home as a solo project. 'There are brilliant examples of designing small spaces and that's how many Japanese people live. Beds get folded away, everything gets stored in cupboards and rooms become multifunctional.'

Gledstone met his wife, Patricia, who has Japanese family, when he was studying architecture at Oxford Brookes University. He went to Japan for a year between his studies and now returns annually to see Patricia's relatives in Tokyo. When he decided to create a family home, it was inevitable that influences from these travels would feed into the project. The architect managed to pack four bedrooms into the floor plan of the house, with three family sleeping spaces positioned at the front. There was even enough space on the ground floor for a combined study and play room. However, the real drama of the house is saved for the living room to the rear, with windows overlooking the courtyard and doors opening to the rear boundary. All the spaces make full use of the irregular shape of the site; the open-plan seating area, dining zone and kitchen are surprisingly light and fresh, enhanced by the connections to the internal secret garden.

DESIGN INGREDIENTS

· Accents of colour

· Cohesion

· Eco-friendly

· Internal courtyard

· Numerous light sources

[2] SPLASHES OF COLOUR On the sofa – manufactured by Italian industrial design specialists Zanotta – the sequence of cushions adds accents of colour. They are made with vibrant mid-century fabrics, designed by Josef Frank for Svenskt Tenn, which stand out against the organic colours of the leather and timber furniture.

[1] COMPACT KITCHEN Given the restricted nature of the site, space-saving ideas have been essential to the design of the house. At one side of the open-plan living room, the kitchen is compact but elegant, with appliances, sink and storage recessed within an alcove and complemented by a slim island. The units and steel-topped work surfaces are by bulthaup and the integrated appliances are by German manufacturer Gaggenau.

[3] <u>FILM POSTERS</u> Gledstone has collected a number of posters promoting classic films. By their very nature, these artworks are colourful, impactive and large in size and scale; consequently, they bring these qualities into the space. Illuminated by the narrow skylight above, they add drama to the expansive side wall, while their slim black surrounds echo the door frames. Iconic and rare period posters have become as collectable and valuable as some original artworks, and Gledstone has made a feature of film posters in other rooms in the house.

[4] <u>GARDEN LIGHT WELL</u> With the exception of the front facade, the only sources of natural light had to be found within the boundaries of the site itself. The addition of a long skylight and a slim light well on the rear boundary provides a key source of light for the living room. This wall of glass opens onto a miniature garden and a bamboo screen, which soften the impact of the high brick wall. Together with the courtyard at the opposite end of the room, these sources create a light-filled space within a land-locked part of the site.

COURTYARD LIVING

The internal courtyard was crucial to the success of the restricted site. It provides an essential source of light to many parts of the building, while also creating an outdoor room and compact garden, complete with planting, seating and a modest lap pool. It is also a fresh air space for the children and a source of natural ventilation for the building. The white Chair_ONE is a design created in 2004 by Konstantin Grcic for Magis.

California Greenhouse

DESIGNER	MARC BRICAULT
COMPLETED	2008
LOCATION	LOS ANGELES, CALIFORNIA, USA

NESTLED IN VENICE BEACH, Paul and Cicek Bricault's house has a life of its own. This is because much of it is actually living and breathing, including a large rooftop garden – complete with a highly productive vegetable patch – and outer walls of flowering sedum. The stylish eco-friendly building is a unique proposition for Los Angeles, where it has attracted a lot of interest in the neighbourhood. Other common sense green measures used in the house range from natural ventilation to solar panels on the roof, which are a source of electricity.

When the Bricaults first bought the house, it was a relatively ordinary home that had begun life as a bungalow, dating from about 1910, and had been extended by a developer. However, with a growing family the owners began to think about extending again. They turned to Paul's brother, Marc Bricault, an architect and furniture designer based in Canada. Marc came up with ideas for a dramatic two-storey extension – complete with green zones of all kinds – that would allow the house to grow into the back of the site towards a rear alleyway. The new elements of the house wrap around a courtyard garden that provides a secure play area for the children and also leads into a long 'breezeway' through a set of glass doors. This open hallway has many functions, one of which is to draw in cool air.

The new extension holds extra bedrooms on the upper level, including a master suite, complete with a large bathroom lifted by a window of translucent glass tiles. At the back of the house, the new master bedroom is a quiet haven, while the old main bedroom at the front has been turned into guest quarters. 'Marc did a great job at designing a family house,' said Paul. 'There is a lot of whimsy in the house. There is quite a level of seriousness in the design as well, but it doesn't overwhelm you. It's balanced by a sense of fun.'

The rooftop vegetable garden has been a big hit with the children. It takes Paul back to the days of his own childhood in Canada, when he used to help his father with the gardening, but it also feeds into the whole family's love of cooking. 'If I buy something from the vegetable store, [the kids] will turn their noses up at it,' said Paul. 'But if I say that it came from the roof their eyes light up, they get excited and they want to try it. It has dramatically extended their vegetable portfolio.'

DESIGN INGREDIENTS

· Contrast of linear
  and sculptural forms

· Inside–outside connection

· Minimal furniture

· Playfulness

· Sustainability

[1] BREEZEWAY LIVING The breezeway forms a link between the old and new portions of the house, but also offers a flexible living space that can be used as a playroom or a secondary sitting area. In addition, it functions as a garden room, connecting directly to the enclosed courtyard alongside via a sequence of pivoting glass doors. This unique space provides a key source of natural cross ventilation, which cools the house in the summer months, and it also enjoys a vast amount of natural light.

[2] WINDOW SEATS A long plinth alongside the windows to one side of the breezeway creates an integrated bench. It provides additional seating when the space is used for entertaining, enhanced by its free-flowing connection with the enclosed garden. The thick pile rug helps to define a soft, flexible relaxation and play zone; the plywood chair is a design by Charles and Ray Eames.

[3] SCULPTED STAIRCASE The staircase by Marc Bricault forms a dramatic focal point. Its design recalls the architectural forms of buildings such as the Sharp Centre for Design by Will Alsop in Toronto. The stairway serves a number of purposes, linking the two storeys and the roof garden, and also acting as a conduit for warm air, which is vented from the top of the stack.

GLASS BATHROOM

Close to the rear boundary, at the very back of the house, is the master suite. The generously proportioned bathroom features a wall of glass blocks, inspired by Pierre Chareau's iconic Parisian house, the Maison de Verre (1932). These translucent bricks introduce natural light but still provide complete privacy. They create a dramatic grid that forms a backdrop to the made-to-order twin sinks and vanity unit.

[4] GREEN WALLS Much of the new section of the house is wrapped in a living green coat of sedum. In addition to serving the environment, it softens the outline and provides a natural blanket that freshens and protects the building. This vertical garden is complemented by the green courtyard and roof garden, which includes a much-loved vegetable patch. The Bricaults have had so much interest in their living walls that at one point they hung up a small dispenser containing leaflets that explained the Canadian planting system that they had used.

Metropolitan Loft

DESIGNER	VICENTE WOLF
COMPLETED	1993
LOCATION	MANHATTAN, NEW YORK, USA

DESIGNER VICENTE WOLF's Manhattan apartment is in a process of constant and creative change. Situated on the eleventh floor of a 1920s building on the edge of the Garment District, the loft is an amalgamation of two separate apartments with large windows that offer both plentiful light and views of the city. The space serves as an open canvas for Wolf's eclectic mix of furniture, art and photography, which blends periods and provenance within a contemporary and engaging melange.

'My work is elegant and relaxed, with very mercurial colours,' said Wolf. 'There is a blend of different periods and elements, but the result is always a modern environment. The first time I entered this space it just felt so New York with the right light and the right views. I wanted a loft because I didn't want to live in a conventional apartment.'

Wolf was determined to preserve the sense of space and wanted to avoid partitioning where possible, as well as anything that might undermine the semi-industrial character of the original interior architecture. Walls and floors were painted white, and the banks of steel-framed windows were left intact and uncovered, with the exception of the master bedroom, which features curtains and blinds. The master bathroom is separated by a frosted glass wall that still allows natural light to filter through.

The open proportions of the main living room have been respected and preserved. Here, Wolf has created a series of lightly delineated zones, crafting areas for relaxing, sitting and dining through the arrangement of furniture and art. Self-designed pieces blend with period treasures, such as a painted 18th-century Swedish folding table and a Louis XVI bench. An emphasis on natural materials and organic tones ties these disparate pieces of furniture together in rounded compositions. Many of Wolf's finds are sourced during his travels, which usually take up a few months each year. 'There are always things that are coming and going,' said Wolf. 'There's a new favourite that I fall in love with and then on my next trip abroad there's something else. I like things that are unique and have a twist to them and I often look outside the interior design world for inspiration.'

Other zones within the apartment include a library and guest quarters, arranged within a flexible setting. This space can be used for reading and relaxing and fits within the open and adaptable design philosophy of the apartment as a whole.

241

[1] REFLECTIVE FLOORS All the floors of the apartment are painted in white deck paint, which gives the surface a reflective sheen. This helps to circulate natural light throughout the space and ties the apartment together with one cohesive treatment. The white floors and walls also provide a neutral backdrop for Wolf's enviable collection of art, furniture and furnishings. Partial walls and monolithic partitions are utilized to anchor particular zones, without compromising the sense of openness and volume within the loft apartment as a whole.

[2] CORNER SEATING In the loft there exists a balancing act between the need to preserve the open-plan layout and the desire for more intimate seating zones and escapes. Wolf has achieved this equilibrium by using a number of devices to define particular areas, including a semi-partition wall that grounds the daybed. Here, he uses the natural intimacy of one corner of the apartment to define a sitting room. It offers a degree of enclosure, enhanced by the arrangement of the sofa and chairs, without impeding the fluid dynamic of the loft.

HOME GALLERIES

Within the apartment, Wolf has designed a number of home galleries, created within crafted corners and upon internal walls, for the display of photography and art. They include this small area, where prints and artworks are displayed on slim shelves mounted upon the wall, where they receive plenty of natural light. The gallery idea is repeated in the master bedroom.

[3] CUSTOM DAYBED The daybed is a design by Wolf that references the notion of a four-poster bed within a contemporary steel-framed cubic piece. It is used for visiting guests as needed, but for much of the time offers a more intimate sitting and reading spot set somewhat apart from the rest of the open-plan apartment. The photograph above the daybed is by Wolf.

[4] ART AND PHOTOGRAPHY
Wolf has created an unusual chair gallery that features several of his favourite artworks, displayed in an eclectic array of frames. He can rearrange his gallery whenever he likes, moving the pictures from the chairs to the narrow shelves nearby. The designer is a respected photographer in his own right and has been collecting prints for some time, including pieces by Edward Weston, Edward Steichen and Richard Avedon. A number of photographs from the collection are displayed at various points throughout the apartment.

Staircase House

DESIGNER	MOUSSAFIR ARCHITECTES
COMPLETED	2011
LOCATION	PARIS, FRANCE

OWNER ERIC DE RUGY works in a creative industry, designing communication strategies for brands and companies. Not surprisingly, he wanted his Parisian home to be all about communication and creativity, with each and every space connected to one another, as far as possible, without any solid doors or divisions. On a modestly scaled urban site, this presented quite a challenge. The solution forged by Jacques Moussafir of <u>Moussafir Architectes</u> was to create a staircase house, with interconnected spaces arranged around a central service core. The result is a vertical loft, where de Rugy's living areas flow freely into one another.

The house is sandwiched between two larger period buildings within a desirable quarter on the Left Bank. De Rugy bought the original 19th-century building, which was in poor condition after being left unused for many years, and thought that he would replace it with a modern home. However, the site faced a number of restrictions: at least two existing walls had to be retained and flood risk planning provisions meant that any living areas needed to be elevated above ground level. At the same time, de Rugy was clear that he wanted a fluid home, full of light and free from partitions. 'To me, liberty is the most valuable treasure and when I was a child I felt sorry when people closed themselves in with doors, walls and fences,' said de Rugy. 'That's probably why I decided to make a career in communications. I wanted the house to be bold but warm, environmentally friendly, with big volumes and large windows, and it was mandatory that there should be no solid boundaries.'

The owner turned to the architect, who developed the idea of a staircase home, with each space in the house representing an extended landing within a spiralling stairway that rises steadily upwards. The basement is devoted to an office; the entrance zone is on the ground floor, followed by an elevated living space and then a sequence of interconnected rooms topped by a roof terrace at the summit of the building. These landings or half-levels are arranged around a service core that contains the kitchen, bathroom and integrated storage elements. In some respects, the concept is a simple one, but it makes for a home with a complex floor plan and a variety of volumes, with glimpses of and connections between the different spaces throughout.

DESIGN INGREDIENTS

· Complex floor plan

· Continuity

· Contrasting textures

· Filtered light

· Rhythm and flow

[1] SHADOW PATTERNS The lace-like pattern of the steel screens, which are used to protect the glass facade, adds a new dimension to the interiors, as well as to the exterior. When drawn across the windows, the screens filter the natural light and create a filigree pattern of shadows across the walls, furniture and floors.

[2] CUSTOM ELEMENTS The interiors of this highly tailored home feature a range of custom-designed elements, such as the concrete-framed shelves attached to the masonry wall in the sitting room. This idea is repeated elsewhere in the house, providing storage and library space. Other custom elements include the latticed screens.

OPEN BEDROOM

Significant areas of colour lift the bedroom, where the integrated bed and headboard unit is picked out in lime green. The colour stands out against the white masonry walls, and a skylight brings extra light from above. A fitted storage wardrobe has been arranged against one wall and the bathroom is tucked into the central service core.

[3] CONTRASTING TEXTURES

The pre-existing masonry walls expose the texture of time and age. These raw surfaces are juxtaposed with the vast expanses of glass and the warm locust wood used for the floors, ceilings and panelling around the service core, which contains the kitchen, bathroom and other elements. The organic character of the dark wood helps to enrich and invigorate the living space.

[4] REPEATED HIGHLIGHTS

Organic greens make their way into the interiors in the form of a variety of potted plants, while the laser-cut filigree pattern of the metallic screens echoes their leaves and branches. A more vibrant lime green is utilized as an accent colour throughout the home. In the living room, this standout shade is used for the coffee table and within the fitted shelving unit. It is repeated in the storage niche by the front door and in the bedroom, and also finds its way into the dining area via the injection-moulded Moroso dining chairs.

Viewpoint House

DESIGNER	WARREN TECHENTIN ARCHITECTURE
COMPLETED	2008
LOCATION	LOS ANGELES, CALIFORNIA, USA

SITTING WITHIN THE LEAFY neighbourhood of
Los Feliz, Warren Techentin's self-designed home
maximizes the open vista across the city of Los
Angeles. The architect and his wife, Mimi Won
Techentin, bought the hillside site with a rather
forlorn 1950s bungalow in situ and embarked on
a radical rebuild. Their new family home is clad
in redwood, stained and painted black, with a
montage of distinctive windows framing the views
of the city. The main living spaces revolve around
a dramatic stairwell library that sits at the heart
of the house and doubles as a snug retreat,
surrounded by books.

To some extent the design of the house was dictated
by the bungalow footprint, then liberated by a
two-storey layout, with key living spaces positioned
on the raised ground floor and bedrooms above.
'As we are not on a wholly private site, we had to
balance the need to open up the house and create
indoor–outdoor connections with maintaining
privacy,' said Techentin. A lightly delineated
entrance area leads directly into the great room,
which is the pivotal living space of the house. Here,
a window seat faces south towards the green tree
canopy. Nestling at the heart of the building to one
side of the sitting area is the library, with a staircase
wrapping around it as it ascends. The stairway
doubles as a light well, lit from above by a skylight,
while operable windows on the skylight turn the
library into a natural ventilation stack.

Furnishings mirror the eclectic feel of the
neighbourhood – a mix of styles and periods – and
add to the rich character of the house. The brick
fireplace in the library was salvaged from the
original bungalow, although the chimney was
removed and the brick covered in beautifully
textured tiles. In the great room, tailor-made pieces
by Techentin mix with Florence Knoll armchairs and
a contemporary dining table and chairs, as well as
period pieces such as a Victorian chair upholstered
in red toile fabric. The kitchen is also a highly
tailored space, with a custom design by Techentin
that includes a diner-style breakfast alcove. 'Diners
were definitely an inspiration,' said the architect.
'They are prominent in Los Angeles and the period
diners have these small alcoves with fixed table tops.
Having created the circulation routes in the kitchen,
this [space] seemed to make the perfect breakfast
area with built-in seating.'

DESIGN INGREDIENTS

· Cosy corners

· Defined zones

· Dramatic flourishes

· Eclectic mix of styles and periods

· Statement lighting

[2] FEATURE FIREPLACE The fireplace is a delightful remnant of the original bungalow, set into one wall of the library and coated in textured hand-made tiles from Heath Ceramics in San Francisco. It plays upon the idea of a library as a special kind of sitting and reading room – rich in warmth and comfort – with a soothing and uplifting character. A music room and study are accessed via inset doorways set discreetly among the library shelves.

[1] LIBRARY WALLS At the heart of the floor plan is the library: a key space around which many elements of the house revolve, including the staircase that ascends alongside the tall book shelves. This custom-made shelving is picked out in a sky blue accent colour, which complements the poplar staircase. The armchair is a design by Hans J. Wegner.

[3] STATEMENT CHANDELIER A focal point of the library and stairwell, the porcelain chandelier was designed by Los Angeles-based artist Pae White and it is a key piece within an eclectic mix of new and vintage furniture and lighting. The five-tiered Baroque-influenced design lends the double-height library added drama, thus reinforcing its importance within the house as a whole.

[4] KITCHEN DINER The kitchen is a self-contained area to one side of the main sitting and dining room, next to the library. This crafted space contains an integrated breakfast booth, inspired by diner-style banquette seating. The seating and marble-topped table are made-to-order pieces by Techentin, whereas the wallpaper is a design from Cole and Son.

WINDOW SEATING

The living and dining room has generous proportions and a dramatic picture window, complete with an integrated window seat for making the most of the open vista. 'The house is just perfectly placed,' Techentin said. 'On the lower floor you feel as though you are in the treetops and upstairs you are above the trees. It has a really good feel to it.' In the great room, the trees and greenery bring something of a tree house feel, while the cylindrical installation artwork in the corner – by Canadian artist An Te Liu – recalls the design of Alpine stoves. The sofa is a custom-designed piece by Techentin and the two armchairs are mid-century Knoll designs; Italian design firm Paola Lenti supplied the green ottoman.

Bondi Wave

DESIGNERS	TONY OWEN PARTNERS/PEARL TODD INTERIOR DESIGN
COMPLETED	2008
LOCATION	BONDI, SYDNEY, AUSTRALIA

IN THE BONDI DISTRICT of Sydney, this dynamic residence is defined partly by its sinuous form. The roof line rises from a modest street facade to an open and expansive rear elevation, which opens onto a secluded garden. This sweeping roof echoes the waves of nearby Bondi Beach, but it is also emblematic of the increasingly energetic and sophisticated character of the area itself.

The two-storey house, designed by architect Tony Owen with interiors by Pearl Todd Interior Design, sits on a slim urban site where every square foot of space has been maximized, both inside and out. Sandwiched between neighbouring residences, the Wave House offers a simple face to the street, with a discreet entrance zone and an integrated garage. The hallway is bordered by an enclosed study, plus a playroom, at the front of the building, but towards the heart of the home the space begins to open out in dramatic fashion.

As the ceiling height lifts to follow the wave of the roof, the living spaces below are arranged in an open plan, combining a kitchen to one side, a dining zone to the other and a seating area at the rear. The lounge sits at the back of the house, alongside a tall wall of glass that folds away to offer an instant connection with the terrace and garden. This outdoor space may be relatively small in scale, but it provides another important room, an amenity space and a key source of natural light. 'Because of the mild climate the garden is considered as much a living space as the interior,' said Owen. 'We design to embrace the climate and this is done for environmental reasons, but it is also a fundamental part of the lifestyle, especially for a house so close to the beach. In Australia these days the design of most houses starts with examining this relationship between inside and outside.'

Built for a supplier of architectural glass, the house makes ample use of glass walls and expanses of windows wherever possible. This includes the main living area, which features glazing at eye level and sequences of glass at clerestory height. Upstairs, the house has four bedrooms. Again, the sequence of spaces expands in volume and scale towards the rear, where the master suite opens out onto a terrace overlooking the rear garden. Here, too, the use of glass is extensive, forming part of the ongoing contrast within the house between openness and enclosure, solidity and transparency.

DESIGN INGREDIENTS

· Dynamic shapes
· Extensive use of glass
· Inside–outside flow
· Neutral tones
· Sinuous curves

[1] ISLAND WAVE The sculptural, custom island in the kitchen, made with polished concrete, echoes the sinuous curve of the roof. Cantilevered from a single pedestal, the island wave is used as a breakfast bar and serving counter as well as an additional preparation surface that complements the rest of the kitchen. The transparency of the three Ghost stools from Kartell – designed by Philippe Starck and made of polycarbonate – allows the wave to remain the prominent feature, with the seating having only the lightest visual impact.

[2] FLOATING FURNITURE
The house features many custom-made elements and fitted pieces of furniture. Among them is a long, wall-mounted console that provides storage for home technology and other items. The black unit appears to 'float' on the white surface of the wall. Wall-mounted elements such as this save space and liberate the floor area, creating the impression of free space and open volumes. The artwork above introduces a splash of colour that stands out all the more against the whites and greys of the walls and floors.

[3] LIGHTING Close to the staircase, the high windows are milky and translucent, ensuring privacy from the neighbours while still introducing additional sunlight. The quality of natural light throughout the space is rich, enhanced by a multitude of windows filtering sunlight from different directions. Artificial light is largely provided by recessed ceiling lights, which are discreet and allow the clean contours of the interior architecture to be fully appreciated. The exception is the large pendant ceiling light that floats over the small dining table.

[4] INTEGRATED TERRACE The polished concrete floors and the folding sequence of glass doors at the back of the house allow for a seamless transition between the interior living space and the terrace, as well as the garden beyond. Complete with a barbecue and kitchenette to one side, the garden provides an outdoor room, while mature trees offer a degree of summer shading.

[5] LIGHT STAIRWAY In certain buildings the staircase assumes particular importance, serving as a crafted, sculptural focal point. Here, the focus is on the dynamic shape of the roof and ceiling, as well as the way in which these curves contrast with more linear elements seen elsewhere in the house. The stairway, therefore, becomes a simple, subtle and functional structure, with a lightweight frame that resembles an elegant ladder, and a glass balustrade that allows the eye to pass straight through.

Chelsea Town House

DESIGNERS	WINKA DUBBELDAM/ ARCHI-TECTONICS
COMPLETED	2011
LOCATION	CHELSEA, NEW YORK, USA

TUCKED AWAY BEHIND the elegant row houses and brownstones of Chelsea, there is a secret world. This is where the hidden gardens of the town houses meet, forming a green oasis that is quite a rarity in Manhattan. Winka Dubbeldam of Archi-tectonics and her fashion designer client wanted to make the most of this verdant enclave within their wholesale reinvention of this New York home. Key to the success of the project is a generously scaled ground-floor living space space – combining a seating area, dining zone and kitchen – that overlooks a private outdoor room.

From the street, the early 19th-century town house looks pretty much as it always has. The house is protected as a historic building, so it was essential to preserve the neat facade. Initially, everyone assumed that the structure of the building was sound and suited to renovation and a gentle reworking. However, when Dubbeldam and her team began looking more closely, they realized that many of the supporting beams were failing and that the floors were tilting. They had to gain planning permission for a dramatic rebuild.

Behind the original facade, Dubbeldam has in effect created a new house, rebuilding in contemporary style. The reworked layout offers a natural sense of progression through the house down to the banks of glass at the rear, which tie in dramatically with the tree canopy and greenery of the hidden garden. 'I love the combination of the house and the garden,' said Dubbeldam. 'It's a calming, beautiful and contemplative space. . . . The garden is really a green room – another living space connected to the house.'

The ground floor holds the main living areas in a largely open-plan layout. This is given added flexibility by a series of custom-made sliding oak doors that can be used to separate off the entrance hall and stairwell. Designed around a custom-made fireplace finished in French limestone, the sitting room flows straight into the dining area and kitchen at the back of the house, with a wall of glass opening out to the treescape and steps leading down to the garden itself. With its crisp kitchen, wooden floorboards and walls painted a cool, calming grey, the house is rich in contrasting textures and characterful finishes, complemented by the client's eclectic mix of furniture – both vintage and new.

DESIGN INGREDIENTS

· All about the views

· Characterful textures
  and finishes

· Flexible living

· Gallery of photographs

· Vintage modern

[1] KITCHEN VISTA The sleek kitchen, by innovative Italian specialists Valcucine, arranges the space in two parts, with a galley against one wall complemented by an island close by. These elements form parallel lines facing the glass wall, which looks out onto the garden and its tree canopy. This elevated position recalls tree houses, and the greenery adds a fresh, organic dimension to the room and to the house as a whole. 'We really wanted to create this picture wall and frame the beautiful view,' said Dubbeldam. 'You get this stunning plane of vivid green.'

[2] VINTAGE TOUCHES The architectural character of the living space is sophisticated and crisp, illuminated by the rich quality of natural light. A number of vintage pieces soften the linear nature of the room and create more eclectic interiors. They include the mismatched dining chairs by the window and the row of vintage cinema seating against the side wall, as well as the antique rattan rocking chair. This mixture of styles adds individuality and character to the space, while also introducing complementary textures.

[3] <u>MONTAGE GALLERY</u> One wall to the side of the dining table has become a home gallery, with a collection of photographs forming a striking montage. This sequence of pictures is arranged in a grid formation, supported by slim timber display shelves. The photographs were taken by the owners themselves and they form a dynamic focal point within the dining zone.

[4] <u>FEATURE FIREPLACE</u> In the seating area, the fireplace provides a natural anchor point. The chimney breast is a monolith coated in Gaudi marble from Stone Source, with a seductive colour and pattern that stand out against the cool grey of the surrounding walls. The armchair is by Brazilian designers the Campana Brothers; the floorboards are in Russian oak from Siberian Floors.

COCOON BATHING

The master bathroom is a well-proportioned space. It has the feel of a sophisticated hotel suite or exclusive spa, with its generous scale, thoughtful detailing and fine finishes. This indulgent room features a custom sink and vanity unit made of Corian®, a sculptural and ergonomic bathtub, textured tiles and a double shower. The floors are in timber, apart from the area around the bath, which is picked out in stone.

Eclectic

Spanish Glade

DESIGNER	SELGASCANO ARCHITECTS
COMPLETED	2006
LOCATION	MADRID, SPAIN

TUCKED AWAY IN A TRANQUIL and leafy spot on the outskirts of Madrid, Silicone House is a decidedly modern and contemporary building, designed by architects José Selgas and Lucia Cano of SelgasCano Architects. They successfully injected character into the new building and designed a home that is layered with colour, texture and an eclectic mix of furniture and custom-made elements, seen to best effect in the sitting room and adjoining dining area.

For many years Selgas and Cano made their home in the heart of Madrid. However, they were drawn to La Florida, on the very edge of the city, by the temptation of creating a different life for themselves and their children. Here, they came across a leafy glade of pine and plane trees, acacias and laurels, where they could build a calm and inviting haven as well as an office for their architectural practice, which is situated close by. 'We wanted to protect and preserve the trees and the landscape, and that drove the design of the house,' said Selgas. 'We didn't really worry about the form of the house but positioned it where the land permitted us to put it.'

The house was designed as two single-storey pavilions, one containing the main living and social spaces and the other holding the bedrooms. Although the two structures are interlinked by a glass hallway and share a common visual language and design approach, each has its own identity, partly defined by the use of colour. The 'daytime' pavilion, holding the social spaces of the house, is dominated by a vibrant orange. This shade is used for a number of features throughout, including the ceiling beams and the flooring in the kitchen; the same colour is also used for the recycled rubber coating on the roof of the pavilion, which doubles as an elevated terrace. The main sitting and dining area is a largely open-plan space, with the two rooms defined by changes in floor level and the use of low bookcases to define the zones. Made-to-order elements blend with mid-century pieces and vintage finds to great effect.

In the master bedroom, within the 'blue' pavilion, Selgas and Cano designed an intriguing Heath Robinson-inspired system of cedar wood shutters, operated by a pulley system. The bathroom is dominated by a unique cement bath and shower unit, with a skylight above and views into the woods from another bank of windows.

DESIGN INGREDIENTS

· Changes of levels

· Colour repeats

· Custom-made and mid-century furniture

· Pavilion-style living

· Retro styling

[1] TAILORED FURNITURE
Selgas and Cano designed a number of custom pieces of furniture and other elements that are cleverly integrated into the house. These include the trestle dining table, the island of low-slung bookcases and the banks of integrated sofas, arranged around the edge of the sitting room. Such tailored pieces are not only made to measure – and therefore more in tune with the space as a whole – but they also represent a welcome opportunity to inject individuality and character into the home.

[2] VINTAGE MODERN
Colour, character and contrasting textures are provided by an eclectic collection of 1950s and 1960s furniture by Verner Panton, Pierre Paulin and Charles and Ray Eames. Some of the pieces, such as the orange coffee table and the iconic yellow and blue fibreglass Eames chairs inject vibrant notes of colour, whereas the sofas are more subdued. All the elements provide sculptural shapes and tempting textures that resonate throughout the space. Their height in relation to the ribbon windows means that there is a constant sight line to the landscape.

[3] STATEMENT FIREPLACE One of the standout elements in the sitting room is the steel fireplace, flanked by two low shelves with ornaments. Designed by Selgas and Cano, it forms a sculptural yet traditional focal point and suggests the ongoing importance of the hearth, even within a very contemporary building. The striking hood and flue provide a vertical contrast to the low levels seen elsewhere in the room. Furthermore, the lacquered white finish ties in with the walls and floors, creating a subtle and considered impact on the space as a whole.

[4] MODERN LIBRARY Despite the digital age, libraries remain a vital ingredient within homes that have a true sense of individuality and personality. Here, a floor-to-ceiling wall of books adds warmth, interest and delight, while complementary shelving serves as a way of displaying art, objects and personal curios alongside. Like many of the walls in the house, the library wall forms a gentle curve, echoing the shape of the pavilion itself. The half-height windows wrap around the entire building, reinforcing the close connection between interior and exterior spaces.

ZONED SPACES

Open-plan living offers numerous delights, including free-flowing spaces, unrestricted perspectives and the easy circulation of light. However, sometimes it is desirable to create distinct zones, suited to particular activities, within one larger space to avoid the risk of an open 'prairie' feel. Here, Selgas and Cano have created a number of different seating areas, denoted simply by the arrangement of furniture. In addition, a distinct dining zone is demarcated by a change of floor level and the use of low shelving to provide a degree of separation.

Stable Conversion

DESIGNER	DAVID KOHN ARCHITECTS
COMPLETED	2009
LOCATION	NORFOLK, UK

GALLERY OWNER STUART SHAVE was searching for silence when he came across Stable Acre in Norfolk. He had been hunting for a country retreat for weekends and holidays as an alternative to his working week in London. He found this stable block at the end of a winding farm track, some distance away from the nearest village, and converted the building with the help of architect <u>David Kohn</u>. The reinvented house celebrates the big East Anglian skies and open countryside, and also offers the perfect setting for Shave's collection of mid-century furniture. The result is a welcoming blend of simplicity and sophistication.

'All of us live in this very accelerated day-to-day atmosphere and when I first came here and turned down the track it did feel like leaving the world behind and arriving somewhere different,' said Shave, whose London gallery – Modern Art – was also designed by Kohn. 'I am really drawn to the Norfolk countryside and the house looks over a large pine forest. It's amazing to me to have this almost cinematic outlook and incredible how much more aware I now feel of the changing seasons.'

The single-storey stable block had been poorly converted into a house in the early 1990s, with a warren of rooms and a set of French windows leading out to the garden. Initially, Shave thought that he would commission a simple renovation and update of the building, but he was soon tempted by a more complex plan to radically reinvent the house. Kohn designed the new interiors within the remnants of the brick shell of the stable, with a large, open-plan living and dining space at the centre of the building. 'When I bought the stables I imagined a home where you could almost walk right through from one end to the other without having any doors,' said Shave, 'but where you could still create these separate spaces.'

To one side of the generously sized, light-filled living area sits a modest kitchen and to the other the entrance area, as well as a long and open hallway leading to the master bedroom at the far end of the house. This room can be separated off by a sliding door and – like all the spaces in the house – it savours the vista across the open countryside. Two guest bedrooms filter off from this dramatic corridor, as well as a bathroom with a tailor-made concrete bath, designed by Kohn and positioned to maximize the view.

DESIGN INGREDIENTS

· Architectural details

· Cohesion

· Fluid inside–outside living

· Informal, rustic quality

· Neatly defined areas

[1] INDOOR GARDEN

A collection of cacti, succulents and other small potted plants – some displayed on rustic benches and stands – runs alongside the windows. The organic simplicity of this composition softens the living space and contrasts well with the sophistication of the furniture and the minimalist purity of the interior architecture. The indoor garden is sheltered by a bank of glazing, which offers a suitably greenhouse environment for the plants, while the greenery links the interiors with the landscape beyond.

[2] **OPEN OFFICE** The open-plan living room is large enough for a dining table at one end and a comfortable seating area at the other. In addition, Shave and Kohn created a small home library and study area against the spine wall of the building, defined by a tall recessed bookcase. The Pierre Jeanneret desk with drawers is accompanied by a simple vintage Jean Prouvé chair. 'My favourite era of design is the 1950s, especially French designers such as Jean Prouvé, [Charlotte] Perriand and Jeanneret,' said Shave.

[3] WHITE WALLS The interior of the spine wall at the rear of the building has been coated with rough sawn timber and painted white. This lends a rustic, textural quality to the space, in contrast to the concrete floors and the banks of steel-framed Crittall windows looking out over the grounds and open fields. The brick walls and fireplace have also been painted white, making the interiors coherent but still allowing for contrasting textures.

MINIMALIST BEDROOM

The master bedroom contains furniture with a contemporary rustic character. London-based furniture designer Jona Warbey made the bed, storage drawers and side tables from reclaimed timber. They sit well with the wood panelling, while the high, pitched ceiling lends the space volume. 'I would say that being up at the house is pretty much about the simple things of life: sleeping, walking, cooking,' said Shave. 'It's just that you have the opportunity to be so much more mindful about it.'

[4] VINTAGE FURNITURE
The owner assembled a personally selected collection of furniture with great care and consideration, informed by a particular interest in mid-century design. Key pieces include Chandigarh library chairs designed by Pierre Jeanneret and a white daybed by Charlotte Perriand. A number of items were bought through dealers, but there are also characterful eBay purchases such as the Danish sofa from the 1950s. Each piece has provenance and purpose, adding an extra layer to the composition.

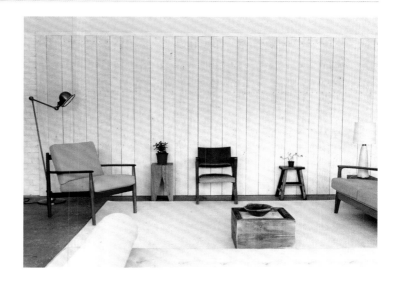

Palmeraie Escape

DESIGNER	MERYANNE LOUM-MARTIN
COMPLETED	2001
LOCATION	MARRAKECH, MOROCCO

DESIGNER AND HOTELIER <u>Meryanne Loum-Martin</u> chose a peaceful spot among the palm groves outside Marrakech to make her home. Here, she created both a hotel and a house for herself and her family, while her husband – a botanist and anthropologist – worked on the surrounding gardens. Their home is an eclectic mix of Moorish and contemporary influences, designed around the mature palms that inhabit the land. The most dramatic space in the house is the generously proportioned sitting room, which features many tailor-made pieces by the designer, as well as treasures and art sourced both in Morocco and during her travels.

Loum-Martin grew up in Paris, where she trained and practised as a lawyer. However, she always nurtured a love of architecture and design, and after falling in love with Morocco she decided to change careers. She first visited the country looking for land to build a house for her parents and spent a decade living between France and Marrakech. Eventually, she decided to settle in the Moroccan city full time and, with her husband, Gary, bought 7 acres (2.8 ha) in the Palmeraie district. Loum-Martin opened her hotel, Jnane Tamsna, in 2001 and built a family house nearby at the same time.

'I wanted the house to have a more modern approach to Islamic architecture using the elements of light, perspective and water,' said Loum-Martin. 'You have all these aspects of Moorish architecture, but each with a twist. We made a map of all the palm trees on the land and then designed the hotel and the house around them.' The courtyard entrance boasts a water feature and contemporary interpretations of traditional arched doorways. It creates a processional approach to the two-storey house, with a generously sized hallway leading to the main living spaces. Chief among them is the sitting room, which flows out to the swimming pool and a choice of welcoming outdoor rooms created among the greenery.

Like the rest of the house, the living room is largely fashioned out of tadelakt. This traditional Moroccan material consists of lime plaster, which is then polished with stone and olive oil soap to give it both a lustre and a water-resistant finish. The tadelakt walls and floors – the latter of which have been scored to create a flagstone effect – have a pleasing sheen to them, while the custom fireplace has a rounded, organic character.

DESIGN INGREDIENTS

· Architectural influences

· Myriad curios and artworks

· Organic character

· Proportion and scale

· Tailored designs in local materials

[1] CORNICING Loum-Martin struggled to find a suitable treatment for the cornicing. Given the high ceilings, she regarded the cornice as a key element, and inspiration finally arrived during a drive through the medina in Marrakech when she spotted an old oven on a carriage being pulled by a donkey. She replicated the pattern of the oven door in tadelakt, introducing a fresh decorative element and lifting the space. The three-dimensional quality of the cornice combines geometry, texture and shadows, which help to define the proportions of the room.

[2] SEATING CHOICES In addition to a comfortable family space, Loum-Martin wanted a sitting room generous enough for entertaining friends and for hosting occasional hotel events. The scale of the room fully allows for this, with a choice of seating areas at both ends plus an easy flow to the complementary outdoor rooms. 'I like a global, eclectic mix,' said Loum-Martin. 'With the furniture, I often design it myself and have it made by local craftsmen. . . . With the sitting room in particular I love the sense of space and the light.'

[3] CRAFTED FIREPLACE The fireplace is one of Loum-Martin's favourite elements in the sitting room. It is a unique design, made out of polished tadelakt, with rounded edges and a tactile quality. This traditional material has been given a contemporary twist here and in many other parts of the house. The eclectic mix of pieces on the mantelpiece includes a carved wooden head from Cambodia, a glass vase with locust pods from the garden and an African sun mask.

[4] UPSCALE ARTWORK The blend of art is as eclectic as the house itself, with a mixture of works brought over from Loum-Martin's former apartment in Paris and pieces sourced and commissioned in Morocco. The large painting above the white sofa is by Belgian artist Philippe Deltour, who has worked extensively in Morocco and in other parts of Africa. The scale of the piece adds a touch of drama to the room, while the image and colours sit well with the themes and tones of the interiors.

ROMANTIC BEDROOM

All the bedrooms have a romantic and atmospheric quality. This room features a parquet tile floor, an in-built fireplace and soothing colours. Framed by the niche above the bed, the collage of pictures creates a miniature gallery that has the equivalent visual impact of a headboard, helping to anchor the bed and thus the bedroom as a whole. The fabric canopy introduces colour, pattern and theatre, and the vibrant Moroccan textile has been embellished with hanging corner tassels to create an effect reminiscent of a canopied four-poster bed.

California Lux

DESIGNERS	MARK RIOS/RIOS CLEMENTI HALE STUDIOS
COMPLETED	2009
LOCATION	LOS ANGELES, CALIFORNIA, USA

DAVID BOHNETT'S HOME in the 'flats' of Beverly Hills is an elegant and playful mixture of its 1930s roots, mid-century furniture and a contemporary edge. This glamorous house of white-painted brick sits among generous grounds – with a swimming pool, tennis court and guest house – in a neighbourhood once favoured by old-time Hollywood stars, such as Lucille Ball and Jack Benny. Here, Bohnett has experimented with colour, pattern and furnishings to create a home that is both sophisticated and highly individual.

Bohnett is a philanthropist and technology entrepreneur who bought the house with his partner, Tom Gregory, an actor and radio host. 'It was an opportunity to take on a fun and interesting architectural and design project and ensure that the house remained an icon in Beverly Hills,' said Bohnett. 'We were looking for each room to have its own character, but for the house to also tie together as a whole. To do that, each space needs to be distinctive without being inconsistent with the overall design. It was a balancing act but also fun.'

They turned to architect Mark Rios of Rios Clementi Hale Studios, with whom they had collaborated on earlier projects. The house had been updated by a previous owner and was in good shape structurally. However, the roofing was replaced with slate tiles and the services and systems were also upgraded. There were few structural changes, apart from the reintroduction of an original terrace on the upper level of the building. The marble floor was retained in the entrance hall, but in many of the key living rooms the flooring was replaced with dark timber boards to tie the spaces together. The majority of the furniture is from the 1950s and 1960s. Rios and Bohnett collaborated on assembling a noteworthy collection that includes pieces by Billy Haines, Edward Wormley and Karl Springer. These choices have been combined with custom-built designs and contemporary touches throughout.

DESIGN INGREDIENTS

· Flexible seating compositions
· Furniture by legendary designers
· Harmony and glamour
· Maintaining balance
· Pleasing proportions

[1] ICONIC FURNITURE

The sitting room features a range of mid-century pieces of particular provenance and rich character, which lend the room layers of depth, personality and interest. They include a cabinet by Piero Fornasetti, red chairs by Billy Haines and a number of pieces by the legendary Giò Ponti, including the circular coffee table and the matching chairs and sofa by the fireplace, upholstered in a fabric by Mariano Fortuny. The large modernist sofa beneath the window is by Edward Wormley for Dunbar.

[2] COMPLEMENTARY SEATING

The seating has been arranged in two distinct zones, which sit easily within the generous proportions of the room. One area is illuminated by its proximity to the large window, while the other is focused upon the fireplace. Red accent colours stand out against the pale tones of the walls and curtains and help unite one seating ensemble, whereas soft lilac tones tie the other arrangement together. There is considerable flexibility as to how the two areas are used – whether during the day or the evening.

[3] MIRRORED WALL The mirrored wall around the fireplace lends definition to this part of the room, while helping to reflect and circulate light. A regular feature of Art Deco interiors in particular, mirrored glass tiles add drama and a degree of glamour to more contemporary and eclectic spaces. Smoked, distressed or aged glass prevents the effect from becoming too stark and intense.

[4] RUG DEFINITION The large antique carpet sitting upon the wooden floorboards was sourced from Mansour Fine Rugs. It adds texture and pattern and also helps to soften the space. Reaching almost wall to wall, it gives definition to the twin seating zones at the heart of the sitting room. There is still space for a grand piano in one corner, thus confirming the room's expansive proportions.

GRAND ENTRANCE

Together, Bohnett and Rios designed the interiors to display an elegant sense of scale and grandeur, exemplified by a sweeping staircase that commands immediate attention in the entrance hall. The original polished black and white marble floors reinforce the luxurious feel of the space, while a painted Fornasetti screen, a custom-designed glass table by Blackman Cruz and a FontanaArte wall mirror introduce eclectic notes, directly establishing the unique character and sophistication of the house right from the start.

Mountain Lodge

DESIGNERS	MACA HUNEEUS/JOHN MANISCALCO ARCHITECTURE
COMPLETED	2009
LOCATION	PLACER COUNTY, CALIFORNIA, USA

THIS CONTEMPORARY SKI LODGE is the winter home of interior designer <u>Maca Huneeus</u> and her family. Situated among the pines in the historic Sugar Bowl ski resort, the two-storey house offers dramatic views out into the trees and across the mountains. Designed in conjunction with <u>John Maniscalco Architecture</u>, the building is elevated on a concrete plinth to provide ease of access during the winter when the snow is many feet deep. The main living spaces are on the upper level, which benefits from the best of the light and the views, with an open-plan sitting room and dining area forming the comfortable and inviting hub of the home.

Huneeus has known this California resort for many years. She and her husband – vintner Agustin Francisco Huneeus – and their five daughters live in San Francisco for most of the year, but they have spent many of their winters at Sugar Bowl and have grown to love the area, which is blessed with some of the best skiing in the state. They rented a house here on numerous occasions, but then started to look for a place of their own.

Eventually they found a plot of land in the old village, where access is by gondola and you can ski right from the door. Huneeus turned to architect John Maniscalco to design the building, with the two collaborating closely on the project. She designed many custom pieces for the interiors, aiming for an aesthetic that was informal but also refined. 'I wanted the house to feel calm but to have character as well,' said Huneeus. 'Every fabric and detail was thought out and hand crafted, with blankets from Patagonia and Uzbeki tapestries. I looked at cold climate cultures and drew from there, because I wanted that authentic, hand-made character with lots of texture and warmth.'

The lower level contains boot rooms, guest accommodation and a children's bunk room, as well as the entrance zone and utility spaces. This leaves the upper level free for the master suite at one end, the kitchen at the other and an open-plan living zone at the centre. This inviting space is warmed by the characterful timber floors and ceilings, as well as by the views of the trees through the windows. 'I love the light, the space, the simplicity and how warm it feels,' said Huneeus. 'We love it in the summer when it's very quiet and beautiful and we come a lot in the winter.'

DESIGN INGREDIENTS

· Contextuality

· Contrasting timbers

· Informal but refined

· Maximizing the views

· Sociable living arrangements

[1] BENCH SEATING

Four benches from Portuguese manufacturer De La Espada are arranged around the long dining table, with two iconic Eero Saarinen for Knoll armchairs positioned at either end. The benches make a pleasing alternative to a long procession of dining chairs and create a setting that is more casual and sociable, as befits a winter ski lodge. 'I wanted it to be quiet, simple, warm and refined,' said Hunneus. A number of elements here were especially designed by the owner, including the dining table.

[2] FEATURE LIGHTING

The house showcases several lighting fixtures that add a sculptural quality to the interiors. In addition to a statement chandelier that hangs in the stairwell, the seating area features a solid glass bead chandelier from British firm Ochre. Huneeus custom designed the elegant oval pendant lighting over the dining table. These pieces add drama and a fresh layer of interest to the room, drawing the eye upwards and through the space, while the simple lines of the timber ceiling allow these features to stand out all the more.

BUNK ROOM CHIC

Providing enough space for children
and their friends in ski chalets and
beach houses can be quite a challenge.
Once again the bunk room has offered
a welcome solution to this problem,
and these custom-made beds sleep four
in comfort, with a mesmerizing view
through the picture window provided
as standard. Colour comes courtesy
of blankets sourced in Chile; playful
cushions and bedside lamps are from
Jonathan Adler.

[3] COMFORTABLE SOFAS The house is
designed primarily as a holiday retreat and as such
needs to be comfortable, practical and inviting, as
well as stylish. The seating area features two large
sink-in sofas from Italian furniture designers
Molteni, with plentiful cushions and throws. The
rug – bought locally – creates a soft touch underfoot
and echoes the blues seen elsewhere.

[4] MADE TO ORDER Numerous tailor-made
features add a new dimension to the lodge and
elevate the interiors. Among the many elements
designed to suit and serve the space are the
timber console units beneath the windows and
a large oval mirror. Both pieces were designed
by Huneeus, and they introduce new layers of
personality and individuality.

Marais Modern

DESIGNER	FRÉDÉRIC MÉCHICHE
COMPLETED	1996
LOCATION	PARIS, FRANCE

ART AND PHOTOGRAPHY have always been important to French interior designer <u>Frédéric Méchiche</u>. His father was a doctor, but also an art collector with a passion for architecture and design. Many of Méchiche's private clients have owned major collections, which have been woven into the interior architecture of the spaces that the designer has created. Unsurprisingly, art is also one of the key elements of the Parisian home that Méchiche has designed for himself, in the bustling streets of the Marais district.

Here, Méchiche found three apartments with little in the way of period detailing or architectural features. Together, they offered a blank canvas to create a home that recalls the sophisticated charm of Directory period town houses. The interiors are furnished with a blend of mid-century furniture and custom designs as well as a collection of artworks that includes pieces by César, Jean Arp and Joan Miró. The melange is highly personal but carefully considered and full of character, interest and originality. 'People think that it's enough just to mix anything up, but I'm sorry it's not,' said Méchiche. 'It's about composition, perspective. I wanted to give the impression that I had just arrived here and really found it like this. I just added my books, my sculptures, my paintings. Even if it's a calculated look, that's the feeling I wanted – arriving in an 18th-century apartment, painted very simply with white walls and no curtains, no carpets, very few of the things that people often call "decoration."'

Over two floors, Méchiche combined an assembly of 18th-century wall panelling – partly sourced from a postal staging inn – with cornicing, mouldings and fireplaces. The library, with its sweeping staircase, made of reclaimed timber and iron, is the heart of the house, whereas the dining room has the feeling of a small bistro. Mirrors from the 18th century mix with chairs by Arne Jacobsen and Charles Eames; photography by Robert Mapplethorpe stands out against the neutral walls.

DESIGN INGREDIENTS

· Comprehensive narrative

· Easy circulation

· Informal display of prestigious
  artworks

· Light and bright

· Organic textures

[1] FLUID LAYOUT The library serves as an inviting room. It also functions as an important element in the circulation of the apartment, with the sweeping stairway to one side and double doors and another sequence of doors to the other, feeding through into the hallway and the dining room. These many doorways, surrounded by floor-to-ceiling bookcases, create a free-flowing floor plan, but allow each room to maintain its own identity. The library was created from two former bedrooms, one bathroom and a corridor.

[2] LIBRARY WALLS The old adage 'books do furnish a room' still rings true in the digital age. Here, a personally selected collection of books adds a great deal of texture and personality, as well as offering a source of immense pleasure and well-being. The bookcases line the walls and sit between the windows and around the fireplace and doors, unifying the space and adding depth and richness throughout. A library gives the impression of timelessness, yet its content offers a clear indicator of the unique character of the owner.

[3] ART AND PHOTOGRAPHY The apartment features a collection of 20th-century art, sculpture and photography. The calibre of the works – by well-known artists including Cindy Sherman, Nan Goldin, Anish Kapoor, Jean Dubuffet and others – is impressive and of gallery standard. However, the pieces are exhibited informally, sometimes leaning against a wall or a bookcase, and in this way they become another intriguing layer of the interiors, rather than sacred objects displayed in a gallery-style presentation.

[4] ORGANIC ELEMENTS Designed by Florence Knoll, the mid-century black leather chairs and white sofa sit upon a floor of bare wooden boards. These organic textures stand out all the more against the refined aspects of the painted wall panels and period features, lending the space a loft-like informality.

BATHING BEAUTY

Arranged around an 18th-century bathtub, the bathroom becomes a seductive space. The panels and cornicing are from the Directory period, while the painting is by Jean-Charles Blais, a contemporary French artist who has exhibited widely in Europe, the United States and other parts of the world. Harry Bertoia designed the vintage latticed steel chairs for Knoll, and the chrome ceiling light is from the 1960s. The use of metallics (tub, chairs, light) creates a striking contrast with the period elements, while the juxtaposition between the graphic modern art and the bucolic scenes on the period panels offers an eclectic but effective melange.

Parisian Eyrie

DESIGNERS	PIERRE FREY/MARIKA DRU
COMPLETED	2012
LOCATION	PARIS, FRANCE

EVER SINCE HE WAS A STUDENT, Pierre Frey has made his home on the top floor of a 16th-century building that houses the Paris headquarters of the fabric company that bears his family name. It is certainly an extraordinary location in which to live, with the Musée du Louvre and the Palais-Royal close at hand and other delights of the city within easy reach. Over the years, Frey's apartment has evolved and changed, culminating in the decision to combine the apartment with three offices alongside and transform the space into a larger home for himself and his wife, Emilie, who works in the film industry.

Frey collaborated on the reinvention of the apartment with architect Marika Dru, a friend whom he had known for many years and had worked with in the past. Together they were able to transform this collection of modest spaces into an airy and largely open-plan apartment, pushing upwards into the attic to create a much greater sense of space and light, enhanced by a large new skylight over the central living area.

'We tore apart the entire apartment,' said Frey, who is the head of communications for the family business founded in 1935 by his grandfather. 'The living room and kitchen used to be four separate rooms and a corridor, so instead of five separate spaces we now have one. The structure was changed a lot and because it is an historic building we had to have all these changes approved by the planning authorities. We changed everything: the kitchen became the bedroom and an office became the kitchen.'

Oak floors were installed throughout, walls were painted a neutral shade and the old timber beams were exposed at ceiling level. A mezzanine gallery was created within the attic space, looking down upon the main living area, and now serves as a home office for Emilie. The apartment was then layered with furniture and fabrics from Pierre Frey's recent collections, blended with an eclectic choice of personal treasures and other flea market finds. A dining area sits at the far end of this open-plan space, by the windows, with Pierre Frey chairs surrounding an antique timber table from the St Ouen flea market. Frey's favourite spot in the apartment is the library close by, tucked under the mezzanine gallery, where the custom bookshelves are lacquered in a vibrant crimson red.

DESIGN INGREDIENTS

· Accents of colour

· Comforting textures

· Exposing features and spaces

· Imaginative repurposing

· Punctuation

[1] INTERCONNECTED KITCHEN The kitchen is situated within a separate but interlinked space adjacent to the main living area. It is an effective arrangement, with an easy flow between the kitchen and the dining area. At the same time, the kitchen retains its own identity and character, with the business of preparation and cooking neatly contained within. The ceiling light is by Constance Guisset, based in Paris, and the breakfast table is a custom piece by Marika Dru, who also designed the kitchen units.

[2] SPIRAL STAIRCASE The interiors feature a number of reclaimed and salvage finds, including the vintage spiral staircase designed by Gustave Eiffel, discovered in a Paris flea market. The staircase forms a sculptural focal point and is used to access the modest home office on the mezzanine level. Its wrought-iron construction and twisting form contrast with the organic texture and regular angles of the timber beams.

ATTIC STUDY

A portion of the original attic was removed to create the double-height living room, but one section has been retained and converted into a modest home office accessed via the spiral staircase. The mezzanine provides just enough space for a vintage chair and desk, while the wall immediately behind the desk is picked out in a vivid Bananier wallpaper from Boussac, introducing pattern and colour that illuminates and lifts a modestly scaled room.

[3] WARM ACCENTS Vivid accent colours are used throughout the apartment to add warmth and contrast. The repeated use of vibrant reds – seen in the red rug of the seating area, a crimson feather hat from Cameroon and red shelving in a library inset in an alcove near the dining area – is all the more effective when seen against the neutral Poivre Blanc, or white pepper, used for the painted walls and ceilings.

[4] SINK-IN SOFA In the central sitting room, the generously scaled sofa is a custom design by Pierre Frey. It takes centre stage within the composition of the lounge area and provides an enticing and comfortable point of retreat. The large armchair is also a Pierre Frey piece, upholstered in a colourful Boussac fabric. Both Braquenié, which manufactured the rug, and Boussac are now owned by the Pierre Frey company. The vintage leather-topped coffee table is actually a repurposed gym bench, bought from a Parisian flea market.

Manhattan Duplex

DESIGNERS	TSAO AND MCKOWN
COMPLETED	1995
LOCATION	MANHATTAN, NEW YORK, USA

ARCHITECTS AND DESIGNERS <u>Calvin Tsao</u> and <u>Zack McKown</u> share a love of detail, craftsmanship and custom interiors, and enjoy creating spaces that are both thoughtful and tailored. They draw inspiration from an eclectic range of influences and historical periods and their backgrounds are international. However, their work always possesses great clarity and cohesion, with an emphasis on order and comfort. Their own Manhattan duplex, overlooking Central Park, was completely redesigned to their own taste and specifications, with the living spaces on the lower floor assuming the open feel of a sophisticated loft.

Tsao and McKown were looking for southern light, a park view and plenty of space. The duplex, within a 1930s building, offered all three and also came with four discernible corners that lend it some of the feel of a generously scaled two-storey house. It had been renovated many times over the years and few period features and a confusion of styles remained. The new owners decided to reinvent the duplex afresh, transforming it from a series of box-like rooms into a more open and fluid environment.

Tsao and McKown created a largely open-plan living space on the ground floor, unified by the Brazilian cherry wood floors. The dramatic spiral staircase divides the kitchen from the seating and dining area, which has south-facing windows. 'The staircase was an opportunity to do something sculptural, which was a pleasure,' said McKown. 'Most of the architectural vocabulary was meant to recede so you are not really aware of it right away. With the stairs it's okay to notice it and that's part of its function. We really took the chance to experiment upon ourselves and practically everything is custom designed.' Made-to-order pieces sit alongside an eclectic mix of vintage and flea market finds. Tsao and McKown also have extensive collections of personal treasures. Such pieces are constantly brought out and put away, meaning the apartment is always changing.

DESIGN INGREDIENTS

· Clarity and cohesion

· Dynamic collection of antique and vintage treasures

· Ordered layout

· Sophisticated design styles

· Statement staircase

[1] ANTIQUE MODERN

The interior architecture is ordered, clean and contemporary, yet the blend of furniture is distinctly eclectic and personal. As collectors, Tsao and McKown are tempted by different design styles, and the seating zone alone includes an antique Sicilian cross, fireside lamps made with vintage lanterns from a Venetian gondola and a daybed and hospital tray table found in a Paris flea market. The subtle use of blues and reds softens the masculine character of the space, while the rug and upholstered furniture add layers of texture.

[2] INTEGRATED FIREPLACE

Although the neat fireplace is a focal point for the seating area, it is a subtle one. It is integrated within a smooth run of fitted cupboards, coated in a reflective silver-leaf finish, that provide a wealth of storage for ceramics and curios, as well as hidden bookshelves. This crafted wall provides a textural backdrop for the seating area, which is defined within the open floor plan by a rug on the cherry wood floor. The two Napoleonic stools were bought at the Galerie Camoin-Demachy in Paris.

[3] **LONG TABLE** Given the scale and proportions of the apartment, a long dining table was needed to fill the space. Tsao and McKown designed a piece in cherry wood that would comfortably seat ten and that carries echoes of the traditional 'great table'. The dining chairs are Scottish, dating from the 18th century, and the table doubles as a display surface when not in use. 'We used pieces of furniture that we find beautiful or interesting and then designed extra pieces of our own to complete the composition and provide comfort,' said McKown.

[4] **SPIRAL STAIRCASE** The crafted spiral staircase is positioned at the heart of the apartment and becomes a dominant feature. It is, of course, functional and practical, but it also serves other purposes, helping to separate the open-plan living space into more distinct zones, with the dining and seating area to one side and the kitchen and breakfast table to the other. Manufactured using the same cherry wood as the floors, it is a pleasing, dynamic structure that softens and gently subverts the linear quality of the rest of the apartment.

SUNSHINE BEDROOM

The bedrooms on the upper storey are soothing to the eye. Enhanced by the rich quality of natural light from multiple windows, the golden yellow bedspread adds to the uplifting, sunny disposition of the space. Integrated storage reduces clutter, and only a few select treasures are displayed at any one time, such as the 19th-century models of the solar system either side of the bed. The sun and cloud photograph is by renowned contemporary US photographer Richard Misrach.

Pennsylvania Escape

DESIGNER	TODD OLDHAM STUDIO
COMPLETED	1997
LOCATION	PENNSYLVANIA, USA

DESIGNER <u>TODD OLDHAM</u> has taken his time to get this country retreat exactly the way he wants it. He describes the design process as organic, with a decade of effort and thought put into his house and garden. Even now, furniture and art are often rearranged and new ideas introduced to highly individual interiors that are full of colour, pattern and character. The heart of Oldham's home is the sitting room, with views out into the woods, framed by hand-made murals.

The house is an unusual one and relatively modest in scale. It sits in a clearing in the woods where there was once a three-hole golf course. The architecture is quirky, exemplified by the timber siding combined with a vaulted metal roof. After buying the house as a weekend and vacation retreat, Oldham and his partner, Tony Longoria, spent years planting trees and re-landscaping, as well as adding a number of new follies and terraces in the grounds, including a crafted tree house that forms a residence in miniature for visiting guests.

The interiors have an irregular asymmetric layout: the double-height living room feeds through to a single-height dining area and kitchen, with the master suite above and a den below. Previous owners had painted the interiors white throughout, thereby creating a blank canvas that Oldham then layered with an eye-catching assortment of furniture and art. He utilized bold, broad, painted stripes in several parts of the house, particularly where the different living zones intersect; this technique is repeated in the master bedroom and elsewhere. The kitchen walls, meanwhile, are coated in Japanese silk screen.

The blend of furniture is eclectic, with mid-century pieces – such as the dining chairs by Russel Wright – complementing contemporary pieces and self-designed choices, including the Oldham La-Z-Boy sofa in the sitting room. Here, wall murals add splashes of colour and pattern, as does the grid-like montage of bird images.

DESIGN INGREDIENTS

· Asymmetry
· Complementary organic textures
· Dynamic patterns
· Living among the greenery
· Playfulness

[1] **BIRD MONTAGE** The collection of bird images by mid-century artist and graphic designer Charley Harper introduces colour and interest. Harper's work has a graphic, playful quality that suits the montage treatment and the images have been coordinated within the composition to create triptychs with similar background colours. Harper's art is a particular favourite with Oldham, who has produced a book on his work.

[2] **IRREGULAR TILES** The orientation of the FLOR carpet tiles takes its lead from the dining area, which projects from the body of the house at an irregular angle. This means that the tiles, arranged in a graphic pattern, adopt the same angle as they head through into more linear spaces such as the sitting room. The formation helps to subvert the lines of the room itself, while also suggesting the idea of movement. It establishes a series of pathways through the interiors and ties together the interconnected spaces of the ground floor.

[3] **TABLE ART** Instead of a single coffee or side table, Oldham has opted for a quartet of surfaces at the centre of the room. These pieces introduce different textures and materials as well as a variety of shapes. They offer great flexibility within their arrangement, which can be particularly useful in a modest living space. The sculpted timber diamond was made by local chainsaw artist Jim Shaw to a design by the owner.

[4] **PLANTED SPACES** The house features a wide array of plants, which introduce a fresh, organic element and natural, sculptural shapes to the interiors. A variety of complementary textures is used, as seen here with this miniature garden set in a ceramic bowl on a low cork table by British industrial designer Jasper Morrison.

TREE HOUSE LIVING

Oldham has created a series of decks and outdoor rooms, but most accomplished of all is the tree house. Its fairy tale interiors have a crafted, hand-made quality, using a variety of woods and laminates to create a medley of timber shades and surfaces. This combination of woods offers a sense of cohesion and textural delight. The tree house sits upon a platform, 60 feet (18 m) high, anchored to pine trees and accessed via a winding wooden staircase. It includes a substantial living room and elevated bunk beds reached by ladders.

Melbourne Hideaway

DESIGNER	ANTON ASSAAD
COMPLETED	2009
LOCATION	MELBOURNE, AUSTRALIA

THE CITY OF MELBOURNE is renowned for its creative energy and it is blessed with a rich architectural and design scene. Here, design entrepreneur <u>Anton Assaad</u> founded Great Dane, specializing in contemporary and iconic Danish furniture, lighting and home accessories. The company's base is only a few minutes' walk from his family house – shared with his wife, Emma, and their daughter – where Assaad indulges his passion for Scandinavian craftsmanship and characterful living. The hub of the home is a generous, open-plan space to the rear of the property, flowing out onto an adjoining deck and garden.

Assaad's home is an urban bungalow, which dates back to the 1930s, and it is bordered by hedges, garden walls and mature trees, which offer privacy and a fresh, verdant setting. Bedrooms are arranged to the front of the property, with a hallway between them leading through to a small internal courtyard, which serves as a light well, with the main living spaces beyond. 'The house is simple, clean and understated with good bones and natural light,' said Assaad. 'The free-flowing connection between the living area and the deck is hugely important to us and the main reason why we love the house. It gives us the scope for inside–outside living, even though we are right in the heart of the city. The deck is Emma's favourite part of the house.'

The open-plan kitchen, dining area and lounge are arranged in an L-shaped formation, with plenty of built-in storage in the kitchen and to the back of the seating area. Floors throughout are in hardwood, treated with a dark Japanese lacquer finish. Walls and ceilings are in a soothing, creamy white, while the storage cupboards in the lounge are picked out in grey. It makes for a calm, soothing and flexible environment for family living.

The kitchen island is on wheels and its positioning can be easily adjusted. With a row of stools alongside, it also serves as a breakfast bar. The dining table nearby is a Charles and Ray Eames design, bordered by J. L. Moller dining chairs in walnut and leather. Both the dining and the seating areas look out onto the deck, with floor-to-ceiling sliding windows offering a fluid link between indoors and out, as well as a wealth of sunlight. The deck serves as an outdoor sitting room, with the backdrop of the enclosed garden creating a hidden hideaway at Melbourne's heart.

DESIGN INGREDIENTS

· Careful composition

· Equilibrium

· Fluid circulation between inside and out

· Informality and practicality

· Light and dark

[1] CHARACTERFUL FURNITURE

As expected from the founder of the Great Dane furniture company, the house features a selection of striking Scandinavian pieces full of personality and character. They include a classic Hans J. Wegner Papa Bear chair and a vintage Danish leather sofa. The Swedish rug anchors the main seating area, while its lighter tones and accent colours offer a suitable backdrop for the dark colours and silhouettes of the seating. The coffee table is a contemporary piece by Lex Stobie Design from Great Dane.

[2] HARDWOOD FLOORS

The hardwood floors unify the living spaces, but they also provide a practical surface for a part of the house that sees steady traffic coming in from the deck and garden. The wooden floors are dark and have a high gloss finish, which creates a degree of reflection. This helps to circulate light and allows the colour and character of the timber to shine through. The dark hues also mean that lighter pieces, including the grey cupboards and the bright white kitchen island, stand out against the floors.

[3] STORAGE MATTERS The lounge area includes a good range of storage, which helps to maintain a clean and uncluttered look throughout. There is a bank of built-in storage, shelving and cupboards to the rear of the room – picked out in battleship grey – complemented by a striking sideboard produced by Danish furniture designer Arne Vodder.

[4] DECK LIVING The deck serves as an outdoor sitting room, with the walled garden providing privacy and enclosure. Potted succulents and other plants soften the deck and provide a visual transition between the trees and greenery of the garden proper and the interior spaces. The garden walls have been painted grey, thereby reinforcing the concept of an outdoor room.

FLEXIBLE KITCHEN

Having the kitchen island on wheels creates great flexibility as to how the overall open-plan space is used. In its usual position, beneath the pendant light, the island can be utilized as a storage facility, a preparatory station and a breakfast bar, while the stove, sink and other connected services are contained within the galley area opposite. When the island is repositioned, it creates new possibilities for the living space and allows for a more fluid setting when entertaining.

Period

English Barn

DESIGNERS	DAVID POCKNELL/POCKNELL STUDIO
COMPLETED	1600s/2010
LOCATION	ESSEX, UK

DESIGNER <u>DAVID POCKNELL</u> knows more than most about barns and barn conversions. He has worked on nearly a dozen over the decades, both for clients and for himself. The Essex countryside forms the setting for this dramatic conversion of an early 17th-century timber-framed barn, plus adjoining brick outbuildings dating from the Victorian period. Anxious to preserve the character of the barn and its dynamic scale and volume, Pocknell created a double-height, open-plan living space that swallows the majority of the barn, with a kitchen and guest bedroom to one side topped by a mezzanine gallery holding the master suite.

Before the latest move, Pocknell and his wife, Sally, had lived in a vast medieval barn that he had converted himself. It comprised a substantial home at one end, a design studio at the other and an internal courtyard inhabiting the gap in between. The couple decided to downsize, but wanted to find another barn with space enough to accommodate the studio, which embraces architecture, interiors, graphic design and branding.

When a friend asked Pocknell for advice on obtaining planning permission for a vacant barn next to their farmhouse, the designer realized that the proposal could present the perfect opportunity for him to do another barn conversion for his family. Having secured the site, he designed the main barn to house all the principal living spaces, plus the generously scaled master suite. The adjoining Victorian sheds were adapted into a new home for the studio, as well as a guest annex to accommodate family and friends.

Wide engineered oak floorboards help to unify the vast space, while a wood burning stove forms a focal point in the seating area to one side of the barn. 'The idea that it would be cosy – if a room that is 6 metres by 6 metres can be cosy – was really important to us,' said Pocknell. The central section is left largely open, with the exception of the dining table and a custom-made storage unit that conceals the entrance area by the front door. On the other side of the building, Pocknell excavated the floor level to create a sunken kitchen and utility areas. The master suite sits on the mezzanine above, largely open to the rest of the space. Consequently, the full scale and grandeur of the barn can still be seen in its entirety and fully appreciated.

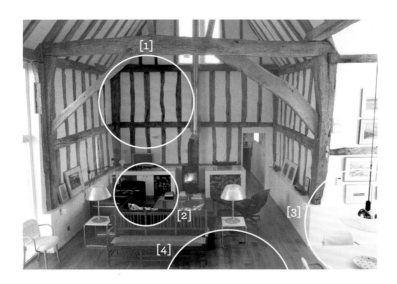

DESIGN INGREDIENTS

· Agricultural character

· Craftsmanship

· Informal lifestyle

· Juxtaposition of old and new

· Open volumes

[1] **EXPOSED FRAME** The original oak frame of the barn has been left fully visible and 'readable' even after the extensive conversion process. It carries great character and the patina of time, and is also an expression of rustic craftsmanship. The exposed rounded beams, in particular, have a sculptural quality and an intrinsic beauty all of their own. 'When you are by the fire or we are upstairs in our bedroom you can see the whole of the building,' said Pocknell. 'You are still aware of the fact that you are in a big space with the frame fully expressed.'

[2] **OLD AND NEW** The timber frame is a key element in the contrast between old and new, which lies at the heart of any successful barn conversion. Rustic period features contrast with more contemporary finishes, such as the expanses of glazing and the new stove. The theme is continued with the choice of furniture, which combines period pieces, such as the Arts and Crafts settle by British furniture designer and architect Ernest Gimson, with mid-century and contemporary designs, including the comfortable sofa from The Conran Shop.

[3] **FLEXIBLE DINING** The dining table sits within the open volume of the barn, in the portion of the building that held the original entrance and a tall doorway for bringing in carts and livestock. Designed by Achille Castiglioni, it is a flexible piece of furniture that folds out to accommodate additional guests, without troubling the space itself. The custom-made, half-height storage unit beyond the table – which includes Vitsoe shelving designed by Dieter Rams – forms a type of vestibule area without closing off the space.

BARN CONVERSIONS

Redundant barns have long been a temptation for those looking for a particular kind of rural home. The countryside equivalent of urban lofts, barns provide characterful spaces that suit a contemporary layout, in which flexible living arrangements preserve the open volume of the original barn, while introducing modern services and insulation. 'This feels more like a loft in the country,' said Pocknell. 'The central part of the timber barn is our main living space and the single-storey buildings attached to it contain all the other things.'

[4] **MEZZANINE GALLERY** The master suite sits upon the mezzanine level above the kitchen and overlooks the living area. The gallery offers an open platform, which allows the scale of the barn and the beauty of the frame to remain apparent. Integrated storage units shelter the bed and provide a degree of privacy, while the master bathroom is tucked away to the rear beyond a dressing area and fitted wardrobes. The central timber stairway is a standout feature, with a crafted quality that echoes the artisanal character of the barn.

Georgian Reinvention

DESIGNER   CHRIS DYSON ARCHITECTS
COMPLETED 1720s/2011
LOCATION   LONDON, UK

THERE CAN BE FEW PEOPLE who know the streets and houses of Spitalfields in east London as intimately as <u>Chris Dyson</u> and his wife, Sarah. As an architect and designer, Chris has spent many years working on historic buildings in the area, patiently piecing them back together and giving them a contemporary twist. The Dysons have also reinvented a number of homes here for themselves and their two children. Their latest – a calm, inviting and character-driven family house over five floors – is their most ambitious project to date.

The family first bought the house in the mid 1990s, but made only basic repairs and renovations before they were tempted by another period building across the street, where Chris has his architectural offices and an art gallery. However, a change of circumstance enabled the Dysons to re-engage with the original house, which had long been rented out to fund its upkeep. They decided to realize their ambitions and perform a radical reinvention, which included removing a plain, mid-century facade and replacing it with a frontage in reclaimed brick that was much more in keeping with the early 18th-century origins of the building.

'We wanted more space and a little more distance from the office,' said Dyson. 'The house had been used as a workshop and was in a terrible state when I bought it. It was really a wreck, so the first time around most of my money went on sorting out basic issues like wiring, plumbing, windows and the structure. I always had the ambition to do more.'

Before the Dysons took it on, the building had last seen use as a leather coat factory. Consequently, few period details remained in the house, inside and out. In fact, Dyson was left with little more than a blank canvas in the interiors. He set about designing a house that is generous and warm, with plenty of living space for all the family. On the ground floor, he created a wide and welcoming hallway, with double doors leading into the main reception area, oak floors and panelled walls. Upstairs, on the first floor, there is a generously proportioned sitting room with bare floors in reclaimed pine. A pair of salvaged pillars lend the fireplace a sense of drama and contemporary furniture brings the space into the 21st century. The children's bedrooms are on the floor above, along with a family bathroom, while Chris and Sarah have claimed the entire top floor for themselves.

DESIGN INGREDIENTS

· Eclectic collection of furniture

· Generous proportions

· Ornamentation

· Period detailing

· Symmetrical composition

[1] THOUGHTFUL SYMMETRY In the interiors there is an emphasis upon neoclassically inspired symmetry, with the sitting room fireplace framed by Corinthian pillars and panelling. The arrangement of furniture echoes the architectural symmetry, with twin chairs on either side of the fire and twin tables arranged around the central window. Dyson created a new facade for the house with a linear grid of windows that is very much in keeping with the neighbouring Georgian buildings.

[2] SALVAGED ELEMENTS Few original features survived within the house so fireplaces, timber panelling, mouldings and floors were all reinstated. A number of pieces of architectural salvage were sourced for the house, including the pine floorboards in the sitting room and the pillars either side of the fireplace. Such period elements add character and authenticity, while serving as cues for newly introduced and custom-made elements.

ATTIC BEDROOM

Positioned on the top storey of the house, the master bedroom offers a good degree of privacy and escape as well as expansive views and a wealth of natural light. The entire floor is given over to the bedroom, thus creating a self-contained world among the rooftops. The attic bedroom features a four-poster bed from Ikea, an antique linen press and a display case of stuffed birds from the attics of Chatsworth House in the Peak District. There is also an inviting bathtub in one corner of the room.

[3] **CONTEMPORARY FURNITURE** The design of the interiors represents far more than a slavish reproduction of Georgian style. There are many contemporary elements and modern touches within a thoughtful and eclectic approach. The furniture is a successful fusion of period pieces and contemporary finds, such as the two wing-back armchairs by British designer Matthew Hilton and the contemporary blue sofa.

[4] **DRAMATIC TOUCHES** In the sitting room there are touches of theatre, such as the French chandelier from Trois Garçons. This makes for a dramatic focal point and it sits well within the generous proportions of the space, with its high ceilings and welcoming sense of volume. Bold and playful elements prevent the house from becoming too serious or museum-like. Other rooms feature ornate, sculptural plasterwork and intriguing vintage finds.

Elephant Farm

DESIGNER	FT ARCHITECTURE
COMPLETED	1800/2005
LOCATION	COLUMBIA COUNTY, NEW YORK, USA

THE PICTURESQUE COUNTRY HOUSE that Brad and Amy Barr use as a weekend retreat has long been a landmark in this quiet enclave of New York State. Known as the Elephant Farm, it was once home to the Adele Nelson Elephant Farm and housed three elephants. They performed at shows, carnivals and circuses, but nearly destroyed the barn one day when they all bolted for the door after being frightened by the hum of electricity cables. Today, life here is much more sedate.

Framed by a striking line of pine trees, this small, traditional, timber-framed and timber-clad building had long attracted the Barrs, who rented the former farmstead for six years before finally buying it. They commissioned Kathleen Triem and Peter Franck of FT Architecture to update the house in a sensitive manner without changing its great sense of character. 'For me, I didn't want it to look as though it had been renovated,' said writer and editor Amy Barr. 'We weren't trying to change the character of the house, just make it bigger. Inside, all I really wanted at first was a bathroom of my own and in a way everything else went from there.'

From the outside, the traditional character of the Elephant Farm – parts of which date back to 1800 – has been preserved, despite some significant changes. To one side an entire extra bay has been added to create a larger kitchen downstairs and additional guest space above. This involved new windows and a sequence of French doors leading from the kitchen to the rear terrace. Inside, the priorities were not only to improve the relationship between outside and in, but also to create a greater sense of privacy and flexibility. A new staircase was added, leading from a reconfigured front hallway up to two guest bedrooms, served by their own bathroom. On the other wing of the house, which Amy and Brad share with their two sons, a redundant section of the old landing was converted to make space for a master bathroom.

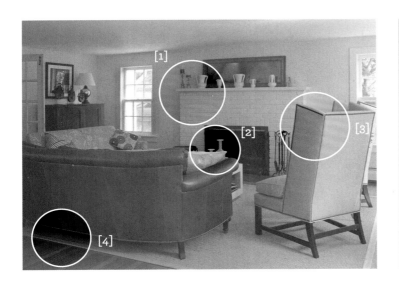

DESIGN INGREDIENTS

· Contemporary twists
· Contrasting patterns and
  complementary colours
· Country modern
· Farmhouse aesthetic
· Organic texture

[1] WHITE FIREPLACE During the winter months, the generously scaled living room enjoys plenty of use and the period fireplace becomes a key feature of the home. The brick surround is original to the house and has been painted white, creating a simple, almost Shaker-like aesthetic in combination with the white walls and wooden floors. The effect is soothing, with the seating arranged around the fireplace partly defined by the hearthside rug. 'It's country modern,' said Peter Franck. 'It's very low maintenance, clean and simple, but also warm with lush, natural materials.'

[2] COLOUR SPLASHES The neutral backdrop creates a subtle framework for introducing accents of colour and splashes of pattern. These include the creamy yellow chairs and the green sofa, bought from the Lounge furniture store. Vibrant patterned cushions and other small touches, such as the brightly coloured vase on the coffee table, stand out prominently within the context of the living room as a whole. The ceramics are mostly flea market finds, whereas the coffee table is from Jonathan Adler; the cabinet against the wall was bought from an antique store in Hudson, New York.

[3] <u>HIGH-BACK CHAIRS</u> In contrast to the organic texture of the wood flooring and panelling, the pair of high-back club chairs from Hudson Home add a contemporary twist. Their colour is engaging, as is their height, and the chairs provide a welcome shift in the composition of the room, drawing the eye. In dark upholstery they might have been too masculine or overpowering, but the soft tone adds a soothing quality. The contrast between the relatively short legs and the tall silhouette creates a striking combination and juxtaposition within the design of the chairs.

INVITING HALLWAY

The generously sized entrance hall was used as a dining room by the previous owners, which was not only impractical but also ruined the impact of the hallway. Now the space has been restored and opened up, creating a welcoming introduction to the house and setting the right tone for the aesthetic style of the interiors. The rounded shape of the bench – bought at the Pier Antique Show in New York – stands out against the timber staircase and the seat provides a useful amenity for changing shoes and dressing for the outdoors.

[4] **OPEN SPACES** The proportions are generous enough to accommodate a seating area at one end and a more formal dining area at the other. In combination, this creates a welcoming space for entertaining and a social hub for the house. It provides a hint of flexible open-plan living yet the room still has a clear identity of its own. The kitchen and other parts of the house remain separate and defined, as expected in a period farmhouse of this age and provenance. 'We do a lot of entertaining up here with friends and family and might have eight to twelve people to dinner,' said Brad Barr.

Parisian Escape

DESIGNER	THOMAS PHEASANT
COMPLETED	1800s/2002
LOCATION	PARIS, FRANCE

INTERIOR DESIGNER <u>THOMAS PHEASANT</u> nurtured dreams of owning a second home for many years. He was looking for an alternative to his main residence in Washington, DC, concentrating his thoughts on the possibility of an escape somewhere in the countryside of Virginia. However, while in Paris he bumped into some friends who had just bought an apartment in the Marais district. It sparked an idea, and a short while later he was looking around a property for sale on the Left Bank. It was in poor condition, but Pheasant could see the potential and soon found himself with a transatlantic renovation project.

The apartment sits at the top of a limestone building dating from the 1800s, just off the Boulevard Saint-Germain. Only the living room had been left intact with its original panelling and moulding, but even this needed work because it had been painted dark green with a burgundy trim. The rest of the apartment had been butchered, with period features removed and pipe work and cables everywhere. 'It wasn't what I expected when I first walked in,' said Pheasant. 'But it was bright because there were windows to both sides and it was quite handsome in terms of scale and I could appreciate the layout of the spaces. Then I looked through the window and saw the Sacré-Coeur in the distance and it seemed like a postcard.'

Pheasant ripped out the existing closets and replaced and concealed the pipe work and other services. He restored the floors and fireplaces and used the period panelling in the living room as a template for creating new panels for the adjoining dining room, as well as for the hallway and bedroom. 'I wanted to make the apartment more fluid and cohesive,' said Pheasant. 'In the hallway we actually lowered the ceiling because it was so narrow and so high that it looked out of proportion. We used mirrored glass doors, from the dining room to the kitchen for instance, to help throw light back and forth and open up the space.'

DESIGN INGREDIENTS

· Cohesion
· Neoclassicism
· Neutral palette
· Sculptural qualities
· Sophisticated composition

[2] INTEGRATED BOOKSHELVES

Either side of the fireplace, the integrated bookshelves offer library space and useful built-in storage, which keeps the room free of clutter. The screen doors allow the outline of the books to remain apparent, while still providing a neat and practical amenity. The neutral palette offers a subtle backdrop for artworks and furnishings, particularly the silhouettes and sculpted forms of the furniture designed by Pheasant.

[1] **WALL SCULPTURE** The living room is infused with interest and excitement by unexpected touches and careful, crafted precision. The wall sculpture by US artist Lisa Scheer is a case in point, offering a surreal punctuation mark upon the sandy walls. Either side of the window, the mid-century Erato wall lights by French designer Félix Agostini also have a highly sculptural, abstract quality, as does the sofa by Pheasant. His furniture designs reflect a passion for contemporary neoclassicism within a 'past present' style.

[3] SCROLL TABLE The 18th-century Chinese scroll table is an unexpected and engaging note, particularly in combination with the low, made-to-order ottoman. Its texture and colour make it stand out all the more against the pale colours of the lightly patterned carpet, the silk curtains and the upholstered sofa and chairs. The cream-coloured paintwork was inspired by the sandy stonework of surrounding buildings. Although much of the wall panelling is new, it was inspired by the period and provenance of the building.

[4] SOPHISTICATED SYMMETRY This inviting room relies upon a neoclassical approach to proportion and symmetry, which lends the space a cohesive and pleasing order. Twin bookcases and twin armchairs sit around the fireplace, while a pair of console tables flanks the tall window. The wall panelling reinforces the linear sequencing of the room. 'Neoclassicism is the foundation of my work,' said Pheasant. 'Both with my furniture and interiors I'm taking that vocabulary and trying to pare it down as much as possible.'

SOOTHING BEDROOM

The bedroom is a calm, restful retreat, with its pale tones and a variety of soft, tactile textures. The new panelling was modelled on the original panels in the living room and forms a canvas for art and standout pieces, such as the image by US photographer Colby Caldwell and the vintage starburst mirror. 'I loved the look of the building itself with the limestone greys and blues,' said Pheasant. 'When I was thinking about the palette of the apartment I was looking out of the window and wanted to bring that same look inside.'

Miner's Cottage

DESIGNER	LYNDA GARDENER
COMPLETED	1850s/2007
LOCATION	DAYLESFORD, VICTORIA, AUSTRALIA

DESIGNER LYNDA GARDENER has a long-standing love of Daylesford. About an hour's drive north of Melbourne, the former mining town, which boomed during the gold rush of the 1850s, has a definite charm. In fact, it was the only place that Gardener considered when she decided to buy a rural escape, settling on an 1850s miner's cottage in need of revival. The more the designer inspected the house, the more she saw that needed to be done, and the result was a radical restoration to the front and a complete rebuild at the back. However, looking at the house today, with interiors that feel cohesive and convincing, it is hard to imagine all the hard work and labour involved.

Gardener grew up in Melbourne and started work as a designer at a young age. She worked at Levi Strauss, designing the interiors of its Australian outlets, before opening a vintage store in the early 1990s. House commissions followed and now she and her partner, Amanda Henderson-Marks, run the Gardener & Marks design studio and shop. Despite being a city girl at heart, the designer was overwhelmed by the temptation to have a country home.

The single-storey, brick-built cottage was being shown for sale at an open day and Gardener went along for a quick look around. The building had been empty for years, the garden was overgrown and an update in the 1980s had left the house with a dismal look. However, the designer could see the potential and the minute she walked in she decided to buy it. 'I could see through it all,' she said, 'and realized that if it was stripped back to its original state then it could be beautiful again. But everything had to come out. So I installed everything from scratch and brought the gorgeous old house underneath back to life.'

Towards the front of the cottage, Gardener created two bedrooms plus a library and a bathroom, complete with a claw-foot bath. The back of the house was rebuilt in the form of a large, open-plan room, which holds the kitchen and dining area to one side and a lounge arranged around a new fireplace to the other. The interiors were repopulated with some of the fruits of the designer's many years of collecting, mixing retro industrial pieces with vintage treasures and finds from abroad. Her unique take on this retro vintage style works perfectly with the original character of the house, creating a home that is highly personal and well rounded.

DESIGN INGREDIENTS

· Industrial influences

· Pared-down country living

· Playfulness

· Repurposed furniture

· Retro styling

[1] CASUAL KITCHEN The kitchen has a casual, semi-industrial and even makeshift character. Arranged around a new Nobel range, the counters are manufactured from a repurposed work bench. The island is made from another bench from a shoe factory and it is fitted with castors so that it can be moved around the space easily. Although the kitchen is serviced with modern appliances, it retains a strong sense of character and individuality. This creates a successful room within a room, while offering a fluid connection with the dining and sitting areas alongside.

[2] PURPOSEFUL PATINA

Many of the pieces selected by Gardener, who has been collecting furniture and other treasures since the age of sixteen, come with the patina of age and a narrative all of their own. Within the context of a characterful period building, these items resonate all the more, adding fresh history. They include the old factory storage cupboard in rugged green and the 1960s dining chairs made by Modern Upholsterers in Prahran, Melbourne. 'Most of the pieces in the house really mean something to me,' said Gardener. 'I am always adding things.'

[3] VINTAGE LIGHTING

A range of vintage lighting adds to the character of the house, creating another layer of interest. The twin lights over the dining table are old factory fittings; their significant scale makes them perfect for an expansive, open-plan space such as this.

The ceiling lights in the kitchen were sourced at second-hand markets in Melbourne. Vintage light fittings should always be checked and installed by a qualified electrician to make sure that they are both safe for use and fully compatible with the circuitry and wiring of the property.

STUDIO BEDROOM

This new pavilion houses a bedroom and bathroom suite. It is a romantic space, all in white, set a small distance from the rest of the house and offering privacy and delight. The high, open ceilings and banks of windows reinforce the notion of an inviting escape. The claw-foot bath, open to the bedroom but raised on a modest platform, is an indulgent extra.

[4] BLACKBOARD WALLS Blackboard paint has been applied to the wall directly behind the kitchen counters, creating the impression of a giant splashback. This wall of matt black contrasts with the neutral walls and ceilings, and also serves as a noticeboard. It can be wiped down easily or repainted if damaged during the cooking process.

Cottage Colours

DESIGNER	SUSAN HABLE SMITH
COMPLETED	1918/2009
LOCATION	ATHENS, GEORGIA, USA

ARTIST AND DESIGNER <u>Susan Hable Smith</u> reinvented this early 20th-century cottage in Athens from afar. Although she and her family were still living in New York when they fell in love with the area, they bought the house and initially regarded it as a second home. The building was in poor shape and the restoration process took three years, as Hable Smith set about infusing the house with colour, art and life. The family room, kitchen and screened porch, as well as three new bedrooms, sit within a new two-storey addition, lifted by rich colour treatments and self-designed textiles. At the end of the adventure, Hable Smith and her husband felt so attached to the neighbourhood and the house that they decided to relocate.

As a textile designer, Hable Smith has a particular passion and flair for vibrant colour and pattern. In 1999 she launched her own company, Hable Construction, with her sister, Katharine, and named the business after their Texan great-grandfather's road construction firm. The company launched in New York initially and has grown over time into a successful design studio producing distinctive textiles and rugs manufactured in New England and North Carolina. Naturally, Hable Smith's own designs feature extensively in the characterful home that she shares with her husband and their two children.

The restoration of the cottage was a time-consuming and complex process that involved installing new foundations underneath the original building and extending outwards in sympathetic style. Hable Smith also created a smaller guest cottage and a studio nearby, taking her lead from the clapboard character of the original building. All three structures are painted a soothing, soft grey. 'The greatest challenge was in renovating the cottage from New York and flying down to manage the project,' she said. 'I do love layering pattern and texture throughout the house and many of the textiles were found on my travels and are so interesting combined with our Hable fabrics.'

Each room in the house has a very distinct interior character, from the vibrant pinks of the dining room to the more subtle, natural tones of the family den, which looks out onto the garden. The screened porch, too, feels close to nature with views of the landscape framed by the vines hanging over the windows.

DESIGN INGREDIENTS

· Close to nature

· Flamboyance and flair

· Influences from around the world

· Layers of texture

· Tailor-made textiles

[1] COOL COLOURS Soft blues and soothing greens dominate the sitting room, or den, which features large windows looking onto the garden. The walls are painted Oval Room Blue by Farrow & Ball, while the George Smith sofa is covered in a fabric by Hable Construction. The Belgian armchairs from John Derian in New York introduce notes of sage to the room and echo the greenery outside.

[2] CUSTOM TEXTILES The Rope curtain fabric was designed by Hable Smith and printed in a shade of blue that was specially tailored for the space. After clients spotted the fabric, it was added to the collection and put into production. The swirling pattern adds a dynamic sense of movement to the space and softens the room's linear qualities.

[3] LAYERED RUGS The textile designer layered two distinctive rugs over the wooden floorboards for added character and texture. 'I absolutely love the texture of the African palm frond mat and then I switch smaller, fuzzy rugs from Morocco to Ethiopia through the year,' said Hable Smith. 'I love to change things around for fun. I usually start with the drapery and floor coverings to set the tone of a room.' The circular vintage cocktail table is a flea market find from Provincetown, adding to the eclectic mix of furniture and other treasures.

[4] THEATRICAL TOUCHES The surreal blue wave by the window is a theatrical prop, originally from an opera house in New York's Bowery district and sourced from John Derian. It adds an unexpected, sculptural element to the space – often prompting a double take – while its colour fits the blue theme perfectly. The découpage bird pictures on the wall are also from John Derian.

SUMMER ROOM

Overlooking the garden, the screened porch serves as a fresh air dining room, used mainly in spring and autumn, as well as an extra family room. This relaxed space offers shelter and shade on the one hand and a direct sense of connection with the surroundings on the other. The fabric used for the banquette is a Hable Construction design called Tumbleweed. The steel chair is an iconic mid-century piece.

Swedish Loft

DESIGNER	THOMAS SANDELL
COMPLETED	1930s/2000
LOCATION	STOCKHOLM, SWEDEN

SWEDISH DESIGNER THOMAS SANDELL renovated this penthouse apartment in central Stockholm for himself and his wife, fashion designer Anna Holtblad. It dates back to the 1930s and was once the home of a textile designer, who used the double-height living room as a studio. Sandell respected the original layout of the apartment, updating the services and restoring the floors, while creating an elegant and sophisticated home.

Sandell's work spans architecture and interiors as well as furniture and product design. He sits within the proud tradition of Scandinavian interdisciplinary design, content to use his imagination in many different areas since founding his own design studio, Sandell Sandberg, in 1995. Naturally, the apartment presents numerous aspects of his work. He was careful to take the original character into consideration when designing the interiors, but also brought them up to date.

The focal point of the apartment is the old studio, with a stretch of windows offering views across the rooftops and waterways of Stockholm. A large sequence of glass bricks above the windows introduces extra light, adding to the vivid and dynamic character of the space. By the windows, within the more voluminous section of the studio, Sandell has arranged a dining area and a simple seating zone with views out across the city. With white walls, plenty of light and occasional bursts of colour, the effect is soothing and peaceful. A similar aesthetic pervades the dining room, kitchen and other complementary spaces.

The main seating area is arranged around a corner fireplace tucked under the mezzanine gallery. This creates a more intimate retreat, in contrast to the double-height portion of the rest of the studio. Here, a number of self-designed pieces of furniture blend in with 20th-century classics. A bookcase has been added to the rear wall, alongside the fireplace, while artworks include large-scale pieces by Nan Goldin and Alexander Calder.

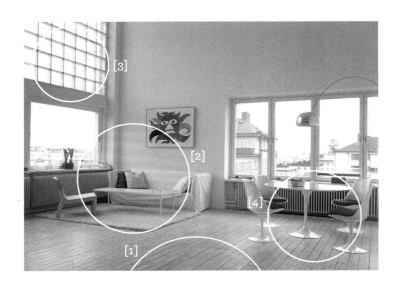

DESIGN INGREDIENTS

· Complementary iconic designs

· Feature glass wall

· Industrial scale

· Scandinavian traditions

· Variations in ceiling height

[1] ROOM WITHIN A ROOM Towards the rear of the studio, the lower ceiling height, created by the introduction of a mezzanine level above, establishes a room within a room that has a more intimate and inviting quality. The formation of comfortable seating around the corner fireplace helps to define the space further, as does the rug designed by Sandell for Kasthall. Twin Italian sofas are by architect and designer Piero Lissoni, complemented by two vintage, cube-shaped Grand Confort armchairs by Le Corbusier.

[2] GALLERY VIEW Here, the mezzanine offers a floating gallery, looking down upon the studio. It provides a flexible extra space, either for relaxation or for use as a study, library or music room. Mezzanines are both separate and connected to their host space at one and the same time, thereby establishing areas that are charming and sociable. The notion of a floating room is always appealing.

SCANDINAVIAN DINING

In the penthouse, the dining room features a pleasing combination of Scandinavian elements from a number of different periods, assembled within one warm and organic space. The tall Swedish clock is from the 18th century, while the plywood dining chairs are iconic mid-century designs by Alvar Aalto. To one side, the bookcase adds a graphic element and serves as a display centre for artworks, curios and personal treasures. The marble-topped dining table is a one-off design by Sandell.

[3] GLASS BRICKS A part wall of glass bricks forms a dramatic feature to one side of the double-height studio. It draws in diffused light but also offers character and texture as well as a graphic grid pattern. The use of glass bricks was particularly popular during the 1920s and the 1930s, when the apartment building was designed.

[4] LIMEWASHED FLOORS
Limewashed timber floors offer an attractive alternative to painted floorboards. Here, the floors have a subtle white finish that allows the grain and character of the timber to remain apparent while still providing a light coating that lifts the floors and the space itself. Deck paints and thick floor coatings can sometimes eradicate the character and charm of the timber. The Tulip dining table and chairs are by Eero Saarinen for Knoll; the bright red seat pads stand out against the neutral backdrop of the floors and walls.

Thirties Miami

DESIGNER	APARICIO + ASSOCIATES
COMPLETED	1930s/2013
LOCATION	MIAMI, FLORIDA, USA

ARCHITECT AND GALLERY OWNER Carlos Aparicio has reinvented this 1930s house in Miami as an oceanside retreat. Having bought the period property in Surfside sight unseen, he set about tailoring the house to his needs and updating the interiors for 21st-century living. Key to the success of the project is the new sitting room: a large and well-proportioned space flowing out to the rear garden and pool terrace.

When Aparicio decided to buy this Miami house, two factors sealed the deal. One was its location close to the ocean in the Surfside district of the city; the other was the alluring symmetry of the facade, with its neat portico over the entrance and neoclassical influences. He could see the potential immediately, and it did not take long to decide what to do to improve the single-storey dwelling. The architect embarked on a wholesale renovation project and reinvention of the building, but ensured that the sense of symmetry and the simple perfection of the facade were preserved. A new guest suite was created by converting a garage at one side of the house, and the courtyard garden to the rear was transformed by the addition of a new swimming pool, terraces and landscaping.

Perhaps the most dramatic change came with the main living space at the centre of the house. Here, Aparicio swept away a series of smaller individual rooms in favour of a large and open living area. 'People lived differently back in the 1930s and wanted all of these different rooms,' he said. 'I rebuilt it with the principle of creating beautiful, bright, open spaces and added the double doors to the outside.' In addition to a number of custom designs by Aparicio, the home offers a perfect setting for the numerous treasures that he already owned. The architect has been collecting 20th-century furniture and artworks for many years, with a particular passion for 1920s and 1930s design from the Art Deco period and beyond, including early modernist furniture.

DESIGN INGREDIENTS

· Complementary textures
  and colours

· Inside–outside living

· Neoclassical grandeur

· Sophisticated artworks

· Subtle zoning

[1] GRANDEUR OF SCALE

Although the single-storey house is quite modest in size overall, the reinvention of the main living spaces has lent the interiors a grandeur that is in keeping with the neoclassical qualities of the exterior. Opening up a series of smaller spaces to create a well-proportioned living area at the centre of the building has produced a room that truly pleases the eye, with its sense of perspective and scale. It also means that the space works as a fluid circulation hub, flooded with natural light from windows on both sides.

[2] HARMONIOUS COLOURS

This inviting room feels cohesive and well ordered, tied together by the pale flooring and the creamy white walls. Curtains and much of the upholstery sit within a harmonious colour range, thereby creating a degree of serenity and a brightness that suits the warm climate. Against this light, subtle backdrop, the organic textures of wood and leather stand out all the more, as seen in key pieces of furniture. The rugs are Swedish, from the 1950s, and add a softer layer of texture over the limestone floors.

[3] ICONIC FURNITURE As a collector and gallerist specializing in Art Deco and 20th-century furniture, Aparicio was well placed to assemble a collection of provenance suited to the house. Some of the most prominent pieces are by French interior designer Jean-Michel Frank, such as a pair of chaise longues and a cocktail table that combine Art Deco influences with a geometric purity associated with early modernist design. This makes them not only highly collectable but also very fitting for contemporary spaces such as this.

OUTDOOR ROOMS

A key aspect of the reinvention of the 1930s house was establishing a more successful and practical connection between the main living areas and the courtyard garden to the rear. The garden was redesigned completely and includes a number of 'outdoor rooms' that are well suited to the benign climate of Miami. There is a curtained seating area at one end of the pool and another arranged around an outdoor fireplace, both with custom-built sofas by Aparicio.

[4] ART AND HOME The interiors of the house play host to a number of eye-catching artworks and statues, which add another layer of interest. This is enhanced by the fact that the pieces are displayed informally and presented as an integral aspect of the room, rather than given the gravitas of a gallery setting. In this way, they become a sophisticated element of the overall character of the home, as seen in the 1930s statue by Danish sculptor Jens Jakob Bregnø.

Deco Moderne

DESIGNERS	KEMP & TASKER/RUNDELL ASSOCIATES
COMPLETED	1936/2010
LOCATION	LONDON, UK

ARCHITECT AND DESIGNER MIKE RUNDELL had little interest in Art Deco or suburbia until he paid a visit to a unique Art Deco building in Herne Hill, London. He found himself completely seduced by the house and by the end of the tour had decided to buy it. Designed by Kemp & Tasker and completed in 1936, the house had been well preserved and retained many of its original period features. Rundell embarked on a sensitive restoration process, which confirmed his appreciation not only of the house but also of the Art Deco period.

The building had been constructed for a pioneering developer called H.C. Morrell, who also built an Art Deco apartment block nearby. At the Ideal Home Show in 1935, he presented a 'house of tomorrow' and built sister versions for a series of clients. He collaborated on all of these projects with architects Kemp & Tasker, best known for a collection of Art Deco cinemas that they built across London and the Home Counties. When Morrell wanted to build a family residence, naturally he chose Kemp & Tasker to design it.

Fortunately, after Morrell, the house had only one other owner, a judge who had endeavoured to preserve as much original detailing as he could. From the emerald tiles around the front door to the startling entrance hall and stairway, as well as the highly crafted onyx master bathroom, the level of period detailing that remains is astonishing. 'The previous owner had only ever mended things,' said Rundell. 'So with the house I got a complete repair kit of spare parts for anything that had been taken out and replaced, with the originals in sealed and labelled plastic bags.' The designer had all he needed to restore the house, while also making it suitable for 21st-century living for himself and his family.

Rundell updated the kitchen with a design of his own. The dividing wall between the kitchen and dining area was removed to create a more open-plan space conducive to contemporary living, and a new folding screen of walnut wood was installed to allow for maximum flexibility. He also designed a number of sympathetic pieces of furniture for the sitting room, which is graced by artworks by well-known 20th-century artists. Other items of furniture were bought at auction or from antique markets. The Art Deco character of the house is emphasized in all its glory.

DESIGN INGREDIENTS

· Accents of green
· Large-scale artworks
· Linear qualities
· Plethora of original features
· Precision finishes

[1] DECO FIREPLACE The period fireplace in the sitting room is original. It combines geometric precision and symmetry with crafted materials, including marble bordered with characterful timber. On top of the fireplace is a sculpture by Damien Hirst. 'I have really got to appreciate Art Deco since I bought the house,' said Rundell. 'It's pretty restrained and there's nothing about it that is heavy. The quality of design of the building is extremely good.' The master bedroom also features an original fireplace, with integrated lighting that illuminates the glass surround.

[2] CRAFTED CORNICES
The decorative cornices are original to the house but they still feel fresh and contemporary in character. They bring texture and interest and also provide a visual framework for the room itself. The relatively broad dimensions of the cornice sit well within the generous proportions of the space. French doors at the far end of the room lead out to a modest loggia, which offers a sheltered spot for breakfast, lunch or dinner during the warmth of the summer months. The parquet flooring is also original.

[3] **CUSTOM SEATING** Rundell designed both the sofa and the matching armchair especially for the room. They are tailored to the proportions of the space, but also combine a contemporary aesthetic with Art Deco influences. The rounded, comfortable sofa features an integrated book shelf to the back, complete with sunken niches for vases of flowers. Lime green accents add a more vivacious element to the interiors, as seen in the cushions and the twin green chairs sourced from Alfie's Antique Market in Marylebone, London.

[4] **IMPACT ARTWORKS** The scale of the room calls for a number of large-scale works of art, as well as smaller treasures and objets d'art. The large photograph over the console unit (which was a choice discovery in a charity shop) is by Sam Taylor-Wood. There is also a Damien Hirst painting by the door to the entrance hallway.

MAKING AN ENTRANCE

The entrance hall is one of the most impressive spaces in the entire house, with many original period features throughout, including the intricate nickel banisters, the parquet flooring and a chandelier. There is also an original fireplace to one side. The vestibule doorway and the doors to the cloakroom and closet either side are faced with a frosted glass, which allows light to pass through while still offering plenty of privacy.

Mid-century Classic

DESIGNERS ANDREW GELLER/LARSON AND PAUL
ARCHITECTS

COMPLETED 1958/2007

LOCATION FIRE ISLAND PINES, NEW YORK, USA

ARCHITECT AND PRODUCT DESIGNER <u>Andrew Geller</u> was employed at the legendary Raymond Loewy/William Snaith design studio in New York, working on everything from compact cameras to department stores. However, he became better known for his second career, designing a series of imaginative beach houses along the shores of Long Island. One of the most endearing of these mid-century gems is a house that he built for Rudolph and Trudy Frank in 1958 in Fire Island Pines. Known as 'The Cube', the house has been restored with great sensitivity by painter Philip Monaghan.

Geller's architectural career took off after he designed a house for Elizabeth Reese, Loewy's director of public relations. It was a modest cabin but packed with ideas and originality; Reese was so pleased that she fed Geller and the house into her publicity machine and soon the commissions started coming in. They included one from the Franks for a house in Fire Island Pines. The couple had recently taken a trip to the Yucatán Peninsula and were inspired by the region's Maya ruins.

Their home borrowed from the imposing shapes and forms of Maya architecture, peeking over the trees from its hilltop location. However, rather then being made of stone, it was a lightweight house of timber and glass sitting on wooden piles. It was dominated by a glorious double-height living space, complete with an elevated catwalk. By the time Monaghan bought the house in 2003, it had been through another two owners and had suffered from poorly designed additions, as well as many winters exposed to salt-laden sea winds. 'The house really became my mission,' said Monaghan. 'I do feel very comfortable here, which is a real tribute to Geller's design. It's like a tree house, or a ship.' Monaghan turned to architect Rodman Paul of <u>Larson and Paul Architects</u> to help renovate the house. Ultimately, the project was so extensive that it became a virtual rebuild.

Inside, the focus was on creating a sympathetic update, although internal changes were also made to the layout. The positions of the kitchen and guest bedroom on the ground floor were reversed. Monaghan and Paul have been careful to respect the spirit of the house, collaborating on a choice of period furniture mostly from the 1950s and 1960s, while a new log burner in the living room is in the exact position where Geller placed the original stove.

DESIGN INGREDIENTS

· Cohesive textures

· Dramatic mezzanine

· Flexible layout

· Living in the trees

· Sympathetic furnishings

[1] ORGANIC TEXTURES Surrounded by a forest of pines, oaks and American holly, the house has a natural, organic character, with some of the qualities of a tree house. Cedar boards have been used extensively, and these expanses of timber add to the feeling of warmth. The window frames and structural elements of the cabin are also made of wood, creating a cohesive and harmonious aesthetic.

[2] FLEXIBLE KITCHEN The kitchen is a new design, but one that respects Geller's original ideas. It features a sliding timber screen that can be pulled across to separate the kitchen from the main living area; it is perfect for concealing any clutter during a meal. The arrangement offers all the benefits of open-plan living, with a refreshing unrestricted feel, combined with flexibility and choice.

[3] SCULPTED CLASSICS

Monaghan and Paul sourced a number of sympathetic pieces of furniture, designed in the 1950s and 1960s, that suit the space perfectly. Many have a sculpted, rounded and tactile quality to them, as befits the period, such as the vintage coffee table by Eero Saarinen. Other classics include the Tulip dining table also by Saarinen, the Artek kitchen stools by Alvar Aalto and the George Nelson ceiling light. A small artwork by Shirley Geller, wife of the original architect, hangs above the contemporary sofa from Minotti.

ROOFTOP VIEW

Monaghan and his architects created a series of decks, terraces and outdoor rooms around the house, as well as a new swimming pool. One of the most dramatic outdoor spaces is the roof terrace, complete with a hot tub, which forms an extraordinary viewing platform with vistas out across the tree tops and towards the ocean.

[4] HEIGHT AND LIGHT
The main living and dining area is a double-height space, overlooked by a suspended walkway and a mezzanine gallery. This introduces a dramatic sense of volume and transparency, as well as a rich quality of natural light via the vast expanse of windows. In this way, the tree canopy that surrounds the cabin becomes an integral part of the interiors, with a strong inside–outside connection throughout.

Minimal

Tribeca Loft

DESIGNER	FEARON HAY ARCHITECTS
COMPLETED	2009
LOCATION	MANHATTAN, NEW YORK, USA

NEW ZEALAND ARCHITECTS Jeff Fearon and Tim Hay have taken a fresh approach to loft living with this Tribeca apartment, where the design places an emphasis on choice and flexibility. The loft is not only open and light but it also offers intimate retreats, with tracked curtains and sliding doors used to divide interconnecting spaces. It dispenses with an entirely open floor plan and compartmentalized interiors in favour of an original middle ground.

The apartment takes up most of one floor of a former textile warehouse, with glazing to three sides offering views across Manhattan. 'This is a retreat,' said Fearon, whose practice – Fearon Hay Architects – is based in Auckland. 'It's about having a space where the owners can be themselves as a young family and have a place away from the intensity of the city. There was a lot of emphasis on calmness.' In order to leave enough space for walkways and dramatic sight lines around the perimeter of the loft, Fearon Hay gently pushed the living spaces inwards. Where more intimate, private areas were needed, they created pavilions and pods, like miniature buildings sitting within the overall floor plan.

Every other area of the loft apartment beyond these neat shelters is essentially open plan. The master bedroom is positioned in one corner, the dining area in another and the living zone in yet another, all without the need for solid divisions. These give onto a large and open central entrance area and hallway, which doubles as a gallery space for displaying some of the clients' art collection, including a video work by Bill Viola. A steel-and-glass pavilion resembling a crafted jewelry box contains a further three bedrooms. 'The character of the empty loft volume was something that we didn't want to lose,' said Hay. 'Maintaining that openness around the edges of the apartment was critical to us, so that you could still walk around and appreciate the views without being cut off by divisions or smaller chambers.'

At the same time this is a highly individual and crafted home, with many features specially designed for the space. 'Almost every element in the loft was custom built,' said Fearon, 'and the level of detailing just wouldn't have been possible without the artisans involved. It took a lot of time, but the ambitions of the client to achieve those kinds of high standards were the driver for all of these things.'

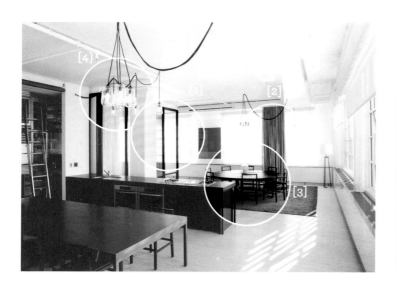

DESIGN INGREDIENTS

· Clusters of lights

· Floating pavilions

· Industrial scale

· Juxtaposition of sculptural
  and linear forms

· Well-ordered zoning

[1] LIVING ZONES The idea of zoning different living areas partly evolved from the popularity of warehouse and loft conversions, which began to take hold in the 1970s and 1980s, drawing upon the notion of the 'free plan' developed by post-war architects and designers. Here, a number of common design devices – the positioning of rugs, furniture and fixed elements such as the kitchen counters – have been used to delineate the various spaces within the loft; more unusual are the diaphanous fabric 'walls'.

[2] CURTAIN WALLS Curtains mounted on ceiling tracks have been used in a number of areas throughout the apartment to isolate particular sections of the interiors. They are most effective around the main seating area, forming floating fabric dividers that provide a degree of privacy and flexibility without the need for solid partition walls.

[3] CIRCULAR ELEMENTS

The nature of the building and the internal shell of the loft create a linear plan, reinforced by the window grid. Fearon Hay has worked to soften the geometrical precision of the interiors by introducing more sinuous shapes, including a circular table and other sculptural elements. The large walnut dining table, custom-made by US furniture company BDDW, is a key example. Its crisp black finish not only stands out against the neutral walls and floors but also ties in with other key pieces of furniture throughout the apartment.

[4] FEATURE LIGHTING

A striking sequence of character pendant lights by New Zealand-based glass artist Katie Brown is strung across the ceiling. Bunching these lights in clusters above key points, including the dining table and breakfast table, creates a contemporary chandelier effect, while other strings of lights have a necklace aesthetic with illuminated 'jewels'.

JEWEL BOXES

Three bedrooms are contained within a floating glass pavilion that forms an escapist home within a home. Designed to be used by children and guests, these spaces sit upon an elevated platform above the main floor. They form a sequence of more intimate rooms, set back from the windows and allowing for a circulation hallway alongside. Floor-to-ceiling curtains are used, once again, to shroud the pavilion without disturbing the purity of the undressed windows and the vista beyond.

Waterview House

DESIGNERS	BRIAN ZULAIKHA/TONKIN ZULAIKHA GREER ARCHITECTS
COMPLETED	2006
LOCATION	SYDNEY, AUSTRALIA

THE HOUSE THAT ARCHITECT Brian Zulaikha designed for himself and his partner, mixed media artist Janet Laurence, in the cosmopolitan suburb of Balmain in Sydney is full of surprises. It reveals its delights by degrees, gradually opening up to views of Sydney Harbour and the busy city skyline. Every aspect of the design – from an integrated veranda on the upper level to an outdoor bathhouse overlooking the terrace – makes the most of the setting. And for a house that has such a lightness of touch and such flexibility, one of the greatest surprises is that a concrete and brick gunpowder store, dating back to 1918, sits right at the core of the reinvented building.

A principal at Tonkin Zulaikha Greer Architects, Zulaikha has lived on the same cobbled street for about thirty years and he was aware of an old gunpowder store at the end of his road from the beginning. Twenty years ago the building was converted into a house, when living space was added on the ground floor and three bedrooms were built above. When the residence came up for sale in 2003, Zulaikha and Laurence did not hesitate to buy it. The architect designed lightweight, timber-framed living spaces around the old concrete core, introducing sliding walls and retractable glass panels throughout. These open up the building to the outside during warmer months, but can also be closed down in the cold of winter.

In addition to the kitchen downstairs, Zulaikha designed a generous dining room with a made-to-order staircase. There is also a garden room over the entrance area, where concrete steps lead up from the lower-ground level on the sloping site. Most enticing of all, perhaps, is the bathhouse that projects out into the rear terrace. Here, glass walls retract to offer a direct relationship with the terrace and garden as well as a view of the harbour.

Upstairs, Zulaikha originally planned for three modest bedrooms, but during the construction he saw the quality of the views from upstairs and changed his mind. Instead of three bedrooms he designed only one, plus an upstairs living room and a long balcony that connects to both spaces. 'It's actually like being in a penthouse when you are here, looking out over this very wide view of the harbour,' said Zulaikha. 'There's nothing like that sense of peace that you get when you are looking out over the water.'

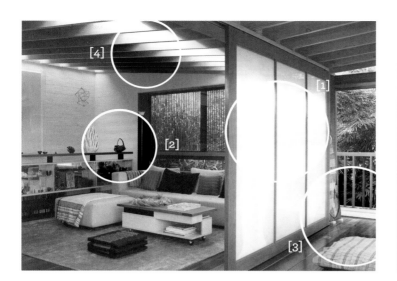

DESIGN INGREDIENTS

· Informality

· Inside–outside living

· Japanese influence

· Light sources from many directions

· Repeated framing

[1] SLIDING SCREENS The translucent sliding screens that divide the main sitting room from the integrated veranda on the upper level are reminiscent of Japanese *shoji* screens, originally designed to conserve space. Here, they provide not only subtle separation between the two spaces but also privacy, while still allowing a degree of natural light to filter through. They are part of a flexible living strategy that allows various portions of the building to be opened up or closed down accordingly.

[2] INTEGRATED DISPLAY The custom staircase is a multifunctional design. On the upper level, the balustrade that separates the stairwell and the sitting room doubles as a display unit, featuring glass-fronted cases topped by a floating timber shelf. These cabinets exhibit numerous personal treasures and objets d'art, and they are supplemented by additional storage units lining the walls around the sitting room in keeping with the minimalist design.

INDOOR–OUTDOOR BATHROOM

The sheltered garden terrace features a bathhouse with sliding windows that allow for fresh air bathing. It is contained within a modest single-storey pavilion, attached to the main house, with a green roof rich in foliage. As with a number of other elements in the house, the pavilion suggests a Japanese influence. 'It is a wonderful room,' said Zulaikha. 'We have a heated floor in there, so even in the winter the bath gets heated up.'

[3] **ELEVATED VERANDA** The integrated veranda on the upper storey is a flexible and elevated space from which the waterside view can be appreciated fully. This minimalist but alluring area also serves as a reading room and an extension to the sitting room in the summer months, when it helps to provide natural ventilation via retracting windows. During the winter, the windows and screens can be closed to insulate the house.

[4] **FILTERED LIGHT**
The soft light that is diffused through the screens is supplemented by natural light from a number of other sources and directions, thereby creating an airy and inviting atmosphere within the space. Light floods into the sitting room via a split-level end window – with a *brise-soleil* (sunshade) protecting its upper portion – and the long, slim skylights set into the ceiling. The white walls and screens help light to circulate throughout the interiors, as does the reflective surface of the lacquer-finish timber floor.

Rural Modern

DESIGNER	GREGORY PHILLIPS ARCHITECTS
COMPLETED	2011
LOCATION	BERKSHIRE, UK

WITH A LOVE OF FRESH AIR and open countryside, Max and Paula McNeill are outdoor people. Consequently, when it came to building their family home in Berkshire – on a stunning location set in 12½ acres (5 ha) of grounds overlooking the Thames Valley – making the most of the connections between inside and outside was a priority. This tailored contemporary home of flint, steel and glass opens up to the landscape, flows out into the garden and connects with a swimming pool to one side and a tennis court to the other.

Designed by <u>Gregory Phillips Architects,</u> the house sits on the very edge of a village, resting on a plateau overlooking the valley below. The McNeills were living in the village itself and were about to start another round of work on their old home when they heard that the site had come up, along with a modest, late 1930s house. Realizing that they might be able to custom build a modern country house to replace the existing building, they asked the Royal Institute of British Architects to arrange an architectural competition. Four architects produced ideas and Gregory Phillips was the one who most impressed them.

Working with project architect Ralph Hill, Phillips designed a building that was orientated towards the valley and the vista, with a fluid relationship between indoors and out via banks of glass and vast sliding doors that open up to the garden. Balconies and a roof terrace at first-floor level reinforce the links to the landscape. The master bedroom and bathroom are among the key rooms that face the views.

The contemporary, linear outline of the five-bedroom house is softened by the abundant use of organic materials, such as stone, timber and flint. Flint walls form a dramatic entrance courtyard at the rear of the house, while water pools front and back add another natural element that connects the house to its setting. The layout of the interiors offers generous living areas, especially the well-proportioned family kitchen, with space enough for a dining area and seating zone. There is also a formal dining room, with the entrance area to one side and the main stairs to the other. However, these large spaces are balanced by more intimately proportioned retreats, including a study, family room and media room.

DESIGN INGREDIENTS

· Context

· Contrast of textures

· Formal and informal areas

· Landscaping

· Rhythm

[1] INDOOR–OUTDOOR CONNECTIONS The design of the house establishes a strong relationship between the interior spaces and the landscape beyond at every opportunity. Large expanses of floor-to-ceiling glass offer extensive views of the open countryside, while sliding windows provide a seamless connection between the interiors and the terraces. The lighting is designed by Christian Liaigre and it creates an atmospheric backdrop to the space in the evenings in particular, while task lighting illuminates the kitchen nearby.

[2] ROOFTOP LIVING The open vista of the English countryside can best be appreciated from the elevated position of the roof terrace. This is a fully furnished outdoor sitting room looking down upon the gardens and the swimming pool. Robust outdoor seats and sofas from Dutch firm Val-eur are complemented by cushions that can be removed when not in use. 'The idea was to design a building that sat in the landscape in a discreet fashion and allowed the family to really take advantage of the location and the views,' said Gregory Phillips.

[3] FAMILY HUB A combined kitchen, breakfast room and family lounge offers a spacious home hub for everyday living. With open views of the gardens and grounds and easy connections to the adjoining terraces, this multifaceted space is informal in nature and elegant in character. The sofa and daybed are by Christian Liaigre, while the rug adds colour and texture as well as helping to define this area as a relaxation zone. This family space is complemented by a more formal dining room at the centre of the house and a dedicated sitting room beyond.

[4] SOFT LANDSCAPING The crisp outline of the house is softened by the gardens and landscaping around the building, designed by Creative Landscape. This includes many gentle grasses and low planting with a naturalistic quality that contrasts with the more linear pathways and gabions that connect the grounds to the house. In this way, the landscaping forms a middle ground between the house and the countryside setting.

BED AND BATH

The master suite on the upper storey also benefits from open views of the countryside. Here, the contrasting desires for open bathing and a degree of privacy are catered for within a flexible arrangement of bedroom and bathroom, offered by a sliding timber wall that can be pulled across to divide or connect the two. The marble was sourced in Verona and the fittings are from Alternative Plans in London.

Istanbul Eyrie

DESIGNERS	SEFER ÇAĞLAR/AUTOBAN
COMPLETED	2012
LOCATION	ISTANBUL, TURKEY

For designer <u>Sefer Çağlar,</u> home is a light and airy apartment in the Gümüşsuyu district in the heart of Istanbul. It sits within a 1970s building – named the Opera Palas by the original owner, who had a love of music – on the fifth floor, where it commands views out across the city and the Bosphorus. A substantial portion of the apartment is devoted to an open-plan living space, with white walls, white painted floorboards and custom-built storage cupboards to one side. Neatly contained within an open-sided timber pavilion, the kitchen is the key focal point. Here, a sequence of latticed wooden doors can be closed to contain the space.

'The building had been used as offices and many different partition walls divided the space into a whole series of rooms,' said Çağlar, a founding partner of the Turkish design studio <u>Autoban</u>. 'So we wanted to take down all these useless walls and really open up the space. At the end we were left with a white cube and that was an important starting point for us.'

Çağlar shares the apartment with his wife, Merve, who works in the field of contemporary art, and their young daughter, Sera. The living area has been lightly arranged into zones for seating and eating, with a quartet of floor-to-ceiling carousel bookcases providing a subtle distinction between them. Many pieces here, including the bookcases, are custom Autoban designs or prototypes. They include a 1950s-inspired Box sofa and matching armchairs as well as a Cloud dining table. These contemporary designs complement mid-century classics, such as the grass-seated dining chairs by George Nakashima and a coffee table by Charles and Ray Eames.

One of Çağlar's favourite elements within the minimalist apartment is the rich quality of natural light, enhanced by the white painted floors and walls that reflect the sunlight through the space. They also create a neutral, gallery-like backdrop for his collection of furniture and artworks. 'Since we work in design and art we really wanted an effective space where we could display both furniture prototypes and our art collection,' said Çağlar. 'But it's also about the idea of having an undecorated space and the way it fits with our daily lives. It's more about the simplicity of the space itself.'

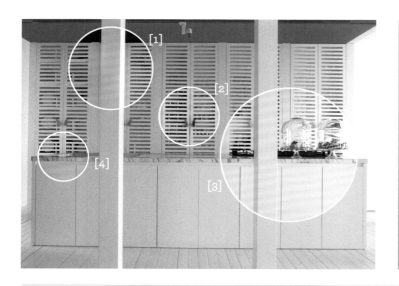

DESIGN INGREDIENTS

· Cohesive elements

· Functionality

· Order and integration

· Purity of forms

· Room within a room

[1] FLEXIBLE LIVING The arrangement of the kitchen pavilion in one corner creates a good deal of flexibility as to how the apartment can be used and enjoyed. The light timber structure creates a room within a room, defined by a sequence of lattice doors at one end where it meets the open-plan living space. These doors can be closed to disguise the business of preparation and cooking or kept open to maximize the social connections between the different areas of the apartment.

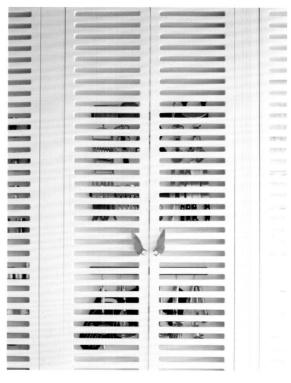

[2] LATTICED DOORS Within the kitchen, the latticed doors disguise a long sequence of shelves and storage cupboards to the rear. These cupboards help to minimize clutter and kitchen chaos, while the lattice design brings unity, cohesion and clarity to the space as a whole. This crafted geometric pattern also adds character and individuality. The custom design of the delicate brass wing handles was inspired by the Çağlar family monogram.

CHARACTER BATHING

The generously proportioned shower room makes extensive use of the same Marmara marble seen in the kitchen for the walls and floors, as well as for a custom-built vanity island floating in the space. The design draws upon the idea of a wet room, with drainage recessed into the floor between the timber slats of the shower tray and minimal partitioning. A mirrored wall provides an effective tool for bouncing light through the room, enhancing the impression of space and proportion.

[3] ISLAND KITCHEN Another key component of the kitchen is the long island, which provides a generously sized surface for food preparation as well as additional storage. The gas cooktop is set into the marble surface, thereby providing a practical work station with implements and ingredients close at hand. The black ceiling provides a dramatic contrast with the whites and greys elsewhere.

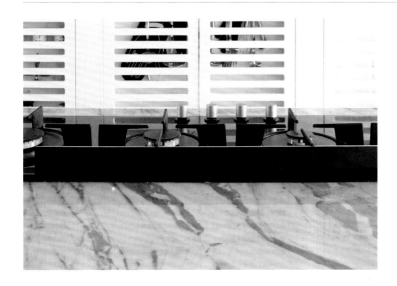

[4] MARBLE SURFACES
The counter is coated in Marmara marble veined with a combination of soft greys and whites. Within a minimalist environment, such expressive materials – and the way that they are finished – become more apparent and important. Here, the grey veins lift the space, add interest and stand out prominently against the white floors and joinery. 'The kitchen is an important contribution to the clarity and harmony of the apartment as a whole,' said Çağlar. 'It's about light, form and materials co-existing in this minimal envelope.'

Bronte Belvedere

DESIGNER	ROLF OCKERT DESIGN
COMPLETED	2012
LOCATION	BRONTE, SYDNEY, AUSTRALIA

OPEN OCEAN VIEWS and a restricted site, bordered by neighbours, were the drivers for the design of this striking two-storey house in Sydney's eastern suburbs. The arrangement of the main living area on the upper level makes the most of the vista out across the sea, with the open plan offering a direct sense of connection with the outdoors and the powerful panorama. The house combines simplicity and restraint with the owners' desire to feel like they were on holiday every day of the week without ever leaving home.

The house in Bronte is a radical rebuild of an existing 1930s brick residence, and only one room of the original building remains. Rolf Ockert's design in effect provides a completely new house, re-orientated towards the sea views. In order to maintain privacy from the neighbouring buildings, concrete boundary walls were introduced to the sides. They create a feeling of isolation and are topped by a continuous series of high clerestory windows, which complements the expanses of glazing that connect the front of the house directly to the ocean. 'The panoramic, elevated ocean view is what makes the site and setting so special,' said Ockert. 'The views were the key factor in the design, together with catching the breeze for natural ventilation. The indoor–outdoor connection is a great way to take advantage of the wonderful climate that we have here.'

Although the plot is relatively modest in size, the upper level of the house contains two bedrooms, a study and a spacious open-plan main living zone, which opens onto an elevated terrace and balcony. With high ceilings and floor-to-ceiling glass framing the ocean panorama, this part of the residence feels sophisticated and inviting, with room enough for dining and seating zones plus the kitchen. This is a custom design, with a run of units and a long counter to the side wall complemented by a marble island.

The lower storey is devoted to a generously sized master suite, flowing into a private lounge that leads out onto the adjoining deck and infinity pool. Again, the ocean view is maximized, with the bed positioned to face the water. The combination of outdoor rooms across the two levels creates a choice of fresh air zones, while extending the available living space dramatically, given the easy flow between inside and out.

DESIGN INGREDIENTS

· Framing

· Maximizing the ocean vista
  and views of the sky

· Multiple light sources
  and directions

· Simple earthy palette

· Sophistication

[1] MULTIFUNCTIONAL FURNITURE The kitchen by Rolf Ockert Design features a monolithic island integrated with a breakfast table made of wenge timber. It is an unusual but effective combination. The 'cockpit' Conch chairs are by Decoma Design for Italian firm Porro, whereas the black and white photographs displayed above the kitchen units include images by Henri Cartier-Bresson.

[2] PENDANT LIGHTING The twin pendant lights in the kitchen are complemented by a larger version of the same design over the dining table. The Allegretto lights are produced by Italian firm Foscarini and designed by Swiss collective Atelier Oï. Made from aluminium rods and lacquered steel, they are particularly effective in a space with high ceilings, where they draw the eye upwards. The rods chime gently when touched by the breeze.

[3] CLERESTORY WINDOWS

The sequence of clerestory windows allows natural light to filter through from multiple directions, adding to the rich illumination of the living space. These windows also draw attention to the height of the ceilings, which was the only available spatial dimension that could be easily exploited by the architects. 'I also wanted a lightness to the roof and the appearance that it is floating above you,' said Ockert. 'And the high ventilation via the glazed louvres gets the breeze into the house in summer.'

[4] ELEVATED TERRACE

The terrace and balcony on the upper level offer a prime vantage point for appreciating the sea vista. There is space for an outdoor dining area that sits conveniently close to the indoor kitchen, although there is also room enough on the terrace for a barbecue. The balcony itself is manufactured in clear, super-strength glass that allows an unimpeded view of the water. The slatted timber bench and table are both elegant and practical for outdoor use, well suited to the demands of the sun and the salt air.

POOL TERRACE

The new swimming pool is sited on the lower level alongside another terrace and the landscaped gardens. This terrace is partially sheltered by the overhang of the balcony above and therefore contains shaded seating zones. Comfortable sun loungers are arranged adjacent to the infinity pool, which offers the sensation of swimming out towards the ocean as the blue waters of both combine into one. The tall planting to the boundary edge of the property maintains a degree of privacy for the outside spaces and also provides a verdant green backdrop.

Riviera Sunshine

DESIGNER	JASON MACLEAN
COMPLETED	2009
LOCATION	CANNES, FRANCE

DESIGNER <u>JASON MACLEAN</u> TRANSFORMED this period villa on the French Riviera into a minimalist retreat over the course of only ten weeks. The sunshine yellows of the sitting room are repeated elsewhere in the house, including on the sculptural staircase that has a balustrade picked out in the same vibrant tone. These bursts of colour are complemented by accents of pattern that lift the interiors. This combination of restraint and warmth sits well with the original architecture of the house, which is fully explored and expressed.

The London-based designer began his French adventures with a crumbling farmhouse in the Lot-et-Garonne region, which he bought and restored with his partner, creating contemporary interiors that still allowed the original character of the building to breathe. He took a similar approach with this project in Cannes, although the character of the house in question was wildly different. Here, MacLean was tempted by a substantial villa dating from the 1870s. 'The house is on a hill in a quiet corner of Cannes overlooking the sea,' said MacLean, 'and only a ten-minute walk from La Croisette. It sits in these beautiful, secluded gardens surrounded by high walls, which makes it extremely private. But the villa was in a pretty rough state and many of the original features had been lost over the years.'

The design and restoration process was rapid but considered, with due respect paid to the proportions of the spaces within and the distinctive period facade without, painted in a characterful peach pink and 'cat lick cream' palette. Large windows introduce a wealth of light and open the living areas to the Riviera view. This is particularly apparent in the main living room, which is a generously scaled space with a quartet of tall French windows. Here, MacLean designed a new fireplace with a terrazzo surround, with a tall library bookcase to one side. Although the bold yellow seating arrangement dominates the room, it is complemented by a select number of less vibrant additional pieces. A wall of vivid pattern at the back of the room adds interest and lifts the space.

Outside, a double staircase leads down to the new kidney-shaped swimming pool, with black and white Eley Kishimoto mosaic tiles. In the grounds MacLean converted a garage into a fifth bedroom, which serves as a romantic pavilion set a little distance apart from the rest of the villa.

- Accents of pattern
- Continuity
- Minimal furnishing
- Purity
- Stark contrasts

[1] PATTERNED WALL This expanse of pattern on the back wall brings a dynamic quality to the space and adds movement and character. At the same time the subtlety of the pattern is not at odds with the minimalist approach to the interiors. The design is by fashion house Eley Kishimoto, which has expanded into the realm of interior design with a range of wallpapers – many with an Op art influence – and home accessories.

[2] INTEGRATED DOORWAY The door that leads through to the dining room is subtly integrated into the joinery that is repeated on both sides of the fireplace. The insertion of the doorway within this arrangement allows for a degree of symmetry around the central fireplace and creates a neat composition that ties in with the dark timber floors. At this end of the room, the slab stone surround forms an anchor, and the dark woodwork holds shelving and display niches.

[3] BEACON FURNITURE The Tufty Time sofa system by B&B Italia, designed by Patricia Urquiola, is an informal modular piece that can be arranged in various combinations. Here, the sectional seating has been divided into three distinct components, which could be easily combined for more intimate social occasions. The bright yellow is offset by the polished dark timber floors and the patterned wall that forms a backdrop behind the main sofa. The same accent colour is also used within the entrance hall, including additional seating by Urquiola.

[4] COMPLEMENTARY SPACES Alongside the sitting room is the dining room, which has been designed as a complementary space, using the same materials and language. The joinery is repeated, here providing a ready storage space for glassware and ceramics. The geometric Eley Kishimoto wallpaper also makes a return, highlighting a sense of continuity between the two rooms, although the proportion and scale of each is very different. These interconnected spaces offer an engaging alternative to a more open-plan way of living.

STATEMENT BATHROOM

The master bathroom is again minimalist in design. However, here a sense of drama and luxury is provided by the striking and streamlined bath and sink combination set against walls and floors of matching pale blue mosaic tile. The Ebb bath and basin unit is a design by UsTogether, a collective of UK and Irish designers who sell their work through C.P. Hart in the United Kingdom, as well as via international dealers. The fluid form of the design is suggestive of a wave of water washing through the space.

Mountain Vista

DESIGNERS	MARMOL RADZINER/ KIM ALEXANDRIUK
COMPLETED	2011
LOCATION	NORTHSTAR, LAKE TAHOE, CALIFORNIA, USA

During the summer months, the mountain resort of Northstar in California attracts hikers, mountain bike enthusiasts and golfers. In the winter, it comes alive with skiers and snowboarders, who can enjoy ninety ski runs and a vibrant winter scene. However, the greatest allure is the landscape itself, with its forests and mountain peaks, as well as the alpine waters of Lake Tahoe close by. The natural beauty of the region was the main draw for architects Marmol Radziner and their clients, who commissioned this family home as a country retreat that could be used in all seasons.

Naturally, the design of the house makes the most of its relationship with the extraordinary mountain landscape. The approach is from the north, but the main living space and adjoining terraces face south, taking great advantage of the mountain panorama and drawing in the southern sunlight. Stone, timber and zinc cladding lend the house an earthy, organic quality. 'It's a beautiful site and it's always our goal to try to fit the house into the natural topography as much as we can, so the building actually steps down the slope very gently,' said Ron Radziner. 'That adds to the rhythm of the house and helps define the different zones, but it's all very gentle.'

The house is largely arranged on one level, apart from the master suite, which sits on its own within the upper storey. At the far end of the building, the children have two bunk rooms and a large playroom. The living area flows outwards, via giant sliding glass doors, to a sequence of outdoor rooms and terraces that step gently down the site. These include an outdoor dining area and a sheltered veranda holding a lounge, with a modestly scaled plunge pool alongside.

The dining area and kitchen lead directly into the main sitting room, which allows the light to circulate freely between them. In the lounge area, the timber-clad ceiling is lower, thus creating a more intimate, cosy environment. Marmol Radziner collaborated on the interiors with Kim Alexandriuk and the blend of furniture includes pieces by Alexandriuk herself as well as contemporary designs and mid-century finds by Italian firm FontanaArte and others. The palette is warm and organic, with stone walls and timber ceilings and cabinetry, complemented by comfortable furnishings in earthy hues.

DESIGN INGREDIENTS

· Context

· Contrasting textures inside and out

· Distinct zoning

· Rustic feel

· Vintage furnishings

[1] CHANGING LEVELS

Although the house has a fluid and cohesive layout, shifts in floor level create a meaningful degree of separation between the main seating and dining areas, reinforced by a custom-made storage cabinet at mid level. In this way, the two spaces have their own identity but also maintain a natural connection to one another. The height and scale of the furniture reflect the nature and function of the space in which they sit, with low-slung seating for the sitting room and taller pieces for the dining area and kitchen.

[2] RECESSED KITCHEN

In keeping with the open-plan layout, the kitchen is only partially separated from the rest of the living space by a long, tailor-made counter by Marmol Radziner. The floating custom unit over the island hides an extractor fan, but the addition of a timber wrap turns this practical element into a feature. The moulded plywood bar stools are iconic mid-century designs by Norman Cherner and the Beat Tall pendant lights in black over the counter are by Tom Dixon. Made from brass, they are hand-beaten by craftsmen in northern India.

[3] ORGANIC TEXTURES Despite the relatively minimalist character of the house, there is a great deal of warmth provided by the choice of materials. These include natural stone around the fireplace, ceilings in Alaskan yellow cedar, and oak joinery, panelling and stairs. Such an organic palette links the house to the natural context of its mountain setting, while providing a contrast to the more man-made elements, such as the concrete floors and the expanses of glass.

FIRE TERRACES

Arranged around a plunge pool that doubles as a hot tub in the colder months, the tiered terraces at the front of the house offer a choice of relaxation areas. There is a large outdoor fireplace and a fire pit, which means that these inviting outdoor rooms can be used during the evenings and even in winter. The arrangement of the terraces and the outdoor furniture echoes that of the indoor spaces, thus reinforcing the connection between the two.

[4] VINTAGE TOUCHES
The house features integrated elements by Marmol Radziner and designs by Kim Alexandriuk, such as the sofa. However, there are also expressive vintage pieces that add character and patina, including the copper cocktail table by New York-based interior designer Jay Spectre and a pair of vintage slipper chairs with leather upholstery. 'I used pieces with clean lines and organic forms, with rustic and natural materials,' said Alexandriuk. 'We wanted to keep the tones in similar hues to the trees and mountains outside.'

Islington Duplex

DESIGNER	PAUL ARCHER DESIGN
COMPLETED	2011
LOCATION	LONDON, UK

A LARGE VICTORIAN PUB in the north London borough of Islington has been transformed into a series of spacious apartments. This duplex, by Paul Archer Design, spans the ground and lower-ground floors and features a generously sized, open-plan living and dining area overlooking the rear garden. A new pavilion was added to the back of the house, containing the kitchen, while the lower level was extended and the gardens were re-landscaped. The aesthetic is minimal but the spaces are highly flexible and lend themselves to a range of permutations and functions.

Originally the project was commissioned to provide a bachelor apartment for Paul Archer's client: a businessman who was based in Asia for much of the year but who also wanted a *pied à terre* in London. However, as the design moved on, the client found himself with a partner and then children, so the duplex needed to be suitable for a family home. Although the requirements and specifications changed, the overall design approach remained the same. 'The client was clear straight away that the big open space on the ground floor should remain open, so the trick was to know whether or not to put the kitchen into that space and how to get more daylight down to the lower floor,' said Archer. 'Because it worked so well as an open-plan living space we decided to put the kitchen in the new glass extension.'

The architect effectively rebuilt the back of the building, banishing low ceilings and wasted space, and dramatically increased the total floor area of the apartment. The process involved excavating a section of the garden and extending the living space on the lower-ground floor, where two of the three bedrooms are situated. A tiered garden of planted ziggurats allows light to permeate down to this floor, where large expanses of glass offer a strong inside–outside relationship.

The new kitchen pavilion sits at right angles to the main body of the apartment, pushing out over the garden, and it is linked to the open-plan living zone on the ground floor. The bridge-like addition floats over the sunken garden below, while the sheer glass walls establish a close connection with the outdoors. 'The garden is really another room in the house,' said Archer. 'The place really only came alive when the garden was done, as it allows the apartment to breathe.'

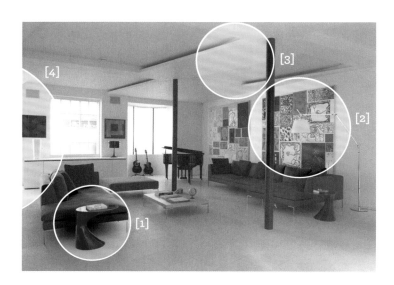

DESIGN INGREDIENTS

· Abstract art

· Dramatic accents of colour

· Linear qualities

· Pavilion kitchen

· Restrained palette

[1] ACCENT COLOURS Within minimalist interiors characterized by restraint, neutral tones and a carefully edited palette of refined materials, splashes of colour stand out in dramatic fashion. Bursts of red from the pair of Tod side tables from Zanotta contrast with the dark tones of the sofas from B&B Italia, designed by Antonio Citterio.

[2] BOLD ART In addition to the expanses of crisp wall space and limestone flooring, the quality of light from front and back makes the open-plan living and dining room a perfect setting for large-scale artworks. Two abstract paintings by British artist Bernard Cohen dominate one wall, complemented by smaller pieces elsewhere in the room that draw the eye.

[3] IRREGULAR CEILING The irregular pattern of the ceiling and the diagonal aperture in the wall break up the extent of the white and introduce a sense of movement and abstract dynamism. The ceiling design also softens the linear quality of the room. Niches for concealed lighting are provided by the recessed slots within the design.

GARDEN PAVILION

The kitchen is housed within a floating glass pavilion that projects out into the garden, forming a bridge over its sunken, tiered profile. This minimalist rectangle of light and space is distinct from the open-plan sitting and dining room, and has a sliding pocket door that can be used to separate the two spaces. A galley-style arrangement to one side is complemented by an island. There is floor-to-ceiling glass on three sides, which offers great transparency and an intimate sense of connection with the garden.

[4] LIBRARY WALL To one side of the living room, the dining area is framed by a custom-built wall of shelves, holding the owners' library of books and providing display slots for a collection of ceramics and household treasures. The irregular grid pattern of the shelves prevents them from becoming too formal. Made by British furniture designer Adrian Swinstead, the dining table doubles as a work station, so the shelving is also used to accommodate paperwork and reference tools. The hand-woven leather Klasen dining chairs are by Italian firm Minotti.

Wight House

DESIGNER	FLETCHER CRANE ARCHITECTS
COMPLETED	2012
LOCATION	RYDE, ISLE OF WIGHT, UK

PROPERTY DEVELOPER MALCOLM BECKETT and his wife, Nisha, first fell in love with the town of Ryde when they took a holiday on the Isle of Wight with their children. Over a number of visits, they developed such an affection for the island that eventually they decided to abandon London living to make their home in Ryde. After they found a sea view site on which to build a new family house, their desire to start afresh found clear expression with the help of <u>Fletcher Crane Architects</u>.

The site for the new house sits in a conservation area, with a listed building next door, and it originally held an undistinguished 1930s home that Beckett and his wife, a journalist, planned to knock down and replace. In order to solicit ideas and to settle on an architect, the couple decided to launch and fund their own design competition. Eventually they opted for Fletcher Crane Architects. The family house the firm created fits into the existing streetscape gently and discreetly, softened by the original stone walls that border the site and the backdrop of mature trees.

The family decided to place the bedrooms on the ground floor, with easy access to the gardens, and to position the main living spaces on the first floor to make the most of the light and the edited views out across Ryde and to the Solent. Here, a large contemporary fireplace, open to both sides, forms a striking centrepiece. At the top of the house there is a generously sized study and roof terrace.

In the main living area there are two separate spaces. 'We decided that we wanted to be able to close off the kitchen and didn't want it to be fully open plan to the living room,' said Beckett. 'We cook Indian food sometimes and it can be pungent, but secondly, if we are having friends for dinner, then I don't like preparing food and washing up in front of them – I like the meal to appear as if by magic. But there is still a very good flow to the layout and we love the fact that you can really open the house in summer and have this connection to the leaves and greenery of the garden.'

The house is lent warmth and character by the use of exterior latticed brick screens, which are reminiscent of traditional Indian screens. The triple-height stairwell brings natural light deep into the house and a side wall of milky glass with a skylight above makes silhouettes of the swaying forms of the trees outside.

DESIGN INGREDIENTS

· Continuous connection
  with the outdoors

· Crisp whites

· Lattice screens

· Narrative and flow

· Play of light

[1] LIVING ARRANGEMENT

The layout of the two main levels of the house inverts the traditional Western floor plan by placing the sequence of main living spaces on the upper storey. Here, the flow of gallery-like spaces makes perfect sense, because only the upper section of the house connects with the sea views. A balcony wraps around the main living areas upstairs, while floor-to-ceiling glass windows slide back to offer a more direct sense of connection with both the garden and the sea view. Accents of colour add warmth and character.

[2] DEDICATED KITCHEN

Separate from the combined sitting room and dining area alongside, this dedicated zone has space enough for an informal dining table and a long kitchen island, with sculptural bar stools from Essex-based company Alexander & Pearl. The distinctive marble counter top for the island stands out against the crisp whites of the other units, which appear to recede into the walls in places. Great thought was given to the circulation routes around the kitchen, with fluid and easy access to the main living spaces from either end.

LIGHTBOX HALLWAY

The entrance hall and stairway are bordered by a side wall of Linit glass. This translucent, dynamic material introduces a rich quality of natural light but also offers privacy for the main circulation route in the house. Throughout the day, light shifts and alters in this space, offering a sense of movement and interest in what could otherwise have been a more mundane area. The result is an engaging compromise between enclosure and transparency.

[3] **BRICK SCREEN** The tower of brick serves many functions and becomes a characterful element of the building, echoed in the low garden wall. It separates the processional entrance zone from the rest of the house, and the lattice design offers privacy for the spaces on this side of the building. This is particularly important on the roof terrace, which overlooks a public footpath. The pattern of the latticed brickwork recalls Indian *jali* screens or Arabic *mashrabiya* panels, both of which were ornamental features designed to create privacy while allowing light to filter through.

[4] **FIREPLACE DIVIDER**
The main living space is open plan and benefits from balconies running the length of the building on two sides. The lounge and more formal dining zone are lightly divided by a double-sided fireplace in the form of a punctured monolith at the centre of the room. This unusual fire surround is a distinctive feature and echoes the white box-like form of the living space as a whole. The sofas and the coffee table are arranged around the fireplace, forming a comfortable enclosure that is reinforced by the colourful patterned rug.

Jigsaw House

DESIGNER	DAVID JAMESON ARCHITECT
COMPLETED	2009
LOCATION	BETHESDA, MARYLAND, USA

THE JIGSAW HOUSE is in constant motion. Architect <u>David Jameson</u>'s family home changes throughout the day and over the seasons as the light travels around this building of many windows and varied volumes. Arranged around a central courtyard, Jameson's residence in Bethesda, Maryland, has a dynamic quality that comes from its mix of different apertures and spaces, like a three-dimensional jigsaw puzzle.

'Light can be an architectural material in itself,' said Jameson, who shares the house with his wife, Nancy, and their two children. 'It is an active, organic space that is totally different at different times of day and you can feel the changing weather even when you are inside. With this house, it was partly about carving away at the interior and creating this outdoor room at the heart of it – the courtyard – and having a feeling almost of implosion rather than focusing the house outward to the street beyond.'

The building sits on a suburban corner site with a front garden exposed to the nearby cross streets. Jameson's solution to this lack of privacy was the courtyard formation, which not only brings light into all of the main living spaces but also creates an integrated outdoor room that is secure for the children. 'It is a very busy street corner, so we didn't want to have windows looking out to the road and see cars passing by,' said Jameson. 'We wanted to have openings that re-orientate you to the sky and the landscape and the courtyard itself.'

Initially, the Jigsaw House was commissioned by a client back in 2005 and it was designed to replace an existing 1950s ranch house with a 1970s addition. Although the previous structure was levelled, Jameson worked within the original footprint to create a new and very different style of house. When the client decided to move on, some years later, Jameson opted to buy the property for himself. He moved in with his family and immediately added a number of new elements, including a swimming pool and pool house. He also completed the basement and converted a motorcycle garage into a studio. Furthermore, Jameson added new features in the garden, including a sculptural front gate, and custom designed cabinetwork for the main seating area, which is open to the dining room and kitchen. With its irregular floor plan, the Jigsaw House remains one of the architect's most dynamic projects.

· Asymmetry

· Complementary textures
  and timbers

· Continuity and flow

· Large-scale artworks

· Vintage character

[1] CHARACTER JOINERY The open-plan living space is minimal in character but warmed by the use of organic materials, as well as by its connections to the planted courtyard. Storage cupboards and the long kitchen island are custom designs by David Jameson made of teak, which is rich in natural warmth and patina.

[2] APERTURES AND WINDOWS As the name suggests, the Jigsaw House is an arrangement of irregular contrasting spaces with varying heights and volumes. It features windows and openings of different sizes, including the sequence of glazing looking into the courtyard. Lantern skylights and slot windows offer a range of light sources that enhance the overall illumination of the interiors.

[3] VINTAGE MODERN

The house features many custom-built elements and contemporary touches, as well as a number of vintage finds. The dining chairs are 1940s Hans J. Wegner designs, bought at auction, while the dining table is a mid-century piece by Florence Knoll. The many vintage touches act as a foil to the crisp purity of the architecture and add character and provenance. Items of furniture such as the Wegner dining chairs, with their woven rattan seats, also introduce texture and complement the crafted timber used for the kitchen.

[4] BIG ART

The crisp white walls and numerous skylights lend certain parts of the house a gallery-like quality. Jameson has taken the opportunity to introduce several dramatic pieces of art, such as a Richard Serra work in the sitting room and this large-scale piece by Steven Cushner in the playroom upstairs; the moulded pink chairs are mini versions of Arne Jacobsen's classic Series 7™ design from 1955.

COURTYARD LIVING

The integrated courtyard serves many purposes within the design of the house. It offers a sheltered outdoor room at the heart of the plan, complete with an integrated fireplace. A fresh air sitting room with connections to nature and the skyscape, it also serves as a light well, filtering natural light into the interior spaces that surround it. Lastly, the courtyard creates a buffer zone that softens the impact of the noise from the nearby access road.

Global

Italian Palazzo

DESIGNERS	SABRINA BIGNAMI/B-ARCH
COMPLETED	2007
LOCATION	PRATO, TUSCANY, ITALY

Casa Orlandi sits at the heart of the Tuscan city of Prato, close to the cathedral. For many years the palazzo – built in the late 18th century by a wealthy family of textile merchants – lay neglected and largely forgotten. Architect Sabrina Bignami of B-Arch was taken by the atmosphere, proportions and character of the building and began a sensitive renovation, during which she found a series of striking frescoes under layers of whitewash. During the project, Bignami preserved the essential character of the interiors but introduced contemporary furniture and installations that stand alone within the space, forming a vibrant contrast between old and new.

The palazzo needed a great deal of work. Bignami focused her attentions upon the *piano nobile*, which held some of the largest salons in the building, arranged around a central courtyard. 'The atmosphere really impressed me but the whole building was in a state of degradation,' she said. The frescoes presented the biggest challenge because they had to be uncovered and then painstakingly restored. They were produced between 1790 and 1815 by Luigi Catani, a Tuscan painter who worked for the grand duke of Tuscany at the Palazzo Pitti in Florence and also decorated several villas near Florence. The richly patterned tiled floors were renovated, too, adding to the drama of the spaces. This combination of frescoes and tilework provides a vivid backdrop for the simple furnishings.

Bignami exercised particular restraint with all of her new additions. The kitchen – for example – is composed of 'floating' counters and a big kitchen table, both of which feel as though they are visitors in a noble space, rich in provenance. The same is true of the sitting room, where contemporary seating, lighting and bookcases sit within the grand proportions of the room, coated with Catani's frescoes. Although Bignami's preference is for contemporary designs, they sit in an environment shaped by history.

DESIGN INGREDIENTS

· Architectural features
· Contrast between old and new
· Historic frescoes
· Sense of grandeur
· Simple symmetry

[1] INSERTED ELEMENTS Continuing with the design philosophy of adopting a light and sensitive touch to all the new additions, Bignami has designed a series of custom storage elements that are inserted into the spaces without interrupting the frescoes. These include the open-fronted wardrobes in the master bedroom – alongside the sitting room – the clean, contemporary geometry of which contrasts with the ornate original detailing.

[2] WHITE SEATING Given the rich terracotta colour of the tiled floors and the vibrant tones and imagery of the frescoes, Bignami selected furnishings that are light and inviting, with clean and simple lines. The white chairs are Piero Lissoni designs for Italian firm Living Divani and they can be separated or combined to form sofas. 'I liked the symmetry and simplicity of the space,' said Bignami. 'So I wanted to use as little furniture as possible and keep it central in the room.'

[3] LIGHT TOUCHES Inserting modern services such as heating, lighting and up-to-date wiring into the historic building without disturbing the restored frescoes was a challenge. The central heating is provided by old-fashioned cast iron radiators, found at a flea market, and the electric cabling is left visible, running around the cornice line at high level to avoid inserting the wiring into the walls. Vintage Guzzini standing lamps from the 1970s are used to illuminate the space, rather than fitted lighting that would have damaged the walls.

[4] ITALIAN GRANDEUR Bignami's three-bedroom residence sits within the *piano nobile* at the mid-level of the building. Traditionally, in Italian neoclassical architecture, the main living spaces would inhabit the *piano nobile* and therefore enjoy the best of the views and the light. The proportions of these spaces were usually among the grandest in the house, as can be seen here at Casa Orlandi. The dramatic and colourful frescoes also speak of the grand provenance of this part of the building.

THEATRICAL ELEMENTS

The master bedroom is a theatrical retreat, where the wall paintings, combined with the grand height and scale of the space, create a kind of stage for contemporary living. A four-poster bed sourced from Cyrus Company in Italy occupies an alcove to one side of the room, while tailor-made wardrobes provide storage. A vintage tailor's dummy offers a neat setting for storing Bignami's jewelry, while there is also space enough for a reading table and chairs.

Rio Retreat

DESIGNER	GISELE TARANTO ARQUITETURA
COMPLETED	2012
LOCATION	RIO DE JANEIRO, BRAZIL

SITUATED WITHIN AN EXCLUSIVE part of Rio de Janeiro, Casa Tempo feels a world away from everything, despite its urban location. With inviting terraces, verandas and lush green gardens – originally laid out by Brazilian landscape architect Roberto Burle Marx – the house has a calming, restful character. The architecture and interiors are by Gisele Taranto, whose designs are a radical reinvention of the previous house that stood on the site.

Taranto's clients gave her only eighteen months to complete the project from start to finish, including the restructuring of the colonial-style building, which was not only claustrophobic and insular but also disconnected from the garden and setting. The new layout provides a grand entrance, with a high front door in grapia timber that leads into a double-height entrance hallway and gallery space. There is plenty of scope here for the owners' extensive art collection, which includes pieces by Anish Kapoor and Robert Rauschenberg. 'The clients are art collectors so they needed as much wall space as possible to exhibit the collection,' said Taranto. 'But on the other hand we wanted to open the house up to the garden, so that was the challenge – to do both at the same time.'

The hallway flows into the main sitting room: an inviting space, full of light, with walls of glass to two sides that slide back to provide a direct connection with the terraces and gardens. More sliding panels and doors within the dining area alongside create a high degree of flexibility about how the space is used, allowing it to be included as part of the open-plan living space or to be lightly separated and differentiated.

Flexibility and adaptability are major characteristics of the house throughout, with many moveable partitions, shifting proportions and alternative functions. The studio at the top of the house, which provides access to the roof terrace with views out across the city, can be used as another family lounge, a home office or a guest room.

Arranged around a towering mango tree, the garden was restored and updated by contemporary landscape designer Gilberto Elkis. A swimming pool was added, too. The new two-storey annex at the back of the garden houses bedrooms for staff, as well as a screening room on the ground floor and a gym and spa on the upper level.

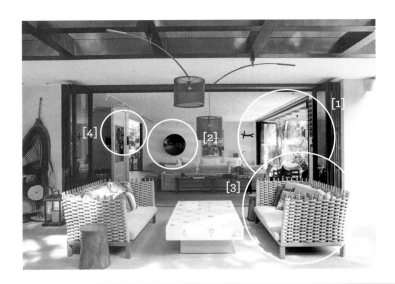

DESIGN INGREDIENTS

· Art display

· Context

· Flexibility

· Fluid connection with the garden
  and terraces

· Private spaces

[1] FLUID SPACES The glass walls to the sitting room retract in gatefold fashion to open up the space to the two adjoining terraces. The division between inside and outside dissolves, with the same floor level and stone tiling uniting the two realms. In this way, the sense of proportion and volume appears to extend outwards, offering a choice of fresh air seating areas that complement the comfortable indoor sofas.

GREEN ROOM

Although the house is surrounded by terraces and verandas, the elevated garden room at the rear of the site is a particularly appealing area. This relaxing space is enclosed by verdant planting set into the surrounding walls and balustrades that border the stairs up to the outdoor room. The landscape design is by Gilberto Elkis, while the Astúrias armchairs, made from recycled timber, are by another Brazilian designer, Carlos Motta.

[2] **INTEGRATED ARTWORK** The house features important artworks and installations by renowned artists, which are woven into the interiors. These include the stainless steel and lacquer disc by Anish Kapoor, which introduces a vibrant injection of colour and forms a distinctive, reflective presence in the space, illuminated by track lighting. There are also minimalist artworks by Sol LeWitt and Fred Sandback installed in the entrance hall; other featured artists include sculptor José Resende and Italian artist and photographer Vanessa Beecroft.

[3] **BRAZILIAN FURNITURE** In addition to pieces by European designers such as Paola Lenti, the interiors feature designs by well-known Brazilian furniture makers. They include several items by contemporary designer Etel Carmona, based in São Paulo, as well as two armchairs by mid-century designer Jorge Zalszupin, who also created furniture for a number of Oscar Niemeyer's buildings in Brasília.

[4] **FLEXIBLE DINING** The relationship between the sitting room and the dining area alongside is very flexible because the sliding door can be drawn across to create greater privacy and intimacy during meal times. The dining table and chairs are by Etel Carmona and the aluminium and plaster pendant Skygarden lights over the table are by Marcel Wanders for Flos.

Thai Tower

DESIGNER	DAVID COLLINS STUDIO
COMPLETED	2012
LOCATION	BANGKOK, THAILAND

THIS PEACEFUL BANGKOK APARTMENT is a calm sanctuary at the heart of Thailand's most dynamic city. The interiors draw inspiration from the colours and textures of Thailand itself, particularly its silks, fabrics and ceramics. However, the treatment is distinctly contemporary and luxurious, with an emphasis on custom designs and finishes, including some seventy-five original furniture and lighting designs by David Collins Studio. This fresh approach creates a highly tailored and individual environment, floating above the urban drama of Bangkok.

Designed by German architect Ole Scheeren, the MahaNakhon tower development contains a five-star hotel and serviced apartments. David Collins was asked to give character and identity to these residences within a model apartment, splicing the sophistication of luxury Manhattan apartment buildings with the unique flavours of Thailand. 'I love Thailand,' said Collins. 'It's a really beautiful country and I love the feeling of serenity and calmness. Thailand is very much about the glazes on the ceramics and the reflective quality of the silks. These are the kind of things that I find inspiring.'

The apartment is arranged around a generously scaled and serene living room, which has been divided into individual zones for relaxation and entertaining. A dining area sits to one side, sheltered within a recessed gallery defined by panelled walls coated in an embroidered silk. A gentle palette of soft blues and greens for upholstery, rugs and artworks stands out against a backdrop of parquet flooring and crisp white walls. 'I felt it was important that the design should be quite subtle and low key,' said Collins. 'It is a very peaceful space, which is what you want a home to be really. Some of the glazes on the walls are subtle reflections of Thai influences and there are allusions in the fabrics and rugs and the whimsical tie-dye curtains in the living room. But we didn't want the Thai influence to be too obvious, more subliminal.'

From velvet sofas to satin chairs and coffee tables coated in shagreen, the original pieces drawn up by David Collins Studio add a rich variety of textures and reinforce the individual character of the apartment. The master suite has been designed as a miniature apartment in itself, with a bedroom large enough for a comfortable seating area and a very indulgent bathroom.

DESIGN INGREDIENTS

- Comfort and grandeur
- Layers of luxury and sophistication
- Statement colour
- Tailored designs
- Variety of textures

[1] REFINED MATERIALS

The apartment contains an array of crafted, custom-designed furniture and features. David Collins Studio has drawn upon a sophisticated palette of materials and luxurious finishes throughout, which layer the residence with complementary textures and introduce a sumptuous level of comfort. The master suite features bedside tables and a console in shagreen, pleated silk curtains and suede and silk velvet upholstery. The four-poster bed posts are coated in leather and the silk bedspread has custom embroidery.

[2] BEDROOM LOUNGE

The bedroom suite provides a choice of relaxation areas. These include a lounge and reading corner, defined by a custom chaise longue with a sculptural profile. David Collins Studio custom made the console, which serves as a discreet media unit, with shagreen drawers and brass detailing. The artwork above it is a local piece, sourced in Bangkok, while the oval coffee table is another tailored design with a marble top and a bronze base. The suite also features a dedicated dressing room and a generously scaled bathroom.

[3] BED DESIGN The notion of a four-poster bed speaks of luxury and indulgence. Custom designs such as this, with lacquered joinery and leather and brass detailing, are distinctly contemporary yet carry romantic, heritage connotations of traditional four-poster beds that were bordered with curtains for warmth and privacy, thereby creating a room within a room. Although this example does not have curtains, it retains the feel of a protective enclosure.

[4] SPA BATHROOM The master bathroom is a statement space, lifted by its generous proportions and the influx of natural light from the floor-to-ceiling windows. The oval Agape Ufo bath – designed by Italian firm Benedini Associati and made of stainless steel with a white enamel interior and a backrest – floats within the centre of the room. The bath is bordered by a custom-made bench by David Collins Studio, while a sea of Arabescato marble unites the floors, walls and vanity unit. The proportions of the room and the quality of the materials are reminiscent of a fine hotel spa.

CRAFTED DINING

The formal dining area sits within a recessed alcove to one side of the main living room. Although for much of the time it reads as an extension of the sitting room, sliding doors can be closed to separate the two spaces. Despite this flexible arrangement, the dining area has a clear identity of its own, and the midnight blue colour scheme, expressed in the custom rug and the wall panels lined with embroidered navy silk, helps to define the space. The dining chairs and the sycamore-topped dining table are designs by David Collins Studio.

Mornington Retreat

DESIGNER	SALLY DRAPER ARCHITECTS
COMPLETED	2010
LOCATION	WESTERN PORT BAY, AUSTRALIA

SITUATED ON THE COAST of Western Port Bay, this vacation home for a Melbourne-based family seeks a constant sense of connection with its surroundings. The house may turn its back on the nearby access road – presenting a wall of blackbutt timber – but to the north the building opens up in dramatic fashion with a series of terraces, decks and picture windows that draw in the landscape. The living room, in particular, maximizes this indoor–outdoor relationship while offering a space that is rich in texture and scale.

The family bought the land on an unused 'farmlet' on a clifftop on the Mornington Peninsula some years ago. With pathway access through a natural reserve down to the beach, the setting is rich in native trees, shrubs and wildlife, including kookaburras, koalas and black-faced wallabies. Architect Sally Draper was commissioned to design the house for use all year round at weekends and vacation time. 'The house acts as a retreat for the family,' said Draper. 'The idea was to create a richly textured space, simple but never minimal. The weather is quite often cold and wet in the region, particularly in the winter, so it needed to be warm and encompassing, while still opening up extensively to the site.'

The two-storey house is divided into three distinct zones, within a rectangular outline and with shifting levels. Glass links holding the main entrance area and a home spa help to separate the different portions of the building. A wing at one end contains three bedrooms and a children's lounge, while the mid section is dominated by the master suite, leading out to a substantial outdoor dining room. The main living space, combining sitting and dining areas plus an open-plan kitchen, is at the far end of the building. Here, the connections to the trees and greenery that surround the house are made vivid. A large picture window looks onto a striking view of the bushland at one end of the room, while a bank of floor-to-ceiling windows retracts to open onto an elevated terrace.

A stone fireplace wall contrasts with the floors, which are in dark wandoo timber – reclaimed from former wool sheds – and the ceilings, in a mountain ash sourced in the region. The extensive use of such organic materials helps tie the house to nature, although the outline of the building remains distinctly linear and contemporary.

DESIGN INGREDIENTS

· Accents of red

· Discovery

· Framing the views

· Inside–outside relationship

· Organic materials

[1] WINDOW SEAT The window seat projects outwards at one end of the living room, with a large picture window framed in wandoo timber. From this elevated position, the feeling is almost one of being in a tree house, with the branches of the trees close by. 'It provides a way of sitting within the view,' said Draper, 'and of being part of the exterior while still being inside, as well as part of the living space but somewhat removed. It's a space between inside and out.'

[2] HOT HINTS The family requested hints of 'happy red' throughout the house. In the open-plan living space, these touches include the red mid-century Plank armchairs by Hans J. Wegner and the loose cushions on the sofa. Solid oak red Toto stools from Melbourne-based Pierre + Charlotte and red accessories on the shelves brighten the kitchen. The antique rug sourced from Loom Rugs also carries touches of red and orange. The interiors were designed in collaboration with Jane Charlwood.

[3] ELEVATED TERRACE The living room and its adjoining terrace have an elevated position, with garaging and storage spaces tucked immediately below. This provides for a striking vantage point looking north across the gardens, while a modest canopy provides a degree of shade from the high summer sun for both the raised terrace and the interiors. This area is but one of a number of integrated outdoor rooms, including a roof deck alongside the master suite.

[4] FEATURE FIREPLACE In addition to the timber floors and ceilings, the house features the occasional use of stone, both outside and in. Here, in the living room, a wall of stone surrounds the fireplace. 'The fireplace anchors the living space and provides a strong symbol of a hearth as well as a warm, textured backdrop,' said Draper. 'The stone is a mixture of Mount Angus and Pyrenees sandstone, the former from eastern Victoria and the latter from the west.'

OUTDOOR DINING

Another wall of stone shelters the outdoor dining room that projects outwards from the mid point of the house. In addition to the integrated barbecue, this fresh air dining zone features a long, sociable table and benches, again with a vibrant hint of red provided by the cushions. The roof deck above offers a sun canopy, while still preserving the notion of an outdoor room. The provision of a number of outdoor spaces with varying degrees of shade and shelter gives different options throughout the day and seasons.

Mexican Palapa

DESIGNER	ALEX PÖSSENBACHER
COMPLETED	1994
LOCATION	CAREYES, JALISCO, MEXICO

ABOUT TWO AND A HALF HOURS' drive south of Puerto Vallarta, set within surroundings of particular natural beauty, the resort of Careyes feels set apart from the world beyond. Here, architect <u>Alex Pössenbacher</u> designed a family home that re-interprets the vernacular idea of a *palapa* for contemporary living. Largely contained under a striking roof of palm leaf thatch, the house blurs the boundary between inside and outside spaces while opening itself up to enticing views of the ocean.

Traditional *palapas* originated in Central America and tropical Pacific countries, where the thatched roofs cover open-sided huts and houses, mostly made with timber frames. This way of building in warm climates has been around for thousands of years and has now captured the attention of contemporary architects, such as Pössenbacher. 'It gives you this terrace with a hat and a very informal way of living,' said Pössenbacher, who studied architecture and design in Paris and Mexico City before designing a number of houses in Careyes. 'It's an easy way to make a light, large-scale structure.'

At Casa Cayman, the open arrangement allows all of the living spaces to enjoy an ocean view, while cooling breezes and natural cross ventilation keep the house temperate. The building was commissioned by Pössenbacher's father, Michael, an antiques dealer who collaborated closely with his son on the design of the house. Casa Cayman features a number of striking antique elements woven into the fabric of the house, including 8th-century columns that stand by the pool. Although the main living areas below the soaring *palapa* are open-sided, more intimate areas such as the bedrooms are contained in a wing to one side and service spaces are tucked away to the rear. This allows the focus to remain upon the *palapa* and the ocean. 'The garden in Careyes is the ocean,' said Michael Pössenbacher. 'Instead of a park, you have the sea.'

DESIGN INGREDIENTS

· Natural materials

· Open-air living

· Theatre

· Vernacular

· Warm, earthy colours

[1] THATCH ROOF *Palapa* roofs generally use palm leaf thatch around a timber frame; the thatch keeps off the rain and provides shade, but also allows the wind to vent through. Around 56,000 palm leaves were used to make the *palapa* at Casa Cayman. 'It's also very airy,' said Alex Pössenbacher. 'The layers of leaves work like vents allowing the wind to escape through each layer, so it's very flexible in coastal settings like this.' The roof shelters the key living areas and allows a direct connection between indoor and outdoor living because the side walls are left open.

[2] MEXICAN COLOUR

The house features rich, warm colours – such as burnt ochre and rusty reds – that are intimately associated with Mexico. They are seen in many traditional houses and *haciendas*, but they have also been widely used by modernist and contemporary Mexican architects, such as Luis Barragán and Ricardo Legorreta, who favoured soft pinks and other organic tones that speak of the colours of the earth and nature. On the terrace by the pool is a vivid red sculpture by Mexican artist Sebastián, which echoes the colours employed for the interiors.

[3] WICKER SEATING

The organic theme continues with some of the furniture, particularly the rattan seating. The texture of the rattan echoes the thatch of the palm *palapa,* while the rounded shape complements the sculptural *bombas del volcan* – cannon ball stones ejected by volcanoes – that are arranged around the terrace. At the same time, these chairs have an enveloping, ergonomic quality that makes for comfortable seating, with rattan proving a popular choice for outdoor furniture that needs to withstand the elements.

[4] ORGANIC ELEMENTS
In addition to the palm thatch, the house features many other organic and natural elements that tie the house to the land and the setting. These include the timber columns that support the roof, wrapped in curling vine wood, and the stone and mosaic floors. The vast stag fern suspended from the ceiling of the *palapa* forms a living chandelier over the sitting room and breaks up the earthy colours.

INFINITY POOL

The infinity pool, designed by Alex Pössenbacher, adds another natural element to the house and the terraces. From the elevated site of Casa Cayman, overlooking the ocean below, the waters of the pool appear to blend with the vivid blue waves of the Pacific Ocean. The swimming pool also acts as a mirror on calm days, reflecting the sky, while the evaporative effect helps cool the terraces.

East West

DESIGNER	ZEYNEP FADILLIOĞLU
COMPLETED	1987
LOCATION	ISTANBUL, TURKEY

INTERNAL DESIGNER <u>ZEYNEP FADILLIOĞLU</u>
lives in the desirable Büyükdere district of Istanbul
in a late 18th-century house, which was once the
summer residence of a clockmaker to the sultan.
The clockmaker lived on the upper storey, while
his carriages and horses inhabited the ground
floor. Zeynep and her husband – restaurateur
Metin Fadillioğlu – were able to buy a crumbling
orangery next door, too, and set about combining
the two buildings into one enticing and thoughtful
house. Their striking sitting room, layered with
ceramics and textiles, best sums up Zeynep's
considered East meets West approach to design.

'After the work was finished I moved into the
house with a lifetime of art, objects and collections
and some antiques from my grandfather,' said
Zeynep. 'For me the most important qualities in a
space are soul, taste and the rhythm between colours
and objects, as well as the lighting that contributes
to a sense of harmony in colour and texture. I like
the feeling of living in a house with traces of lives
left behind.'

Zeynep has created a rich choice of living areas
within the house in a breadth of colours, using a
crisp celadon for the walls in the dining room and
intense ochre for one of the salons. Central and
circulation sections of the house are painted a rustic,
earthy cream, with patina and character upon every
surface. Accent colours, such as startling red for the
upholstery of a pair of armchairs and other bright
shades for various textiles and rugs, stand out
against this carefully conceived backdrop. Textiles
are an important part of Zeynep's design philosophy,
adding drama and theatre but without overwhelming
a layered space. 'There is a different feeling to each
space and I use each one according to my moods,'
she said. 'But I do love colour and texture – I could
never be a minimalist.'

The welcoming sitting room sits within the
rebuilt portion of the house that once formed part
of the orangery, with a sequence of double doors
leading out onto the terrace. The textured, cloudy
blue walls were inspired by a colour that Zeynep
found in the original orangery and replicated in the
completed room. The space is full of treasures and
stories, arranged around a stone fireplace. With
the collections of ceramics and a blend of vintage
treasures and contemporary touches, it is a vibrant
fusion of sympathetic elements.

DESIGN INGREDIENTS

· Collections and displays
· Discovery
· Layering and contrasts
· Rich textiles
· Romantic atmosphere

[1] FIREPLACE COMPOSITION

The fireplace forms a focal point for the room, while the pieces arranged around it speak of Zeynep's passion for collecting and her original approach to design. The fire surround is a salvaged piece from an Anatolian village, while the ornate clock is a French design from the 18th century. Above the mantelpiece, the abstract painting is by contemporary Turkish artist Tayfun Erdoğmuş, who likes to use ash, coal dust and sand in his work. It is a fusion style of old meets new and nature meets science, as well as East meets West.

[2] CERAMIC COLLECTIONS

Zeynep has been collecting ceramics for almost forty years and the fruits of her treasure hunts cover almost every surface. Her finds are complemented by celadon and blue and white pieces inherited from her grandfather. The textured coffee table is largely devoted to her collection, framing the ceramics rather like an open display cabinet but in a more casual style than that of a museum or gallery. Ornate architectural salvage and stonework also sit well with the organic, sculptural quality of the ceramics.

[3] COLOURFUL TEXTILES Much of the strong colour in the room comes courtesy of the richly patterned carpets and kilims, as well as the sumptuous fabrics used to upholster the sofas and for the cushions. These vivid reds and crimsons stand out against the more subtle backdrop of the burnished pale blue on the walls. For Zeynep, colourful textiles are a key part of a layered interior space, and she has used kilims in place of artworks on the wall, helping to soften the space and add texture as well as vibrant tones.

[4] MIRRORED MOMENTS Mirrors are used in several places around the room, reflecting light and creating a sense of movement throughout the space. Tall twin mirrors are positioned either side of the fireplace in a symmetrical arrangement, while a third larger mirror sits on the wall behind one of the sofas, reflecting both sunlight and greenery from the terrace and gardens opposite. This simple act of reflection, combined with the crafted quality of the mirror frames, brings a romantic and dynamic touch to the interiors.

FUSION BEDROOM

This evocative and engaging bedroom blends many elements in one sophisticated union. The walls have texture and patina, but also subtle geometrical patterns and calligraphic influences expressed in contemporary forms. The headboard and bedspread introduce stronger accents of pattern and colour, while the slipper chair has a French influence and introduces another note all together. The result is fresh and engaging, with the ochre walls providing a subtle backdrop against which the colours of the bedding and upholstery stand out.

Marrakech Modern

DESIGNER	ANKE VAN DER PLUIJM
COMPLETED	2012
LOCATION	MARRAKECH, MOROCCO

MARRAKECH IS A CITY of winding streets, high walls and secret gardens, where the traditional houses – or riads – are hidden away and inward looking. Dutch entrepreneur, designer and hotelier Anke van der Pluijm knows this way of living well, having opened a riad guest house in the medina fourteen years ago. However, having a private and personal retreat of her own is a more recent luxury. Her modest but perfectly formed home is a soothing sanctuary set apart from the constant hustle and bustle of Marrakech's old town.

Van der Pluijm first fell in love with Morocco twenty-five years ago. She has divided her time between Amsterdam and Marrakech ever since, sourcing and manufacturing tiles, textiles and home accessories for her company Household Hardware and also running a guest house, Chambres d'Amis. She has long-standing experience of collaborating with Moroccan craftsmen and artisans and this came in useful when she began working on her own home, which was little more than a ruin at the start.

She arranged the two-storey house, topped by a roof terrace, around a new courtyard planted with bamboo and a towering rubber tree. The ground floor features a sitting room and kitchen open to the courtyard. This space is brought to life by a wall of soothing green and blue tiles. 'We wanted the courtyard and salon to be one space, which is not something that you normally see in traditional Moroccan houses,' said van der Pluijm. 'In the winter I change the couch and some of the furniture around and close the curtains and use the fireplace, so it becomes a smaller, cosier salon. But then in the summer we open everything up again.'

A distinctive green colour, which stands out against the plastered walls, is used for the wrought iron balconies of the first floor, as well as window and door frames, while flashes of bright Majorelle blue also feature here and there, picking out a pillar or sections of the exterior bedroom walls.

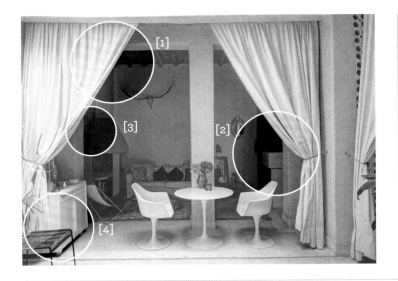

DESIGN INGREDIENTS

· Bursts of pattern and colour

· Courtyard as focal point

· Informality

· Living spaces open
  to the outdoors

· Simple custom-made elements

[1] OPEN LIVING The warm climate of
Marrakech facilitates a more open way of daily
living, with many traditional riads having an internal
courtyard. Here, Anke van der Pluijm dispenses
with solid divisions between the living area and
the courtyard and opts for curtains that offer a
simple wall of fabric to enclose the lounge and the
integrated kitchen during colder evenings. In the
winter, the fireplace gives sufficient heat to warm
the whole room.

[2] SCULPTED KITCHEN At one end of
the open-plan living area is the kitchen: a custom-
made design with a simple beauty and charm
all of its own. The sculpted forms of the counters
seem to grow organically from the tadelakt floors,
while integrated splashback screens hide away the
mess of preparation and cooking. Small areas of
tilework are used to introduce accents of colour
and pattern.

[3] TILED WALL A wall of patterned tiles in pale aqua greens and soft blues brings colour and delight to the lounge. Designed by van der Pluijm and made in Morocco, these tiles are repeated a number of times throughout the house, offering welcome bursts of colour that stand out all the more against the neutral tones of the plaster walls and tadelakt floors. 'In the beginning I knew right away that I wanted a green and blue house and to have a feeling of nature and quiet,' said van der Pluijm. 'The green of the tiles is a very calming colour.'

[4] COURTYARD GARDEN The sheltered private courtyard serves as an outdoor room, extending the available living space of the house. A dining area sits on the border of the inside and the outside spaces, while a miniature garden with tall bamboos forms a wall of greenery. Although the entrance area can be closed off with curtains to enhance the sense of privacy and enclosure, the courtyard remains open to the sky above.

ROOFTOP LIVING

Rooftop rooms such as this have become an essential part of contemporary living in Marrakech, and here the roof terrace has space enough for a seating zone and an outdoor kitchen and dining area. The custom-made awnings provide shade and shelter, while colourful planting transforms the space into an elevated walled garden. Both the kitchen and fitted seating are custom designs by van der Pluijm, while the lanterns and planters were sourced locally in Marrakech.

Bali by Design

DESIGNERS	VALENTINA AUDRITO/ WORD OF MOUTH
COMPLETED	2011
LOCATION	CANGGU, BALI

ITALIAN ARCHITECT <u>VALENTINA AUDRITO</u> settled on the island of Bali nearly twenty years ago, and she shares her home in Canggu with her husband, Abhishake Kumbhat, and their two children. Although Canggu is a quiet enclave, it is not far from the beach town of Seminyak: the bustling epicentre of Bali's southern boutique hotel, spa and fashion scene. With the use of a large garden, swimming pool and generous terraces, the family is able to make the most of outdoor living in this temperate climate. The house itself is an Indonesian 'joglo': a wooden-framed building made up of two pavilions with distinctive sculpted roofs. For the interiors, Audrito embraced the traditional structure of the joglo while introducing a contemporary aesthetic and weaving self-designed pieces into the eclectic mix.

Audrito first fell in love with Bali when she was a child. She grew up living in Italy and Saudi Arabia, but family holidays on the Indonesian island made a big impression on her, and her parents – also architects – set up a satellite office here. Although she studied in Italy and Barcelona and lived in London for a few years, Audrito felt that Bali was always pulling at her heart strings. 'I started my first architectural project in Bali before I had even finished my studies and after a few years I wanted to stay,' she said. 'I set up my own office and I met Abhi in Bali as well. Now our studio is right next door to the house so we spend a lot of time at home. There are days when I don't step out of the house.'

Set in lush green gardens with rice paddy fields just beyond the boundary line, the house is a vernacular timber-framed building, approximately one hundred years old. However, Audrito has updated 'Lalaland' – as the family calls it – in a distinctly contemporary style, creating a striking and individual look that blends custom designs, predominantly furniture from Audrito and Kumbhat's <u>Word of Mouth</u> collection, with art and furniture collected on their travels. One of the pavilions is dedicated to the main sitting room, with the kitchen alongside, and the other pavilion holds the bedrooms, including the generously scaled master bedroom, in which the open timber box at the heart of the space has been turned into a comfortable, intimate lounge area. In each of the pavilions the exposed timber frame creates a natural centre point.

[1]
[2]
[3]
[4]

7

DESIGN INGREDIENTS

- Accents of pattern
- Inside–outside living
- Organic qualities
- Room within a room
- Vernacular

[1] TIMBER FRAME Although there are no solid partition walls in this part of the Balinese pavilion, the timber framework provides a clearly defined setting for the spacious main bedroom, with soaring ceilings and plenty of windows introducing natural light and framing the views. The exposed beams and rustic wooden floors inject organic warmth and character, while the open sense of scale adds drama.

[2] DIAPHANOUS CURTAINS Cascading curtains by Word of Mouth introduce movement, colour and pattern. The curtains are draped over the timber beams of the pergola within the pavilion or sit upon sliding rails elsewhere. They are more decorative than functional, and blinds are used to shroud the windows at night.

[3] INTEGRATED LOUNGE

The structure of the joglo creates a central timber pergola that forms a room within a room. Here, in the master bedroom, the pergola makes the perfect setting for a private lounge, with custom-designed seating by Word of Mouth. The bed sits outside the 'box', with windows to either side of it, which usually remain open. 'It never gets cold here so the house is open all year round,' said Audrito. 'The inside–outside relationship is very characteristic of Bali and nature interacts with the spaces in a very direct way.'

[4] SOFT COMFORT

The master bedroom is a very comfortable and welcoming area, with soft seating and the luxury of space. This makes it a secondary hub for the whole family, complementing the main sitting room. 'The bedroom is a space where we spend a lot of time,' said Audrito. 'The children don't spend quite as much time as we would like in their own bedroom because they prefer ours.'

OUTDOOR BATHING

The master bathroom comprises two sumptuous parts. Inside, there is a spacious area with room enough for a bench opposite the sinks and vanity units. Outside, in an adjoining courtyard, is a custom egg-shaped bathtub. 'The floor tiles are typical, colonial Indonesian tiles from Java,' said Audrito. 'They make them in many different colours and motifs. The bath in the courtyard is one of our designs in fibreglass.'

Hong Kong Belvedere

DESIGNER	YABU PUSHELBERG
COMPLETED	2012
LOCATION	HONG KONG, CHINA

THE OPUS APARTMENT, with interiors designed by <u>Yabu Pushelberg</u>, is a sophisticated and thoughtful response to a landmark new building situated in a unique and prominent hillside position within the verdant woodlands of Hong Kong's Peak District. The twisting glass columns that dominate the outside of the building – the first in Asia designed by Frank Gehry – open up to epic views across the cityscape, while the rear of the Opus gazes over rugged, rising slopes carpeted with lush greenery.

This apartment, designed by George Yabu and Glenn Pushelberg, takes up an entire floor of the building, with the main living spaces to the front making the most of the urban panorama, and three bedrooms plus service spaces such as the kitchen to the rear. Threaded through with many custom elements and pieces of furniture, as well as sumptuous finishes and detailing, the apartment was the perfect project for Yabu and Pushelberg, who have been travelling to Hong Kong for many years and know the city and its culture intimately.

A long sequence of screens was specially designed to create an undulating spine wall, separating the more public sections of the apartment from the private sleeping zone. The screens are both functional and decorative, with an evocative pattern created in collaboration with a small group of artists. The screens serve many uses, hiding storage areas and providing pivoting doors to the entrance foyer and other parts of the home. They also offer a colourful and enticing backdrop to the key living spaces, or 'petals'. 'There is usually a hierarchy of spaces within a home and you find that the living room is larger than the bedroom or kitchen, for instance,' said Yabu. 'But in this floor plan all of those petals are equal.'

The main sitting room is positioned within the central petal at the front of the tower, enriched by the quality of the light and the views. Most of the pieces here are Yabu Pushelberg designs, including the sofas and the circular rug, which help to define the space. To one side of the sitting room is a generous media room that doubles as a study, while to the other there is a dining room, complete with a made-to-order dining table seating twelve. A breakfast area is positioned to one side of the dining space, lightly separated and cradled by a latticed, sculptural divider.

- Concealment
- Petal formation
- Sculptural shapes
- Tactile surfaces
- Touches of opulence

[1] PATTERNED SCREENS Custom-made screens are used throughout the apartment to define the various spaces and to provide separation between the main living zones and other sections of the apartment, including circulation, service and storage areas. However, they also have a powerful decorative role and echo the traditional use of screens in Chinese and Asian homes. Here, a secondary sliding screen of burnished steel can be moved around the breakfast area to create a greater sense of separation from the more formal dining area nearby.

[2] STATEMENT CHANDELIER The main dining zone is dominated by a tailor-made marble table, designed by Yabu Pushelberg, which is surrounded by black lacquered Superleggera dining chairs, designed in 1975 by Giò Ponti and produced in Italy by Cassina. The setting is crowned with a Pastilles chandelier by French designer Hervé van der Straeten, which offers a dramatic and sculptural focal point that lifts the eye upwards. The shimmering golden discs of the chandelier tie in well with the branches of the bronze-finished screens, adding a touch of opulence.

[3] BANQUETTE SEATING

The custom banquette seating suggests a more casual approach to meal times in the breakfast 'room'. The benches recall French cafés and bars, as well as American diners, although expressed here in a highly sophisticated way. The design creates a more sociable and intimate setting, with the semi-circular banquette complemented by matching Cervino dining chairs by Dutch designer Marcel Wolterinck. The vibrant finish and pattern of the painted screens stand out against the more muted tones of the upholstery and the Nota Bene table.

[4] FRAMED SPACES

The fluid floor plan creates a series of interconnected petals. These spaces are partly delineated by the sequence of screens but also by other devices that reinforce the idea of zoning. They include the silk rug and the recessed ceiling dome as well as the arrangement of furniture around the cast-bronze Kailash table. 'The screens that continue throughout the apartment were purposefully designed to accentuate the flow of the building and encourage the eye to follow one serpentine piece of artwork through the entire space,' said Pushelberg.

SHIMMERING RETREAT

The emphasis on characterful, tactile materials and finishes continues in the master bedroom. Here, a dramatic curving wall of shimmering metallic plates forms an anchor for the bed, which looks towards the window. The wall becomes a vast geometric-patterned headboard, complemented by the golden bedside tables. Either side of the bed are pendant lights by glass specialist Caleb Siemon. 'The luxurious, cocoon-like quality of that space was very important,' said Yabu. 'Hong Kong has an insane hustle and bustle and the homeowners need to be able to unplug and recharge in their bedroom.'

Wabi Inspiration

DESIGNER	SEBASTIAN MARISCAL STUDIO
COMPLETED	2008
LOCATION	SAN DIEGO, CALIFORNIA, USA

THE WABI HOUSE, in suburban San Diego, is full of surprises. This individual, tailored building evolved from a collaboration between architect <u>Sebastian Mariscal</u> and his Japanese-born clients. The result is a delightful fusion project, splicing many traditional elements of Japanese architecture and daily living with a crafted and contemporary approach to aesthetics, materials and finishes. A strong and vital relationship between indoor and outdoor living spaces is another key aspect of the Wabi House.

In the beginning, the clients were thinking about remodelling an existing 1970s suburban home but eventually decided on a new project that would deliver a fully tailored and more sustainable two-storey house. The low-slung building has been purposefully tucked into the site not only to enhance privacy but also to create an engaging process of discovery. 'It is a series of surprises,' said Mariscal. 'When you are outside in the street, you have no idea what is behind the line of trees or the charred timber boundary wall. As you enter and pass over the bridge across the water ponds you still have no idea what is ahead when you find the second wooden front door.'

These layers of charred cedar wood walls give the house an enigmatic quality, subverting the suburban context. Over the threshold is a traditional Japanese entrance hall, or *genkan*, where shoes are removed and slippers put on. The entryway leads through to the rear of the house, which opens up in dramatic fashion, with an open-plan living area leading out to a gravel garden via a folding wall of glass. Sliding screens allow a guest bedroom and a study to be read as part of this overall central space or to be separated off and transformed into more private and intimate zones. This creates a welcome degree of flexibility as to how the house is arranged and used on a day-to-day basis. The master bedroom is situated on the upper level, which leads out to a planted roof garden. 'It became clear that the clients wanted to have an introspective home with a peaceful and serene atmosphere,' said Mariscal. 'The gravel garden is another traditional Japanese idea and we even made a rake for them to rake the fine gravel. So you have this sunken garden, which helps maximize privacy from the neighbours, while the glass doors at the back open up and create a frame for the garden as you look outside.'

DESIGN INGREDIENTS

· Close connection with
  the outdoors

· Discovery

· Flexible living

· Reinterpreting Japanese
  traditions

· Serenity

[1] FLOATING KITCHEN

The custom-made kitchen island is read as a piece of furniture, anchored within the open-plan living space, rather than as a room in itself. Although there are no upper cabinets, it contains all the necessary elements of a kitchen within one sleek unit, with a sink and cooktop set into the work surface, which can be used for preparation and for dining. The island also contains integrated storage, which is essential in this minimalist environment, while a discreet extractor unit is attached to the ceiling to remove cooking odours.

[2] GRAVEL GARDEN

The gravel garden forms a serene and textural backdrop to the veranda and to the main living spaces themselves, particularly when the long sequence of glazing that separates the inside and outside realms is fully retracted. Other outdoor elements are woven into the design of the house, including the water pools and the roof garden that adjoins the master bedroom on the modest upper level of the building. The timber veranda appears to hover slightly above the surface of the gravel, suggesting the illusion of a floating deck.

OFURO BATHING

There is a strong Japanese influence in the bathroom. It is not fully integrated with the interiors of the house, and there is a modest open-air passageway that links the two. 'In traditional Japanese architecture you have to first go outside before you go into the *ofuro* and we wanted to refer to that tradition,' said Mariscal. 'That brief contact with nature and the outside helps you to relax by the time you get into the bath itself. It's nice to have this secret, hidden niche with the sunken bath and reflecting pool.'

[3] <u>WATER POOLS</u> The house features a number of water pools, which serve as transitional spaces and sunken 'courtyards'. One of the pools is positioned alongside the main entrance, with the concrete path to the front door crossing the koi pond. A secondary pool sits to one side of the kitchen, also serving as a light well. The water pools are primarily decorative but they also offer a soothing element, while natural cross ventilation cools the house during the summer months.

[4] JAPANESE DINING
The Japanese influence that pervades the house is evident in the dining zone alongside the kitchen island. Traditional floor seating and a low circular dining table are positioned on tatami mats, in close proximity to the doors opening onto the veranda and garden. The seating area at the far end of the room features a colourful Mah Jong modular sofa with hand-sewn padded cushions and corner elements designed by Hans Hopfer for Roche Bobois. Its low profile complements the floor seating in the dining area.

Designers

Jonathan Adler
+44 (0)20 7589 9563
uk.jonathanadler.com

Kim Alexandriuk
+1 310 399 7000
alexandriuk.com

Eric Allart
+33 (0)6 87 61 01 53
ericallart.fr

Aparicio + Associates
+1 212 431 4430
aparicioassociates.com

Paul Archer Design
+44 (0)20 3668 2668
paularcherdesign.co.uk

Anton Assaad
+61 (0)3 9682 2777
greatdanefurniture.com

Autoban
+90 212 243 8641
autoban212.com

Bade Stageberg Cox
+1 718 858 4409
bscarchitecture.com

Shigeru Ban
+81 (0)3 3324 6760
shigerubanarchitects.com

Bates Masi + Architects
+1 631 725 0229
batesmasi.com

Sabrina Bignami
+39 0574 546335
b-arch.it

Ben Bischoff/MADE
+1 718 834 0171
made-nyc.com

Marc Bricault
+1 604 739 9730
bricault.ca

Buro Koray Duman
+1 212 686 6875
burokorayduman.com

Anthony Collett
+44 (0)20 8969 6967
collett-zarzycki.com

David Collins Studio
+44 (0)20 7835 5000
davidcollins.com

Chris Connell
+61 (0)3 8598 2222
chrisconnell.com.au

Mark Dixon Architect
+1 718 974 4498
markdixonarchitect.com

D.mesure
+32 (0)1 42 02 82 72
dmesure.fr

Sally Draper
+61 (0)3 9486 6606
sallydraperarchitects.com.au

Marika Dru
+33 (0)1 75 43 06 86
ateliermkd.com

Winka Dubbeldam/ Archi-Tectonics
+1 212 226 0303
archi-tectonics.com

Chris Dyson Architects
+44 (0)20 7247 1816
chrisdyson.co.uk

Agnès Emery
+32 (0)2 290 86 94
emeryetcie.com

Zeynep Fadillioğlu
+90 212 287 09 36
zfdesign.com

Fearon Hay Architects
+64 9 309 0128
fearonhay.com

Fletcher Crane Architects
fletchercranearchitects.com
+44 (0)20 8546 1640

Found Associates
+44 (0)20 7734 8400
foundassociates.com

Pierre Frey
+33 (0)1 44 77 36 13
pierrefrey.com

FT Architecture
ftarchitecture.com

Lynda Gardener
+ 61 (0)4 1603 2111
gardenerandmarks.com.au

Andrew Geller
andrewgeller.net

Tim Gledstone
+44 (0)7789 203 477
gledstone.com

Gluck+
+1 212 690 4950
gluckplus.com

Gorlin Architects
+1 212 229 1199
gorlinarchitects.com

Susan Hable Smith
hableconstruction.com

Trip Haenisch
+1 323 651 4445
triphaenisch.com

Maca Huneeus
macahuneeus.com

James Huniford
+1 212 717 9177
huniford.com

Jackson Clements Burrows
+1 (0)3 9654 6227
jcba.com.au

David Jameson Architect
+1 202 363 0080
davidjamesonarchitect.com

Diana Kellogg Architects
+1 212 431 1710
dkarchitects.com

Julian King Architect
+ 44 (0)1844 202707
juliankingarchitect.com

Antonie Kioes
+41 22 800 28 28

David Kohn Architects
+44 (0)20 7424 8596
davidkohn.co.uk

Kraus Schoenberg Architects
+49 7531 3805905
kraus-schoenberg.com

Larson and Paul Architects
+1 212 587 1900
larsonandpaul.com

Meryanne Loum-Martin
+212 524 32 84 84
jnane.com

Fiona Lynch
+61 (0)3 9079 2500
fionalynch.com.au

Jason MacLean
+44 (0)7958 505 746
studiomaclean.com

Maison 24
+1 212 355 2414
maison24.com

John Maniscalco Architecture
+1 415 -864 9900
m-architecture.com

Sebastian Mariscal Studio
+1 617 395 1210
sebastianmariscal.com

Lucy Marston
lucymarston.com

Moussafir Architectes
+33 (0)1 48 24 38 30
moussafir.fr

Neeson Murcutt Architects
+61 (0)2 8297 3590
neesonmurcutt.com

Marc Newson
+44 (0)20 7932 0990
marc-newson.com

Nord Architecture
+44 (0)141 552 9996
nordarchitecture.com

Rolf Ockert Design
+61 (0)4 0066 1858
rodesign.com.au

O'Connor and Houle Architecture
+61 (0)3 9686 7022
oconnorandhoule.com

Todd Oldham Studio
+1 212 226 4668
toddoldhamstudio.com

Tony Owen Partners
+61 (0)2 9698 2900
tonyowen.com.au

Pal + Smith
+1 888 725 7684
palandsmith.com

John Pardey Architects
+44 (0)1590 626465
johnpardeyarchitects.com

Thomas Pheasant
+1 202 337 6596

thomaspheasant.com

Gregory Phillips Architects
+44 (0)20 7724 3040
gregoryphillips.com

Anke Van Der Pluijm
+31 (0)20 638 5015
householdhardware.nl

David Pocknell
+44 (0)1371 850075
pocknellstudio.com

Popham Design
pophamdesign.com

Alex Pössenbacher
possenbacherdesign.com

Marmol Radziner
+1 310 826 6222
marmol-radziner.com

Arabella Ramsay
arabellaramsay.com

Chris Redecke and Maryam Montague
peacockpavilions.com

Adam Richards Architects
+44 (0)20 7613 5077
adamrichards.co.uk

Mark Rios
+1 323 785 1800
rchstudios.com

Danielle Roberts Interiors
+1 646 422 0560
danielleroberts interiors.com

Adam Rolston
incorporatedny.com

Rundell Associates
+ 44(0)20 7483 8360
rundellassociates.com

Thomas Sandell
+46 (0)8 506 531 00
sandellsandberg.se

David Scott Interiors
+1 212 829 0703
davidscottinteriors.com

SelgasCano Architects
+34 913076481
selgascano.net

Shamir Shah
+1 212 274 7476
shamirshahdesign.com

Stephen Sills
+1 212 988 6100
stephensills.com

Spratley Studios
+44 (0)1491 411277
spratley.co.uk

Squire and Partners
+44 (0)20 7278 5555
squireandpartners.com

Standard Architecture
+1 323 662 1000
standard-la.com

Studio Arthur Casas
+ 55 11 2182 7500
arthurcasas.com

Studio Catoir
+33 (0)1 42 50 32 46
studiocatoir.com

Studio KO
+33 (0)1 42 71 13 92
studioko.fr

Studio Octopi
+44 (0)20 7633 0003
octopi.co.uk

Gisele Taranto Arquitetura
+55 21 2579 0448
giseletaranto.com

Piers Taylor
invisiblestudio.org

Warren Techentin
+1 323 664 4500
wtarch.com

Techentin Buckingham Architecture
meterbuilt.com/wt-mtr/solo

Vicky Thornton
+44 (0)778 5536 198
vickythomtondesign.co.uk

Pearl Todd Interior Design
+ 61 (0) 410 470 107
11 Wells St, Balmain, NSW 2041

Guilherme Torres
+55 11 2072 0620
guilhermetorres.com

Tsao & McKown
+1 212 337 3800
tsao-mckown.com

Carl Turner Architects
+44 (0)20 7274 2902
ct-architects.co.uk

UXUS
+31 (0)20 623 3114
uxusdesign.com

Miv Watts
+44 (0)1328 730313
wattswishedfor.com

Wells Mackereth
+44 (0)20 7042 8335
studiomackereth.com

+44 (0)20 3735 6460
jameswellsarchitects.com

Vicente Wolf
+1 212 465 0590
vicentewolf.com

Wonder
designofwonder.com.au

Word of Mouth
wordofmouthbali.com

Yabu Pushelberg
+1 212 226 0808
yabupushelberg.com

Zen Architects
+61 (0)3 9482 3504
zen.architects.com

Brian Zulaikha
+61 (0)2 9215 4900
tzg.com.au

Index

Picture Credits

Every effort has been made to trace all copyright owners, but if any have been inadvertently overlooked, the publishers would be pleased to make the necessary corrections at the first opportunity.

Richard Powers

British photographer Richard Powers specializes in interiors, architecture and the built environment. Working worldwide, he has been based in the South of France for several years. Early in his freelance career, Powers focused on the natural environment, developing his skills with a camera extensively throughout Asia, South America and Europe. Once back in London, in 1996, his eye turned to the design world in which he became rapidly established, with commissions from design agencies and shelter magazines such as *ELLE Decoration*. Today his editorial client list includes US and European editions of *Architectural Digest*, *ELLE Décor*, *WSJ*, *World of Interiors* and *Vogue Living*, as well as the international Condé Nast titles. He also works directly with architects, interior designers, hotels and publishing houses, such as Thames & Hudson, Penguin Random House and Octopus. With fifteen books to his name and twenty years of experience, Powers is a true force in his field, bringing equal amounts of enthusiasm, attention to detail and Zen-like calm to his work.

Credits

pp10–13, 14–17, 18–21, 22–25, 30–33, 34–37, 38–41, 42–45, 46–49, 52–55, 56–59, 60–63, 64–67, 68–71, 80–83, 88–91, 94–97, 98–101, 102–105, 110–113, 114–117, 118–121, 122–125, 126–129, 130–133, 136–139, 140–143, 144–147, 148–151, 160–163, 168–171, 172–175, 178–181, 182–185, 186–189, 194–197, 206–209, 210–213, 214–217, 220–223, 224–227, 228–231, 232–235, 236–239, 244–247, 248–251, 252–255, 256–259, 262–265, 270–273, 274–277, 278–281, 286–289, 294–297, 298–301, 308–311, 320–323, 324–327, 332–335, 336–339, 340–343, 346–349, 350–353, 362–365, 366–369, 370–373, 382–385, 388–391, 392–395, 396–399, 400–403, 408–411, 412–415, 416–419, 420–423, 424–427

Mark Luscombe-Whyte

Mark Luscombe-Whyte is a British location photographer who specializes in interiors, hospitality, travel and portraits. He has photographed nine interior design books, featuring work by the world's leading designers, and titles include *Designers at Home*, *American Designers at Home* and *Barns: Living in Converted and Reinvented Spaces*. Luscombe-Whyte lives between London and the South of France.

Credits

pp26–29, 76–79, 106–109, 164–167, 202–205, 240–243, 282–285, 290–293, 312–315, 316–319, 328–331, 358–361, 404–407

Damian Russell

Damian Russell is a leading international interiors and still life photographer who contributes to many magazines and newspapers in the United Kingdom and around the world, including *ELLE Decoration*, *The Telegraph*, *House & Garden*, *Livingetc* and *Vogue Living*. Commercial clients include CB2, Claridge's, Harrods and Liberty. Russell lives in London and Buckinghamshire with his wife and their four children. A self-taught craftsman, he creates evocative images full of texture, life and vivid colour.

Credits

pp72–75, 84–87, 156–159, 190–193, 198–201, 266–269, 304–307, 354–357, 374–377, 378–381

Mel Yates

Mel Yates's commissions range from portrait shoots with Hollywood actors such as Gwyneth Paltrow and Kevin Spacey to photographing industrial landscapes for advertising clients. However, having originally studied product design at Central Saint Martins, it is only natural that the majority of his work is design related. He has shot for *Architectural Digest*, *Blueprint*, *ELLE Decoration*, *Marie Claire Maison*, *The Sunday Times* and *Vogue* among many other titles. He also travels regularly, photographing the new projects of leading designers such as Philippe Starck and Kelly Hoppen, and has shot all the images for Kelly's two most recent books. Yates also works as a video director with clients including the Four Seasons and ME hotel groups. He lives in London with his wife and their three children.

Credits

pp152–155

About the author

Dominic Bradbury is a design writer and journalist. He contributes to newspapers and magazines internationally, including *The Telegraph*, *Financial Times*, *World of Interiors*, *House & Garden*, *ELLE Decoration*, *Dwell* and others. His many books include *The Iconic House*, *The Iconic Interior*, *Mid-Century Modern Complete*, *New Brazilian House*, *Mountain Modern* and *Waterside Modern*. He lives in Norfolk, England, with his wife and their three children.

Library of Congress Control Number 2015938287
ISBN 9781580934343

Designed and produced by
Quintessence Editions Ltd
The Old Brewery
6 Blundell Street
London N7 9BH

Printed in China

The Monacelli Press
236 West 27th Street
New York, New York 10001

www.monacellipress.com